Mathew Hayden

A Man with a Fast Horse

Susan Snyder Lee

Hayden's Legacy

Mathew Antoine Hayden

The Man
With a Fast Horse

Who seeks the way to win renown
Or flies with wings of high desire
Who seeks to wear the laurel crown
Or hath the mind that would aspire
Let him his native soil eschew
Let him go range and seek anew

Sir Richard Grenville (c. 1541-1591) from
In Praise of Seafaring Men, in Hopes of Good Fortune

Table of Contents

To my daughter, Dr. Larissa J. Lee, who bore the courage to battle cancer with dignity. There was never poor me. Larissa worked as a research scientist and physician at Harvard in Boston. She was a well-respected radiation oncologist specializing in brachytherapy at Brigham Women's in Boston. She completed nine unfinished research papers while undergoing a year of cancer treatment. She concluded she belonged at Harvard and dearly loved her colleagues who supported her enthusiasm for saving lives. She excelled in many activities such as violin, piano, swimming, skiing, and hiking being significant in her life. She left two young sons who she had plans to take on international travel experiences and visit the National Parks.

To my husband, John R. Lee, who helped me pay attention to detail and encouragod me to finish Mat's story. Thank you.

Mat Hayden was typical of many people who traveled west. They were hardworking and industrious with strong principles with hope they could achieve their goals. Immigrants sought Mat out for advice. Researching Mat's story increased my awareness of the challenges these people faced as they crossed the land to seek better lives. The immigrants wanted to be accepted in a no-class system and to have the freedom to aspire.

I thank the Oregon Jesuits and Gonzaga University for permitting me to use Mat's papers. James Monaghan, the executor of Mat's estate donated Mat's papers to Gonzaga. All letters are copied as written.

From Ireland to New York

A young wiry Irishman arrived alone in New York in the spring of 1847[1]. Mathew Hayden was nearly 16 years old when he immigrated to the United States. He was 5' 5" tall with dark curly hair, deep indentations for dimples, and fierce dancing hazel eyes. His rail-thin body supported a determined face. He left home with a few coins in his pocket and a tattered valise. He arrived in New York, hungry, tired, and scared but ready to find his way in search of a better life.

Life in Ireland was merciless, as the Irish enjoyed few freedoms while their culture was suppressed. The Irish were being displaced by the English from their ancestral lands and forced to live in hovels made of mud and straw. The English considered themselves superior to the Irish and established the "Popery Acts", which resulted in fewer Irish Catholics owning land or holding political or military offices. Families kept their religion and culture alive by holding mass in secret and hosting illegal "hedge schools." These informal schools were held in the hedgerows of fields where many Irish Catholic parents worked. By holding classes in secret, Irish teachers could teach Irish lessons and avoid penalties. Religious discrimination was common.

To make matters worse, Ireland was experiencing a famine between 1845 and 1850 caused by a widespread potato fungus. Food was so hard to come by that many ate grass to suppress their hunger. An estimated one million people starved to death during this period and were described as dying with a "green mouth" and another million emigrated. The devastated families found virtually no support from the Catholic Church. The English continued to export food from Ireland while allowing the Irish to starve. As the famine grew, the English landlords eventually bought steerage to send the famished to America. The English had the head of a household arrested for minor infractions, leaving their families starving and unable to pay the rent. Given the dire situation in Ireland, the Irish began to emigrate to the United States by the thousands. America offered the Irish an opportunity for jobs that paid a living wage, to own land, to teach the children their faith, and to attend school.[2]

While in Ireland, Mathew worked as a laborer doing menial jobs but remained impoverished. He wandered the countryside of Wexford County and saw fellow countrymen die of starvation, fever, and chills. Several close to him died during the famine and those who survived encouraged him to go to America. Mathew Hayden was born into this environment, but he aspired to live in a place where he could own land, find work, and raise a family.[3] He knew he had no choice but to leave his beloved Ireland for the opportunity of a better life. He would miss the brightly colored wildflowers of spring, the incandescent greens of the moors, and the camaraderie of the noisy, smoky pubs where he met his mates in the village. Most of all, he would miss his family.

Woodcut engraving. 1886 London Times. Irish collecting limpets and seaweed during the famine.[4]

Mathew Hayden boarded a passenger ship to America. He was one of the millions of Irishmen to emigrate. Excitement and dreams of the future overcame passengers as they climbed the steep plank to board. Men and boys made up the majority of the passengers. They spoke of job prospects and enlisting as soldiers in the Army to ensure clothing, food, and money in their pockets. Others hoped to earn enough to send for their families. Steerage costs a laborer £3-£12,[5] more than a year's wage, and many traded their freedom for the fare and traveled as indentured servants. In exchange, they would work for a period of 3 to 7 years for low pay but receive food, shelter, and some training or education. Mathew fell into this category. His father knew that if Mat received training, life would be better in America. He exchanged Mat's papers for his fare. The 13th Amendment abolished slavery and servitude after the Civil War.

The journey across the ocean was a challenge. Mathew was relegated to the crowded steerage section of the ship, under the rudder as an indentured servant. The crawl space was less than five feet high and the cots were barely wide enough for one to turn over. The rancid food and contaminated water were meager with the only light afforded by one small port window. Many died in the crossing of dysentery, cholera, typhus, or starvation and were buried at sea. Diseases spread rapidly and those who survived were left weak and sick after their arduous journey.

When ships docked in New York, many immigrants walked off the ship at a wharf where they landed. America did not have a passenger immigration center until 1855 at Castle Garden. Mat was checked off the ship's manifest.[6] The hungry and disheveled immigrants faced a tough world. When they found that it cost a nickel for a shave, they relinquished the idea of a better appearance. They paid a penny for their barber at home. They could buy a cup of coffee and a cheese sandwich for ten cents. Their introduction to New York City was one of confusion with overcrowded streets and turmoil among hundreds of frightened immigrants. Some mistrusted farming and didn't want to move out of the city. There were street gangs, rivalry for jobs, and people struggling to try to find housing. Typhus and cholera were prevalent, and the Irish were thick as flies around a sorghum mill. The people lived in squalid conditions with barely enough to feed or clothe themselves or their families. Poverty was rampant in the Irish quarters and many women took in laundry or worked as domestics for the wealthy in New York. Mathew didn't spend much time in New York and journeyed 150 miles along the Hudson River. He transferred in Albany to a packet boat on the Erie Canal to a farm in Utica to begin his indentured servitude.

With immigration exploding, settlers wanted to get out of the overcrowded cities. The Erie Canal opened in 1825 and was the obvious choice for travel. Immigrants flooded the area to take advantage of agriculture and industrial growth. The line boats carried passengers, freight, fresh produce, and dairy products. They were guided by two horses or mules and charged one cent a mile, or $1.20 for eighty miles and a meal. When the horses needed rest, the crew exchanged them with fresh ones that were carried in the bow. The packet boats, which were smaller and faster, carried 70 passengers with a berth and meals for the $3.50 passage. Some of the Irish who came over during the famine knew someone to help them move to another part of the country and they traveled by boat on the canals and waterways.

Mathew found himself on a large farm outside Utica, NY. Life as an indentured servant was not easy. Mat learned modern sustainable farming methods, planting and harvesting grains, vegetables, and fruit under his employer. To grow 100 bushels of corn the men had to work eighty hours. Livestock and farm products were shipped to the cities. Mat's employer treated him well. Some landowners physically exploited and punished their servants. If a young girl became pregnant, she was indentured for a longer time and could not marry without permission.

Mat stayed on task and was determined to fulfill his obligation. The time went quickly. His skills improved as he checked on the crops and livestock on horseback. In the winter, he repaired harnesses and farm equipment inside a large workshop in front of a warm pot-bellied stove. Mat had escaped the Great Famine but yearned for his freedom and for the life he hoped to achieve after leaving his home and family. When he completed his contract, he received freedom dues for his five years of indentured servitude. Freedom dues were given as a stipend in land or money.

In 1831 the mechanical reaper, steam engine, and sewing machine helped farmers' productivity.[7]

The Dragoons

After five years, Mathew completed his service on the farm, and on June 3, 1852, he voluntarily enlisted in the army at West Point, NY, to enable him to qualify for United States citizenship after serving five years. He was sworn in by Brevet Major George H. Thomas, the recruiting officer from the 3rd Artillery. Mathew was nearly 21 years old. He was assigned a uniform, equipment, and a bedroll and waited at his living quarters in the town of Cornwall, New York for his orders. He met many other young Irishmen, which gave him a sense of security and belonging. Mat took the oath believing that in America he would have the right to speak and act freely, vote, and worship as he chose. He would obey the orders of the officers and serve honorably. His enlistment record was signed with his mark, an X, his education was minimal.

The Army furnished all necessary expenses, including clothing, food, and medical care. A private's pay was $8 per month or $288 for a three-year term or $480 for five years of service. A soldier received their pay after the Army deducted any outstanding debts. Typically, soldiers owed money to the camp laundress and the camp sutler who would sell provisions in the field. In the 1850s, the government instituted one of the first military pension programs and withheld twelve and a half cents monthly from the soldiers' pay to be contributed to the Soldiers Home in Washington. The Army didn't want the wounded or elderly soldiers to fend for themselves in frontier towns. Many of the soldiers worked hard to learn English, the customs of the military, and how to march. After the morning roll call, the mounted troops cleaned the stables and fed and groomed their horses. In addition to practicing military skills, the troops unloaded supplies, helped build roads, planted and cared for gardens, hauled wood, and cleaned chimneys. They took turns cooking. The men didn't have a pillow and slept head to toe with two in a bed. The army required them to wash their feet twice a week and bathe once a week. Christmas and the 4th of July were the biggest holidays celebrated in the Army. They often pooled their money to buy hams, sardines, pickles, and perhaps champagne for the revelry.

Mat spent his first weeks at Fort Columbus near New York Harbor, then later received orders to report to Jefferson Barracks, Missouri. Mathew began his journey by steamboat to Albany on the Hudson River. The men continued their travel overland to Madison Barracks, located on Sackett Harbor, Lake Ontario. The men were organized into units and assigned jobs by the commanding officer when they arrived at Jefferson Barracks. Mat volunteered to help scout against Indian attacks when they were beyond the Mississippi and was assigned to the 2nd Dragoons. Captain Ulysses S. Grant was stationed at the barracks in upstate New York in 1852 when Mat passed through.

Departing Sackett Harbor by boat, the night fog was thick as they came to a narrow inlet that was the Welland Canal to bypass Niagara Falls, connecting Lake Ontario to Lake Erie. On Lake Erie, the wind became relentless and the captain worried that the waves would swamp them. Most of the men did not know how to swim and grew anxious as darkness fell. The next morning, they continued to Ashtabula where they would disembark. Supply wagons met the men to lead the soldiers on the 132-mile trek to Steubenville. The troops preferred to walk, hoping they would find a spot in the wagon for their packs. The roads that had been constructed in low swampy areas were decayed. The men had to repair the corduroy roads of small trees laid perpendicular to the direction of travel. The uneven road caused the men to be jolted and tossed about making it difficult to rest. The small towns they marched through had sections filled with destitute and indigent people and later these areas became known as" skid row".

After a five-day march to Steubenville, the men were glad to get on a steamer on the Ohio River. It would be over a thousand miles on the Ohio and Mississippi Rivers before they finally arrived at Jefferson Barracks. Mat, was stiff after sleeping on the deck as he stepped out of the overcrowded steamer. The fort was beautifully situated on the Mississippi River, ten miles south of St. Louis, on a large bluff overlooking the river and prairie. The soldiers were housed in barracks extending along the parade ground. The large cottonwood and hackberry provided shade. Scrub oaks grew small and stooped in the direction the wind blew. The land was an open savanna with native grasses and wildflowers. Mat knew by looking at the oak how persistent the wind was and the lack of moisture in the land. He could hear an Irish fiddler playing an old pub song and a drummer tapping out cadence. As he uncurled his body and stretched out, he looked around and took a deep breath. He loved the openness of the country, the rolling hills, and the stark differences from New York

City. The Mississippi River flowed jubilantly as it quickly moved along its course until it passed New Orleans and emptied into the Gulf of Mexico. At Jefferson Barracks, the air smelled fresh. It was warm with a light breeze. Mat was glad that he joined the army despite the uncomfortable journey. A bugle called the men to mess, and Mat was looking forward to a hot meal.

The optimism that Mat felt after he arrived at the barracks soon faded. After dinner, the men were assigned their bunks. The conditions inside the barracks were undesirable. Rats and roaches reigned throughout the buildings. Many men took their plates and bedding outside to spend the night, weather permitting. The mosquitoes were unbearable. The Army had tried to purchase netting, but the head office in St. Louis would not release the funds, calling them unnecessary. Quinine was used by doctors in the cities, but the military rejected that and believed that calomel and bloodletting would be best for the troops. Calomel contained mercury chloride and was also used as a fungicide. Army medical personnel did not realize the dangers of lead. The barracks had a cholera outbreak in 1849 and directives were issued "to pay attention to cleanliness," but little was accomplished. The cisterns were empty as the pipes and necessary guttering were missing. There were problems with desertion and alcohol abuse. Recruiters, of course, painted a picture of adventure for underage recruits when trying to fill their quotas. A mother missing her son would seek them out with a writ of habeas corpus to gain his freedom.[8] Eventually, in 1854, the barracks were considered unfit as old beds and mattresses were broken and two men were assigned to a bed. The roofs and floors were in danger of collapsing and the army requisitioned $24,346 for repairs.

Mat would be assigned to Company C of the Second Dragoons at Fort Leavenworth, Kansas. The men were an elite group and were strictly disciplined. They had two months of rigorous training in the grooming, feeding, and care of horses. The government purchased the best horses they could for the Dragoons. They learned to mount their horses from both sides without a saddle. The horses were assigned according to the regimental order: Companies A and K rode Black, C-D-E and I rode Bay, B-F-H rode Sorrel, and G rode Iron Gray. The colors of the horses made it easier for the men to recognize their regiment in battle. Mathew learned to ride while caring for horses on the Utica farm. He worked well with stocks and had a natural affinity towards them. He quietly spoke Gaelic to his Bay and felt that she understood the language and appreciated his gentle touch. He and most of the men took pride in taking care of their horses to keep them healthy. Inspections were made daily of the saddles and bridles. A man would find himself in the stockade if he abused his horse or used spurs. Mat enjoyed learning about the care and cleaning of his weapons. The troops practiced firing weapons when mounted and dismounted. Taps were played each evening, signaling lanterns to be extinguished. Soldiers were quick to learn the bugle calls as they could have as many as ten in one day. Reveille woke the men in the morning, alerting them for flag raising, roll call, and breakfast. The next call would be for work assignments. To keep in good standing with the City of St. Louis, citizens were allowed to watch drills and routines.

Mat would join his Company C at Fort Leavenworth, which was made up of forty men. The Second Dragoon headquarters were at Fort Leavenworth under commanding officer Lt. Colonel Nathan Boone, son of Daniel Boone. Nathan Boone joined the Missouri Rangers in 1812, and later he served as captain of the Mounted Rangers in 1832. After his years of rugged army life on the frontier, his health was failing. He returned to Fort Leavenworth in September 1848 to recuperate. As an expert in the habitat and trails across the plains, he was promoted to Lieutenant Colonel and commanded the Second Dragoons in 1850. After serving forty-one years, he resigned from the Army on July 15, 1853, at age 52. Nathan Boone owned 1200 acres of land, keeping eleven people enslaved. He was the father of 14 children and passed away in 1856 at the age of 75.

Before his assignment to Company C, 2nd Dragoons, Mat trained at Ft. Columbus, New York Harbor, and Jefferson Barracks, Missouri.[9]

An Act of Congress formed Dragoon Regiments in 1776 and 1833. The Dragoons were a mounted infantry regiment that developed fighting skills on horseback as well as on foot. The Dragoons symbolized courage. Their insignia, the fleur-de-lis, is a stylized lily resembling a spearhead used by military units to show martial power. The Dragoons' motto, "Toujours Pret," means "Always Ready" or "Always Prepared." The first unit was formed during the Revolutionary War under French General Lafayette to protect General Washington, and the second unit was established in 1836 to safeguard Western expansion. In 1861, the 1st and 2nd Dragoons were renamed the 1st and 2nd Cavalry and remain active today.

The Dragoons were known as a moving arsenal and military depot. They carried a percussion breech-loading carbine with limited impact and range. Its great advantage over the previous muzzle-loading rifles lay in the rapidity of fire and a longer lifetime before lead deposits began to degrade the bore. They were assigned a single-shot flintlock Aston horse pistol known to miss most well-aimed shots. The men were required to practice firing quickly without moving their heads. It usually took the soldiers six months to become proficient. The pistols were fired with an arm extended straight out from their bodies. Their last line of defense was a military-issued saber known to warp. A 6.8 lb musketoon with its short barrel served as a shotgun. The barrels were flared at the muzzle and resembled a cannon or blunderbuss. In addition to a 2.8 lb. Aston Pistol and the saber with saber belt, the men were required to carry a cartridge box, sling, swivel, saber knot, forty rounds of ammunition with holster, a curry-comb and brush, spurs and straps, two blankets (one for the soldier and one for his horse), a valise containing one pair of wool overalls, one pair of drawers, one flannel shirt, one pair of stockings, and one fatigue frock, a greatcoat, the horse's nose-bag, a picket-pin to hobble horses and rope. The total weight of each man's gear was seventy-eight pounds.

The Dragoon uniform was a long-tailed blue frock coat with an orange collar and cuffs. A long stripe ran down the seam of the soldier's gray-blue pants. The color soon faded in the hot sun of the plains. The troops were issued two jackets a year and a white wool flannel shirt with long tails. The full-bodied wool shirt was scratchy with its tight sleeves, so the men wore a soft muslin V-neck shirt beneath their uniform. Mathew's coat bore the number two on each side of his collar, designating the 2nd Dragoons. The troops found the coat cumbersome, making it difficult to maneuver on the horse. The shako, or military dress hat with its short visor, looked similar to an upside-down flowerpot perched on one's head. It was adorned with a tall feather or plume and a heavy brass emblem of the American eagle. The shako would often bounce and slide off the soldier's head when they were riding too quickly. In the heavy sleeting rain, the hats would lose their shape, as they were lined with cardboard. In a short time on the plains, the men looked like a pathetic bunch. They discarded the shako for the smaller caps. The uniforms became tattered and ragged after a few months. They were publicized as the finest group of military men in the, but one would not think so looking at them.

The enlisted men were proud to serve despite their appearance. Often, their commanding officers were of English heritage and carried the conceit and prejudices of their ancestors. Some of the officers treated the enlisted Irish poorly, although their families had lived in America for a century.

Being in the military, Mat soon learned the effect that politicians and presidential decisions would have on his life.

Millard Fillmore lost the election to Franklin Pierce who was elected the 14th President of the United States in 1853. President Fillmore acquired new territory that included California, which entered the union as a free state. At the same time, although the slavery question remained unsettled, slave practice in the District of Columbia was abolished, the Texas boundary was settled, and territorial status was given to New Mexico.

There were countless arguments over the expansion of slavery in the West. In 1850, Congress passed the Fugitive Slave Act, which made it a crime to harbor or help escaped slaves. The fine was $1000 and six months in prison. A man typically earned about $1.50 per day, so if the government caught him harboring slaves, it would greatly burden his family. He didn't think he was interested in American politics until he realized how the decisions of the president and the government would affect him. Mat listened carefully as others fervently debated slavery. He soon joined in and let others know his opinions, as he knew what it was like to be an indentured servant and could relate to the slaves' struggles. Slavery was intolerable. He accepted that others may not agree with him but believed as he did that everyone had the right to their opinions and ideas. Mat understood that the United States was founded on principles of liberty and that individuals were equal by law, nationality, and religion. He supported the abolitionists, as most of the Irish did.

Life on the Plains

During the 1850s, various routes of immigration and commerce were developed to connect the growing nation. The Santa Fe and Oregon Trails were the major highways for mountain men, fur traders, soldiers, prospectors and migrants. Mat served as a scout, giving warning and protection to the wagon trains on the Santa Fe and Oregon Trails from marauding Indians. He learned to read the signs left by the horses' hoofs and the broken brush. The troops often found footprints or smoldering campfires and knew the Indians were tracking them as well.

Mat's company had experience negotiating with the Indians and often gained the release of captives. After the war with Mexico ended in 1848, the 2nd Dragoons began to clash with the Indians frequently. In the Treaty of Guadalupe, the Americans paid Mexico $15 million and gained 500,000 square miles of land from Texas to California. The native population was deceived and tricked into giving up valuable possessions. Treaties were signed and promises made, but were driven from their lands. The Indians were determined to fight to preserve their territory as more and more settlers were moving west like locusts over a field of wheat. Military posts were established from the Red River in North Dakota to Galveston, Texas, at strategic points to protect the westward expansion. The 2nd Dragoon Companies garrisoned and protected the soldiers while they built and supplied the forts. Between 1848 and 1861, they rode back and forth between the forts and Western outposts. They pursued the swift Apache and Comanche over the hot, arid plains of Texas and New Mexico. The troops were periodically called upon to disarm filibusters, unauthorized adventurers causing problems on both sides of the Rio Grande for personal gain.

Before Mat arrived at Company C under Captain Hardee, the men conducted a census of 3,952 Indians along the Texas border. They were told that in February of 1852, a group of ten men from Company C set out to penalize a band of raiding Indians. After a two-day pursuit, Hardee's troops killed three of the Indians and wounded one. The men recovered the stolen pillage. A briefing was given to the enlisted men on what their jobs would entail. The men learned to be alert and cautious at all times. During Indian raids, the wagon trains lost a horse or two, cattle, or household items, which included a coveted mirror.

Shortly after Mat joined Company C, he was deployed to Fort Chadbourne, near the center of Texas in what is known as the North Central Plains. The hills were covered with thick vegetation of shrubs and grasses, which made it ideal for grazing the horses in the spring. The Comanche would make friendly visits to the fort, and the troops would engage them in horse racing competitions and gambling. Most of the men were good at cards and picked up the Comanche language easily. The exuberant activities and entertainment at the fort were often followed by wild revelry, with the Indians participating in the fun. One story told of a Comanche brave riding backward on a nag, taunting and beckoning a soldier on a mare to catch up with him. By 1856, the mood had soured. More skirmishes were occurring at the forts, and the Comanche often stole cattle. The winters in Texas were not easy. Mathew's company patrolled several hundred miles along the Rio Grande River each month. The buffalo grass provided good winter grazing for livestock near Fort Chadbourne. When traveling, adequate grazing was scarce, and horses, mules, and cattle suffered.

Although the dragoons were mounted, their travel was slow when foot soldiers accompanied them. Through their travels, the men of Company C also met the tribes of Kiowa, Cheyenne, Arapahoe, and Apache. As time passed, Mathew began to know many of the indigenous people and grew to respect their way of life. Most warriors kept between one and five wives. The women did most of the work around the camp, preparing and gathering food for meals, chopping the wood, weaving baskets for storage or carrying water, and packing up camp when they moved.

One winter, they patrolled the Dakota territories and fought the powerful Sioux. The Sioux's weapons were more effective than the soldiers' carbines when ice fused inside their muzzles. Winter skirmishes, were particularly tough for the troops. The foot soldiers would walk ten or fifteen miles on roads covered with huge snowdrifts from the incessant wind. Remembering the oppressive heat of Texas, New Mexico, and Kansas in the summer months, the men would find themselves struggling to survive the frozen fields on the Northern Plains. The Indians could maneuver their horses without being burdened with equipment as the soldiers were. They took advantage of their mobility.

Colonel Kearny, 1st Dragoons, on the Oregon Trail to Fort Laramie.[10]

The rain could freeze into sleet or hail before it touched the ground. Some experienced snow blindness but after a few days, the pain and symptoms would relent. During the long nights, the soldiers would congregate together for warmth, but some would eventually succumb to the cold. Others would be frostbitten so severely that the commanders would call the troops back to the fort for amputation and respite.

Some of the men carried a flask of strong whiskey to warm themselves. On occasion, they would purchase dogs from the Indians to make stew. Huddling around a smoky fire provided warmth as well as a chance to roast meat which they ate with relish. Conditions were equally bleak for the Indians and settlers. Travel was slow. Caravans would often get stuck in the snow, and the animals would be exhausted. The food stores were often lost or pillaged. The few trees they would see would be used for fires or to repair a wagon when the part wasn't available. Tents often blew down, and wagon covers were swept across the frozen prairie. Mat heard the mules braying and calling out in pain at night as they huddled together, then silence. The previous summer, Mat entered a poker game and won a heavy buffalo robe. He realized that the robe had saved his life more than once, that of a few of his mates. He refused to die on the plains. He had heard rumors that the average Irishman didn't live more than six months. He was determined to survive the conditions, as many Irishmen were often treated worse than other immigrants. Men became sick and died from fever. Mat learned that his enemy on the plains was not the Indians but the environment.

Mat enjoyed watching the bald eagles along the shore of the river. They would soar overhead with a seven-foot wingspan above the river, searching for a meal, and often stand on the ice waiting for a fish to appear in the open waters. The men respected the majestic eagles and what they represented. The snow and frost sparkled in the grass, and Mat thought of his journey and why he was in America. He loved the openness of the country and never regretted leaving New York with its overcrowded slums or the long, continuous hours he worked as a laborer on the farm. The troops somehow managed to preserve the tenuous peace.

The soldiers and immigrants all enjoyed the warmer weather after a harsh winter, however, the travel still had challenges. When the rivers were high from the melting snow, they could lose a wagon and its contents down the river. Continuous rain would turn the roads into thick, heavy clay, and the cumbersome wagons would get bogged down. The speed was approximately two miles per hour. Some immigrants gave up and stayed when they were too tired to move further. The Irish soldiers celebrated St. Patrick's Day with music, dance, storytelling, and copious amounts of whiskey.

Mathew appreciated the warming winds and spring rains. When he saw the wild blowing grasses with the first flowers of the purple-violet colors of the phlox, penstemon, and prairie violets, he felt nostalgic for the hills of Ireland. He quickly learned to identify edible and poisonous plants. In early summer, the prairie was prolific with cornflowers and daisies.

The summer brought sizzling heat and little shade from the sun. The wagon train ran short of water in the summer months. Settlers would fall from the wagons, and the horses would collapse from heatstroke as if being shot. The land was dried and cracked, and the thick dust made it difficult to see. The scouts covered their faces with bandanas as they traveled west. The Little Arkansas riverbanks were fifteen feet high and very steep. The soldiers dug out the riverbanks so they could get the wagons down to cross the river.

Buffalo 1895 Charles Russell.[11]

The cottonwood trees shed soft clouds of fine fibers, and the bleached grass crackled under the hoofs of the horses as they left puffs of dust. The redbud trees grew wild and bent with lush fuchsia against the blue sky. The soldiers often found wild parsley and dandelion greens to boil with their meat. The wheatgrass was very nutritious for the livestock and made good forage. The men kept sharp eyes out in the grasslands, as it provided good nesting for quail, ducks, and turkeys.

The cavalry occasionally hunted buffalo and feasted on the roasted meat. The hide was tanned and offered in a high-stakes poker game. Many of the settlers saw the value in the buffalo and hunted them to sell the meat and hides to make harnesses, shoes, and clothing. By 1872, 3,000 hides and 1.5 million pounds of meat had been shipped by the Santa Fe Railway to the East Coast. Settlers were paid $4 to $6 a ton for buffalo bones to make buttons, combs, dice, and fertilizer. In February 1874, the Daily Nebraska State Journal wrote an article about saving the buffalo and protecting them from slaughter.

Colonel Edwin Vose Sumner established Camp MacKay in 1850 as the first military presence on the Santa Fe Trail. The small camp was important for mail couches, a respite for travelers to resupply, and contact with the Plains Indians. The name was changed to Fort Atkinson in 1851. The troops referred to Fort Atkinson as Fort Sumner, Fort Sod, or Fort Sodom when the sod buildings became infested with field mice. A dozen cats were requested from Fort Leavenworth, which was 370 miles away. Within two years, the garrison had a flea problem. The fort did not have rain in 100 days, and they were left without water and grass. In September 1853, the fort was abandoned, and the walls were torn down to prevent meandering Indians from attacking migrants on the Santa Fe Trail. Col Sumner had a booming voice and an imposing presence. He was well-liked by the men working under him and became known as Bullhead. A story was told that he had survived a musket bouncing off his head. The fort was closed when Major Robert Chilton arrived with a detachment of dragoons. He moved the Dragoons north to survey a new location for a fort overlooking the Kansas River valley. The fort was named Camp Center because the War Department believed it to be near the center of the United States. Later, the name was changed to honor Major Gen. Bennett C. Riley, who led the first military escort along the Santa Fe Trail in 1829. Fort Riley is located in the rolling prairies carved out of the landscape by glaciers in the Flint Hills. The duties of the military were to protect the traders and settlers traveling west along the Oregon and Santa Fe Trails. The routes traversed unsettled land and extended the migration that became known in 1845 as "Manifest Destiny". As immigrants poured into America and the population grew, many sought free and inexpensive land. Companies E and H marched 485 miles from Fort Belknap, Texas, during the hottest days of August 1855 to return to Fort Riley, Kansas. The dragoons scouted the route to protect the marching troops. Life was very dangerous on the plains for the soldiers. Maintaining health was a challenge when a cholera epidemic erupted at Fort Riley, Kansas, in August, killing 75 to 100 men including the commander, Major E. A. Ogden.

During the five years that Mathew was enlisted in the Army, the skirmishes and scouting against the Indians were continuous. On August 17, 1854, a cow wandered away from the Mormon wagon train. A group of Sioux camping near Fort Laramie found and butchered the cow. Lt Grattan, a young Army officer, took 30 men to arrest the man visiting from another tribe who had taken the cow. Lt Grattan, who was inexperienced, handled the situation improperly and was not willing to negotiate with the Chief, who had offered a horse or cow from his herd. The immigrant wanted $25.00. Unfortunately, the owner of the cow shot the Chief in the back, killing him. The tribe reacted by killing Grattan and all the soldiers of his detachment.

President Pierce, in retaliation for the deaths of Lt Grattan and his troops, ordered Brigadier General William Harney and Colonel Philip St. George Cooke to punish the Sioux. Colonel Harney took 600 soldiers to retaliate. They engaged the Sioux on September 3, 1855, at the Battle of Blue Water Creek near Ash Hollow in Nebraska Territory. Blue Water Creek was two miles from Ash Hallow, a popular stopping place for the wagon trains to take respite. Fortunately, Mat was not involved in this campaign. The troops killed 86 Sioux, half of whom were women and children. Seventy men, women, and children were captured. The New York Times called the Army's action the Harney massacre and labeled Harney and his men "butchers." Harney has gained a reputation as a violent, and cruel leader with a lack of concern for his troops. A fragile peace was kept for seven years. The battles with the Sioux's fourteen tribes continued for years. The Sioux were proud, powerful people, and when pushed, they responded with defiance and warfare. They unwillingly signed a peace treaty.

Battle of Blue Water, near Ash Hollow, Nebraska.[12]

Mat knew many of the men from the 1st Cavalry when he trained at Jefferson Barracks. The 1st U.S. Cavalry was made up almost entirely of Irishmen, though one heard a variety of languages. Colonel Sumner arrived at Fort Leavenworth, Kansas to take command in August 1855 to protect the settlers against the Cheyenne and to keep the peace between the pro-slavery and abolitionists, or Free-State groups. Col Sumner was known to be a great leader, and his appearance commanded respect from his troops. Mat felt it would be a privilege to have Col Sumner as his commanding officer. On September 7, 1855, he asked for a transfer to Company B of the 1st Cavalry. The Army noted that Mat was "recommended for favorable consideration. Pvt. Hayden is a good soldier, and I think he will be a useful man wherever he maybe." The 2nd Dragoons were raided by Col Sumner, for good soldiers and Mat was transferred.

Mats units were always concerned with supplies and weather. The heaviest supplies were rations of six pounds of corn a day for the horses and mules. The storms often came from the Northeast, bringing pounding rain, snow, and hard frost. The soldiers made ineffectual attempts to look for grass for their animals in the heat of summer and late winter.

In 1854, the Kansas-Nebraska Act, which effectively repealed the 1920 Missouri Compromise, was passed. It rekindled issues of slavery and resulted in armed conflicts known as 'Bleeding Kansas." It allowed settlers to decide whether to make their territory a free state or a slave state. President Pierce promised his support for the bill if the Senate would support his appointments and foreign policy.

The Dragoons were present with Chandler's expedition against the Navajo and Apache in March and April 1856. Much of the dragoon work was supporting the settlers and wagons moving west. The 1st Dragoons also removed intruders from Indian lands and settled disturbances.

The pro-slavers, abolitionists, and Free-Staters, had violent confrontations in Eastern Kansas and Western Missouri over the issue of slavery. Mat was involved as Captain Sackett's 1st Cavalry would have expeditions on the Kansas-Nebraska border beginning in 1855 during the Bleeding Kansas period. On December 1, 1855, Governor Wilson Shannon of Kansas telegraphed President Pierce for permission to call upon Col Sumner's 1st Cavalry at Fort Leavenworth, Kansas. Col Sumner wrote Governor Shannon, agreeing to move his troops on a moment's notice with orders from President Pierce.

The violence escalated on the 4th of July, 1856. Colonel Sumner ordered the 1st Cavalry to march to the Delaware crossing of the Kansas River. They received a dispatch ordering them into Lawrence to prevent an attack [13] A congressional investigation committee found the elections in Kansas to be unjustly prejudiced by border ruffians. President Pierce recognized the pro-slavery legislature as the legal government of Kansas. He would not recognize the election fraud when it was found that many of the voters were not residents of the state. Col Sumner was tasked with keeping the peace and dispersing the illegally convening Free-State Legislature while pointing a cannon at Constitution Hall. After five Southern states withdrew from the Union, the Senate passed a law to make Kansas a free state on January 29, 1861.

Col Sumner left Fort Leavenworth on May 18, 1857, to engage in a campaign against the Cheyenne. The Cheyenne had attacked a wagon train, killing twelve people and kidnapping two. They traveled with one company of the Second Dragoons, two squadrons of the 1st Cavalry, four companies of the 6th Infantry, and five Pawnee Scouts to Fort Kearny. Mat traveled with this expedition as his five-year commitment was almost complete. He mustered out of the military the day before reaching Fort Kearny at the Little Blue River in Nebraska Territory on June 3, 1857. Mat was pleased to have served. He was given a government draft for his pay and travel fees, payable when the government had funds. He was 25 years old and received an honorable discharge as a private.

Mathew transitioned to civilian life at Fort Kearny, near the Platte River in Nebraska Territory. The fort had been named for Major General Stephen W. Kearny, who helped win New Mexico and California for the United States. The original Fort Kearny, 117 miles to the east, was abandoned and moved to a better location along the Platte River to help support wagon trains. Major General Kearny was appointed Governor of Veracruz, Mexico, where he contracted yellow fever. He returned to St. Louis and died at 54 in 1848. The hemorrhagic symptoms of yellow fever, known as "black vomit," affected the liver and killed 8-12,000 Americans in New Orleans in 1853.

By 1849, 4,000 migrants and gold seekers had passed by the fort. The buildings provided good protection from the dusty wind, summer thunderstorms, and lightning strikes. The barracks were two stories high but quickly became overcrowded with eighty soldiers and frontier men. The soldiers' uniforms were threadbare, and the men were unshaven. The store sold goods at cost, and some supplies were given to the indigent.

The prairie schooner was the preferred wagon, as it was smaller and lighter than a Conestoga wagon and easier to repair. The prairie schooner was two to three feet deep and could be made watertight. Some migrants used prairie schooners or farm wagons with mules to travel faster. The wagon was loaded with wheels, axles, tools, grinding stones, and supplies that helped migrants cross to Oregon or California. The pioneers carried barrels of pickles that were high in vitamin C to help prevent scurvy, as fresh fruits and vegetables were meager. Between 1840 and 1860, fewer than 350 migrants were killed by Indians, and 12,500 to 20,000 migrants died from wagon accidents, gunshots, diseases, and drowning.

Mat traveled with Col Sumner to Fort Laramie with his men, three hundred cattle, and fifty-one wagons. Col Sumner then proceeded to St. Vrain to meet Major Sedgewick on the 4th of July. The two groups confronted the Cheyenne on July 29, 1857, at the Battle of Solomon Fork. They encircled three hundred Cheyenne and attacked, yelling and waving their sabers. The Cheyenne scattered in different directions with the soldiers in pursuit, chasing them for seven miles. The Cheyenne horses were stronger and faster, resulting in a short skirmish. Several of the Cheyenne carried weapons such as rifles and sabers. It was the first battle soldiers had against the Cheyenne Nation. Two of the troops were killed, and eight were wounded. Nine Cheyenne were killed. The troops could not catch them, but they did come upon an abandoned village and burned the 170 lodges.

Mat heard of a large contingent of troops to be deployed to Utah territory. He was hired on as a teamster in July to accompany a wagon train traveling with troops. Mat knew the dangers and the time it would take, but he agreed to be a bullwhacker driving a supply wagon to Fort Bridger. He was pleased to be a private contractor and to have put his years in the army behind him. The Army allowed Mat to keep his Bay and he felt confident they both would survive the journey west. After Fort Bridger, he planned to continue to Oregon Territory, where he heard of land to farm. He knew he would find work and achieve his goals.

Mat worked with the Army to train oxen, mules, and horses to prepare for the arduous journey to Bridger's Trading Post. The oxen ate less forage and were the slowest, taking the pioneers a month longer to reach their destination. The oxen cost about $2.00 a pair, whereas a horse or mule was twice as much. Oxen were male or female cattle educated to be draft animals. They were economical for the pioneers as they would provide milk, and their horns prevented the yoke from sliding over their heads when traveling downhill. Horses were the fastest, but not as strong. They required more feed and were more likely to be stolen. The oxen were better in mud and rough terrain because the hooves expanded for better traction. The mules ate less foliage than horses and were not as strong as oxen. Mat looked forward to trips that usually took four to six months if they did not have to stop for the winter. Families pushed to reach Fort Bridger[14] or Fort Hall before being caught in the winter snow, which could be dangerous for the pioneers and the livestock.

Following the campaign at Solomon Fork, Col Sumner's men proceeded to Fort Laramie to join the military contingent on their way to Utah in the summer of 1857. President Buchanan ordered 2,500 troops to restore government authority to Utah territory. Mormon leaders, distrustful of the government, stated they would defend their territory and organize a militia. President Buchanan wanted to replace Brigham Young as governor of Utah Territory to settle issues with the Mormons, who disagreed with the United States government on the rule of law and polygamy.

Sketch by Eugene Antoine Samuels Lavieille, 1820-1889.[15]

Children of immigrants were expected to help. They collected buffalo chips to build fires for warmth and cooking meals. They fetched water from the nearby streams and helped watch younger children. The older children kept journals, played string games, and guessing games.

Westward Bound

Mat spent evenings with other soldiers at the saloon playing cards. He possessed the "luck of the Irish" and became skilled at bluffing. He kept his pocketbook close to his body and did not tell anyone about the money he carried. Mat was frugal. Camp sutlers sold whiskey and commanders rewarded their troops with a drink. Mat saw what drink did to many of his fellow men and restrained himself from drinking.

Nebraska's rolling plateaus and hot spring weather gave Matt a chance to get away from the Fort to hunt buffalo or pronghorn antelope. He tanned and sold hides to traders for gunpowder, and he hired an Indian woman to make him a new set of buckskin breeches, blouses, and moccasins. Mat considered settling in Nebraska, where many of his fellow soldiers were, but was aware of prairie fires and that the locusts ate everything in their path, including the family's laundry or harnesses that were left out.

Encampment along the Platte by Worthington Whittredge, 1865.[16]

The immigrants had to make three difficult river crossings. The first was on the South Platte, the second was on the Laramie River near the fort, and the third was on the North Platte River where Casper, Wyoming, is today. When the migrants crossed the river, they used a windlass to slowly lower the wagon down the steep slopes. Willow poles were used to stabilize sandbars. In early spring, the rivers were often high. When the water was deeper than four feet, the pioneers converted their wagons into small boats. If trees were available, they made rafts or canoes from logs. Rivers were dangerous, and spooked animals could cause wagons to capsize, resulting in the deaths of animals and travelers.

From Mat's experiences, he was familiar with the challenges the pioneers faced. The pioneers followed Indian and fur trading trails near rivers. They rested in the evening around campfires, cooking and organizing for the next day. They crossed mountain ranges and passed through the territory of several Indian tribes. Fort Laramie, was a welcomed respite as they were one-third of the way. Fort Laramie grew into a large military base to support the influx of travelers in 1849 due to the California gold rush. Unfortunately, prices were outrageously high, and tobacco cost a dollar. The travelers purchased it for a nickel in St. Louis. Many of the migrants wanted to sell their excess baggage, but the people at Fort Laramie were not buying. Abandoned household goods became "Leeverites," meaning "leave it right here." The trail was littered with clocks, books, mirrors, and furniture. The migrants knew that the next step was a long and laborious trek, and the regulars at the Fort took every advantage of them. Many animals died on the trail due to injury.

The Rocky Mountains loomed over the dry plain. Huge cottonwood trees along the river provided shade for the migrants, especially if repairs were needed. Wildlife was plentiful, as jackrabbits, sage grouse, elk, buffalo, and pronghorn antelope provided the sustenance the pioneers needed. By 1860, hunting had become limited as buffalo were scarce. Many carcasses and bones of oxen lined the trail. In dry conditions, migrants would soak their wooden wheels in water to keep them swollen so they would not break the metal rim. A few migrants turned back, while others took their chances by trying shortcuts, but most stayed on the main trails and went on to California or Oregon.

En route to Fort Bridger, news broke that a group of Arkansas migrants that stopped to rest and regroup their head of 800 cattle at Mountain Meadows on September 11, 1857, were slaughtered by gun-wielding Mormon men. One hundred and twenty unarmed migrants died, and seventeen of the children under eight were 'adopted' by Mormon families. The personal belongings of the migrants were auctioned off at the LDS tithing office in Cedar City. Buchanan's administration sought to quell what it perceived to be a rebellion by the Mormons. In October, six men of the Aiken party were captured by Morman militia but released, only to be murdered by them and $25,000 stolen. Mat and his unit were aware of the increasing tensions between the Mormons and the U.S. government. Many of the people became anxious in anticipation of a confrontation.

As a bullwhacker, Mat was driving one of the supply wagons when the Morman militia leader, Lot Smith[17], attacked the supply train at Simpson Hollow, 85 miles from Fort Bridger. Smith's militia stole the mules, oxen, horses, and saddles and raided the supplies. In two days, the Morman militia burned 76 wagons. Two wagons belonging to one of the supply train owners, his father-in-law, were left untouched. The Mormon forces burned down Fort Bridger and stampeded thousands of cattle. [18] The Mormons blocked the army's entrance into the Salt Lake Valley, fearing the army had been sent to annihilate them. The troops were urged to push on to Utah Territory to help stop the resistance by the Mormons. Once again, Mat's valuable buffalo robe protected him from the cold at Fort Bridger that winter.

Most of the men had lost their horses, and there were few food supplies. The soldiers were allowed ten ounces of flour and four ounces of pork per day. It took the remainder of the train a month to go the eighty-five miles to Fort Bridger. The snow was two feet deep, and the people struggled to wrap blankets or anything they could find over their thin clothing. They worried that boulders and large rocks would be thrown down on them. At Fort Bridger, many of the civilian teamsters were assigned the difficult task of guarding the stock in the mountain valleys because the Mormon militia were given orders to annoy and harass the wagon trains by stampeding their cattle, burning the grass before and after the wagons, blocking the roads by cutting trees and stopping the people from sleeping.

The Mormons were fearful of annihilation when President Buchanan sent a large contingent of troops to Utah to replace the governor. In May 1857, President James Buchanan appointed Alfred Cummings, a non-Mormon, as governor of the Utah Territory. His wife, Elizabeth, traveled with her husband and the Calvary in November 1857 to Fort Laramie from Fort Leavenworth. She wrote her sister about the cold and the snow and how her foot was frostbitten and burst. Yet, she told her that there were many discrepancies between what the papers in Boston wrote about the hardships they suffered and what the facts were. Alfred Cummings and his wife spent the winter in a tent along with the contingent of 2,500 soldiers. Brigham Young accepted the terms of the government after negotiating how the territory would be administered. Alfred Cummings became governor on April 12, 1858. Young had 30,000 of his followers prepare to move south and not confront the army. They boarded their houses preparing them to be burned. They buried the stones cut for the temple and prepared food stores to be moved for their evacuation. By July 1858, the threat of war had ended. The press called the Utah War "Buchanan's Blunder."

Upon reaching the Continental Divide at the South Pass, the migrants were jubilant as the water now flowed to the Pacific Ocean, giving them hope of reaching their destination. South Pass marked the boundary between Oregon and Nebraska Territory. It was considered the halfway point after traveling 1000 miles, and they would continue to Oregon City for another 1000 miles. Many of the people preferred to walk, as the uneven terrain caused bumps and bruises when riding in the wagon. A decision had to be made when they reached the intersection known as the "parting of the ways", which was eighteen miles beyond the South Pass. If they did not need supplies and had full water barrels, they could take Sublette's Cutoff, known for its high winds, blinding dust, and lack of grass and water. It was forty-five miles and crossed a barren stretch of the country, but it would save three days of travel. Most migrants went to Fort Bridger.

Spring gave the migrants plenty of forage and clean water for the livestock. They were anxious to leave Fort Bridger after the long, cold winter and were very short on supplies. Early that spring, Mathew left the fort and continued to Fort Vancouver with the wagon train. Many of the migrants were indigent when they arrived in the West and did not plan carefully for ferry and bridge tolls, food, or water. They pressed on. The route was grueling, and it was important to reach Oregon before fall for fear of being caught again in a snowstorm. Everyone looked forward to the hot mineral springs of Soda Springs. The migrants took a hot bath and spent time socializing and relaxing in the warm waters.

Mat enjoyed being a civilian employee with the military but was relieved he did not have to go into Utah Territory and could continue making his way west. The Indian women who were married to many of the French traders had helped the economy by trading flour, clothing, and leather goods. The fort began as a trading post in 1842 and was an important stop for migrants along the Oregon Trail after Fort Hall and Fort Boise closed in 1854.

Fort Hall was sold to the Hudson Bay Company in 1837. James Nesmith, a settler, said the Canadian company dissuaded the migrants from taking wagons west. Fort Hall was a major supply post on the Snake River for travelers and trappers.[19] The Shoshone Indians were hospitable and helpful to the migrants. The forts' adobe walls were whitewashed, a welcome surprise to the pioneers. The food was plentiful along the Snake River. The men at the fort grew turnips, onions, and peas, providing fresh vegetables. The river was teeming with birds, ducks, and geese, as well as egrets, osprey, and cranes. Fish were abundant, as mountain trout and whitefish were easily caught. Fort Boise was closed in 1854 due to flooding and was not rebuilt until 1863 when it was moved 40 miles to the mouth of the Boise River. As tedious as the journey was, there were many beautiful warm days with blue skies and snow in the surrounding mountains. The travelers were beginning to see an end to their odyssey, and some began to enjoy the trail. The people at Fort Hall had told them how beautiful the Boise Valley was with the timber, river, and mountains surrounding it. Blockhouses were at each corner in case of attack, and living quarters and storehouses for the pelts were arranged around the four walls. Mat wasn't sure what was ahead in his future, but he was optimistic because he loved the country he was traveling through. He found the geographic formations fascinating as well as the differences in the flora and fauna as he traveled.

The Pacific Northwest

Washington Territory was an untamed land of rugged wilderness. The Columbia River winds its way 1,270 miles from the Canadian Rockies to the Pacific and is a major travel corridor. Mat loved the natural beauty of the country. His keen mind, energy, and reliable judgment made him a good leader. Most of the men wore full beards or handlebar mustaches. They were mountain men, prospectors, entrepreneurs, gamblers, and farmers who all seemed to have the same goal; to own land and make a living that would provide for their families. The workingmen wore sturdy lace-up boots, heavy work pants with suspenders, large felt fedoras, and a gun. There was an attitude of offhandedness toward the risk the men took with their own lives, and often an argument over a game of cards could be very volatile. There was a shortage of women, and when one moved into the area, she could usually choose among several suitors.

When Mat arrived at Fort Walla Walla, everyone was busy making preparations for Captain John Mullan and his team, who were to build a road to Fort Benton, Montana. John Mullan's road took seven years to plan and build. In 1859, work started on the road, which would be 624 miles long and 25 feet wide. The Mullan Trail was the first northern wagon trail to cross the Rocky Mountains, connecting the end of river navigation on the Missouri River at Fort Benton to Fort Walla Walla. It would usher in a new era of emigration into the Pacific Northwest. Two hundred soldiers and civilians worked for John Mullan. The men cut through the dense forest and blasted through rock, moving slowly. They were discouraged when Mullan changed the route to go around the northern end of Lake Coeur d'Alene. The road they had built in the south was prone to flooding. He gave the civilian and military workers double rations of dried vegetables to help prevent scurvy. The Flatheads and Pend Oreille were sympathetic and friendly toward them. When reaching Cataldo, the Mission built by Jesuits and the Coeur d'Alene tribe between 1850-1853, Mullan used it as his headquarters. The Jesuits and the residents that lived there cultivated 200 acres of land with root vegetables, timothy, and hay for animal feed. They operated a dairy and a flour mill, selling supplies to Mullan's road crew. On the 4th of July, 1861, John Mullan and his crew decided to celebrate at the top of a pass and took time off from building the road. Mullan gave a speech, and the men danced and sang long into the night. [20]

Today, this area is known as the 4th of July Pass. The Spokan Times[21] announced on December 13, 1861, that a hundred men working with Mullan "had cut every stump for one hundred miles, built substantial bridges over thirty-six crossings, and that all the crossings on the Coeur d'Alene forks were bridged." After a snowy and cold winter, all of the bridges needed to be repaired. The roads had extensions of corduroy logs placed perpendicularly over marshes. The roads were very bumpy, and the wheels broke. By 1866, the road was busy as "1500 horses, 5000 head of cattle, 6000 mules with freight, 2000 miners, and 52 wagons left Walla Walla for Idaho and Montana." That same year, 31 wagons came over the trail from the east with 20,000 people and $1,000,000 in cash.[22] When the road was finished, Mullan began farming near Fort Walla Walla. When the farm failed, he moved to California and found employment with a law firm.

Fort Walla Walla, established in 1856, was a spot for travelers to resupply before proceeding on the Walla Walla, Columbia, and Willamette Rivers to Oregon City. There was a wide range of grasses for livestock. The fort at Walla Walla was one of the strongest west of the Rockies. Some of the migrants chose to build rafts to float down the Walla Walla and Columbia Rivers to Celilo Falls, the first obstacle of the twelve-mile Dalles rapids. Near Celilo Falls is possibly the oldest continuously inhabited community on the North American continent. Mid-Columbia Indians have lived in this prime fishing area for 10,000 years. Before 1846, when the wagon trains arrived at The Dalles, everyone had to continue by building a raft or renting a bateau from the Hudson Bay Company for the high cost of $80.00. After 1846, a decision had to be made to float to either Oregon City if The Dalles and Cascades of the Columbia River were not too rough or continue by wagon on the new Barlow Road. This recently completed eighty-mile road went around the southern side of Mount Hood to Oregon City. It was considered the hardest part of the Oregon Trail due to its steep and narrow passages. Immigrants were not too pleased it was a toll road. Travelers who embarked from Fort Walla Walla by raft had 50 miles on the Walla Walla River, followed by a 200-mile challenging float to Oregon City. It wasn't uncommon for a raft to break up in the rushing water, with families losing household goods, animals, and their lives. The river did provide a bountiful food source of coho, chinook, sockeye, steelhead, and Pacific lamprey. Mat continued from Fort Walla Walla with the wagon train, mules, and his horse.

Celilo Falls required a portage[23]

Dipnet fishing at the Celilo Falls Cul-de-sac.[24]
On March 10, 1957, Celilo Falls disappeared under the
water when the floodgates of the Dalles Dam closed.

Fort Vancouver was an important fur trading post established in 1825. It was the Hudson's Bay Company's center of activity in the Pacific Northwest and gave immigrants a chance to purchase equipment to start their homestead. The Hudson's Bay Company provided Fort Vancouver's fur trading post with supplies overland on the York Factory Express from Hudson Bay or by ship up the Columbia River. In June 1846, the British and Americans settled on the 49th parallel as the dividing line between Canada and the US. The Oregon Treaty ended the decades-long land dispute. Oregon Territory included present-day Oregon, Washington, Idaho, and parts of Montana and Wyoming. The Hudson's Bay Company moved its Northwest headquarters to Fort Victoria, Canada. Fort Vancouver was allowed to operate, but activity declined. Dr. John McLoughlin managed the fort for twenty-two years and spoke several native dialects. Against Hudson's Bay Company policy, he provided aid and assistance to the American migrants. He started the first school in Oregon in 1832 and is considered the father of Oregon. He retired in 1846 at Oregon City's Willamette Falls.

In 1849. the United States built Vancouver Barracks on a hill above the Hudson's Bay Company's Fort Vancouver to establish a military presence. Soldiers at these barracks were involved in conflicts with Native Americans in the Pacific Northwest. The Nez Perce signed a treaty in 1855 that allowed them to live on most of their original land. Migrants and gold rushers moved into the Wallowa Valley, and the government demanded a new treaty be negotiated in 1863, which would reduce the reservation by 75 percent. Old Joseph (Chief Joseph's father) told his son to retain their land and never sell. The tribe was forcibly removed from the Wallowa Valley as outbreaks of bloodshed began. In 1877, Chief Joseph fled with his people over the Lolo Pass into Montana. Their flight culminated months later, 40 miles from the Canadian border. After fighting, eight hundred Nez Perce men, women, and children had traveled 1200 miles in 105 days. Chief Joseph surrendered and spoke his famous words: "I will fight no more forever." They were sent to reservations in Kansas and Oklahoma. Many of the surviving Nez Perce died of starvation and malaria. After years in this strange environment, the few Nez Perce who were left returned to Colville in 1885. Chief Joseph believed that "everyone could live in peace if all men were treated alike." He died in 1904, continuing to fight for rights and laws to be extended to his people.

When Mat arrived at Fort Vancouver, he found the area buzzing with activity. The influx of settlers to the Pacific Northwest was promoted by the Donation Land Claim Act, an 1850 statute that allowed any citizen to claim up to 320 acres in Oregon Territory. For a tribal member to claim the land, he had to become an American citizen and sever his tribal affiliation. There were many French Canadian, Métis, and Kanaka Hawaiian workers in the area. Mat hired a few men from the fort and the tribe to help him build a log inn for travelers. The Inn was a log structure and soon became a stopping place for a man in need of a meal and a dry place to sleep. Travelers slept on cots in the attic or near the fireplace on the floor when an ice or snowstorm kept them from moving on. Destitute people were arriving in Oregon territory, many of whom carried a foul smell as they had been unable to wash themselves or their clothes. Their clothing was shabby and tattered, and their shoes were stuffed with scraps of animal fur, fabric, or grass. They paid Mat what they could, but often they would help with chopping wood or cooking.

Below the Cascades, the Columbia River with Indians Fishing, Paul Kane 1810-1871. [25]

Mat decided to hire on as a teamster at Fort Vancouver, realizing that with the flow of immigrants arriving from the East, his own pockets would soon be threadbare. He carried supplies between forts in Oregon and Washington Territories. In 1853, Washington Territory was created from a portion of Oregon Territory north of the Columbia River and the 46th parallel east of the Columbia. Mat enjoyed traveling the countryside, but the trips could sometimes be dangerous if highwaymen thought travelers might have something of value. Mat typically traveled between Fort Vancouver, Oregon City, Walla Walla, and the newly established Fort Colville. It was 242 miles from Vancouver to Walla Walla and another 232 miles to Fort Colville. A trip usually took about 12 days, and he earned three cents per pound for the cargo. He didn't carry extra grain for his horses, as the grasses were plentiful for foraging. Mat would sometimes hire Native Americans to help the wagons travel around waterfalls or traverse rivers. He compensated the men with trade goods, tobacco, or blankets.

Mat paid a woman from the native population to manage his 'boarding house' when he was traveling between forts. At times, he was gone for as long as two weeks. When the Fort received news from Washington, D.C. and the East Coast, everyone was interested in what the government had to say about the Western Frontier and the Midwest. Most of the men were illiterate, and the news was relayed while sitting on benches outside the mercantile. Mat would go to the fort to catch up on the gossip before setting out on his next trip to deliver supplies to Fort Walla Walla. He often met friends he had worked with on the Plains. The Hudson's Bay Company abandoned its Fort Vancouver trading post on June 14, 1860, as the market for furs had declined. The military's Vancouver Barracks remained active.

Mat purchased eighty acres of pasture land and timber six miles north of Fort Vancouver. He had seen promise in Vancouver when he first arrived a few months earlier. Mat received an affidavit for his land purchase there, which was signed in 1887 in Washington Territory, stating:

Fort Vancouver by Gustav Sohon. He arrived at the post in 1854.[26]

Before me, the undersigned a Notary Public for the Territory and County aforesaid came Mathew Hayden personally known to me who deposes and states under oath as follows, I bought on the 11th of October 1878 a piece of property, more particularly described as The South East quarter of the North East Quarter and Lots No. 1 and 2 in Section 12. Township 2 North Range 1 East in the County of Clark, Territory of Washington containing 79 11/100 acres from Aldeay Neel, in consideration of Five Hundred and Fifty dollars ($550)" that Aldeay Neel owned a short time before that made final proof to above named property before the U.S., Land Office at Vancouver W.T. and handed the receiver final receipt to the undersigned, Mathew Hayden at the time made a deed to the above described property, which land is recorded at the Auditor's office of Clark Co. W. T. at Vancouver.[27] I do herewith state under oath that I made a diligent search for that receipt but could not find it and must have lost it and I make this affidavit for the purpose of getting the patent to above described land which is at present in the Land Office at Vancouver W.T. I used the patent for the purpose of having it recorded at the Auditor's office of Clark Co. W.T. to establish the chain of title. Witness: X. (written underneath, the mark of Hayden. Sworn and signed before me this day 1887. [28]

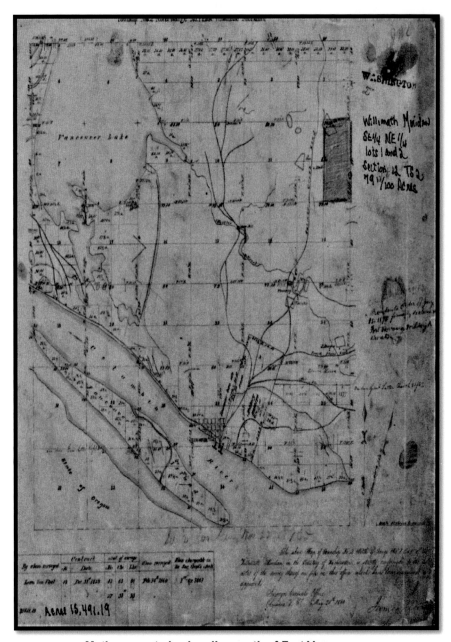

Mat's property is six miles north of Fort Vancouver

After owning his land for 11 years, Mat agreed to sell his merchantable timber in Clarke County to J.W. Maitland for fifty cents per thousand board feet. The official sealer would inspect, test, and certify the weight and measurements. Mr. Maitland was to take the timber clean, whether sawtimber or piling, within eight months of January 8, 1890. The property was valued at $1,200. Mat received a receipt from his friend, the Post Quartermaster, August J. Morritz, at Vancouver Barracks for taxes of $21.26. The real estate broker B.W. Matlack found there was little improvement, and perhaps only six or seven acres were cleared. He said the land was good, with little gravel, and that it was close to the VK&Y RR. He believed the land was held at a higher price than $20 an acre. It was sold to B.L. Morrisson in November for $2,065.25. Mat would be paid monthly according to the returns. He told Mat that the property was not selling as the work on the railroad bridge had stopped. August wished him and his family a "Merry Xmas and a Happy New Year." It wasn't long until Mat's property was sold. The next year, Matlack Real Estate in Vancouver sold the land for $2,085.25.

Mat first met James Monaghan at Fort Vancouver. Their paths often crossed, and the two men would become close friends and business partners for the rest of their lives. James was 21 when he worked for Bates Ferry between Colville and Walla Walla, carrying supplies. He initially lived with a brother in New York after leaving Ireland and came West by ship.

In 1855, the Panama Canal Railroad was completed, and James crossed the Isthmus of Panama in 1858. He worked as a ferryman on the Deschutes River in Oregon and helped to bring the first 125-foot steamer up from The Dalles of the Columbia River to within twelve miles of the confluence of the Clearwater and Snake Rivers at Lewiston. James started a ferry service in 1860 where the Fort Walla Walla-Fort Colville Military Road crosses the Spokane River. Ever business-savvy, he invested part of his income in 1867 in the construction of an eight-foot-wide bridge. Within a few months of finishing the bridge over the Spokane River, twenty miles west of Spokane, James obtained a government contract for hauling military supplies and mail. The mail from Washington, D.C. to Portland usually took thirty days and another ten days to arrive in Colville. He completed the work with a partner, Bill Nix, and the bridge soon netted $5.00 for a wagon carrying three tons with four horses, $1.50 for a horse and a man, $.50 for loose stock, and $1.00 for a pack animal.[29] It costs a quarter to go on foot. The people crossing the bridge were frontiersmen, miners, soldiers, government merchants, stockmen, stage drivers, carriagemakers, and Indians. James greeted the people crossing the bridge and was well-liked and trusted. He sold the bridge to Joseph LaPray, and it became known as the LaPray Bridge. Mat worked with James in his new business venture, helping him carry freight and supplies to the Forts. Mat enjoyed the beauty of the snow and the frost in winter. The snow-covered terrain and trees sparkled with ice crystals in the sunlight.

Native American tribes were shaped by the arrival of the missionaries. Father Joset arrived at the Mission of the Sacred Heart in Northern Idaho in 1845, succeeding Father DeSmet. Father Joset was a small, energetic man of 35 with a charismatic personality. He traveled between missions in the Northwest, settling in Colville from 1850-1857. With tensions growing between the settlers and the Native Americans, Governor Stevens insisted that Father Joset ride with the military contingent in 1855 into the Bitterroot Mountains. Governor Isaac Steven's objective was to obtain more land for the white settlers and to put the Indians on reservations. The seven Stevens treaties were poorly negotiated and misunderstood by both sides.

Hostility increased as miners and immigrants encroached upon Indian territory, which was reduced in size. Col Steptoe left Fort Walla Walla to go to the Hudson's Bay Company's Fort Colville in response to a request from the settlers for military protection. He ignored the warnings and chose a route through restricted Indian Territory onto the Spokane tribal territory by crossing the Snake River.

Father Joset heard of Col Steptoe's plans and rode all night from the Cataldo Mission to warn him of increased tension with the tribes. The troops spent Saturday night at Pine Creek near Rosalie, WA. Tribal leaders, noting the army's big guns, approached Colonel Steptoe and asked about his plans. He stated that they were going peacefully to the trading post at Fort Colville to help the settlers. The tribes said they would not help them cross the Spokane River or give them canoes. Colonel Steptoe decided to return to Fort Walla Walla early Monday, May 17, 1858. Father Joset arrived, sharing with Colonel Steptoe the lack of progress he had made in negotiating with the tribes to allow the Army to cross the Indian lands. He suggested a meeting with the Indian chiefs. Father Joset brought Coeur d'Alene Chief Vincent, but the meeting was unsuccessful as Chief Vincent would not speak for the others. Later Monday morning, the

Indians started to attack. The flight lasted ten hours. Two officers, five enlisted men, and five of Col Steptoe's Navajo scouts were killed on May 17 at the Battle of Pine Creek (Tohotonimme). Colonel Steptoe had been reckless, failing to arm his men properly. He had told them to leave their sabers behind and to carry only 40 rounds of ammunition. That night, Colonel Steptoe's forces abandoned their equipment and

Father Joseph Joset S.J.[30]

retreated undetected. The soldiers heard the beating of drums, and believed that Chief Vincent was giving Col Steptoe and his men a chance to escape.

Four months later, Colonel Wright launched a campaign of revenge against the tribes north of the Snake River for their attack on Colonel Steptoe. He and his men were armed with new long-range rifles that could shoot small balls up to 1,000 yards. He had Nez Perce scouts, volunteers, 200 mule skinners, and 500 troops with him. His orders from General Clark were to "attack all the hostile Indians you may meet with vigor, make their punishment severe, and persevere until the submission is complete." The first encounter with the Indians was the Battle of Four Lakes on September 1. The 200-yard range of the Indian muskets was no match for the Army's new Springfield Rifle Musket. John Mullan volunteered to help Colonel George Wright when he began his war against the Plateau tribes on September 5, 1858. After three days of rest, they proceeded north and fought again at the Battle of the Spokane Plains. The army casualties were minimal, while the Indians suffered significant losses. The tribes tried to burn the grass to keep Wright's men back, but it was not successful.

On September 8, on the banks of the Spokane River near Liberty Lake, Colonel Wright ordered his troops to slaughter over 800 Indian horses his troops had rounded up. The tribes could not comprehend what they were seeing. They burned food caches and fields to diminish the tribe's fighting ability.

Colonel Wright wanted to hang Chiefs Garry, Miklapsi, and Polatkin. Polatkin was the Chief of the Spokane's and had led two battles against the army. Wright wrote Father Joset on September 16, 1858, saying he would release Chief Polatkin, whom he had held hostage after trying to reach an agreement with the tribes. Wright warned Chief Garry if they didn't reach an agreement, their "nations would be exterminated." Many of the young warriors did not trust Colonel Wright, and a large group of them made plans to ambush the soldiers on their return through the 4th of July Pass. The soldiers would have to march single file for twenty miles. Father Joset brokered a peace with the Chiefs not to attack Wright's men. In retaliation, the soldiers took advantage of their firepower and chased the Indians with their sabers, pushing them onto reservations with the Chief's attack. Father Joset saved the Chiefs from being hanged by Wright, convincing the Chiefs to sign a treaty. He knew there were no other alternatives. John Mullan said, "The only constructive assistance given to the Indians came from the Society of Jesus." Mat listened intently when he was told of the ruthless and vindictive behavior of Colonel Wright. His wagon train had made it safely to Oregon by the Barlow Road and not taking their chances on the Columbia River and the Plains.

Qualchan, a Yakima Chief, was unaware that his father, Chief Owhi, was being held by Wright when he carried a white flag, hoping to negotiate peace and discuss the treatment of the Yakima tribe. Peace was not to be. ruthless with his retaliatory force of seven hundred muzzle-loading rifles. At Hangman's Creek on September 25, 1858, thirty miles south of Spokane, Qualchan was murdered by Wright. Colonel Wright wrote, "Qualchan came to see me at 9 o'clock, at 9:15 he was hung." Sixteen other Palouse warriors were hung the next day after surrendering. The tribe quickly learned that many of the whites would lie and cheat to secure the conquest of the land. Lok-out, the half-brother of Qualchan, escaped Wright's hangman's knot by swimming the Snake River with his sister, the beautiful Whistalk, who was married to Qualchan. Owhi was brutally killed a few days later in an escape attempt. Colonel Wright took three days' respite before moving north to the Spokane Plains. Mat was relieved he was not in the Army. Wright's name has been removed from the Mukogawa school campus in Spokane, and Fort George Wright Drive has been renamed Whistalk Way.

The Mullan Road moved toward the Pacific, and immigrants followed, trespassing and settling on tribal lands. Gustav Sohon worked for Captain John Mullan and was important as a surveyor, cartographer, guide, and interpreter. Sohon' was important to John Mullan's success. Sohon learned languages quickly and proved to be a good negotiator and interpreter, preventing many altercations. He had joined the Army as a private in 1852.

Battle of the Spokan Plain, September 5, 1858. The cavalry with infantrymen under the command of Colonel Wright. Gustave Sohon.[31]

Stevens County

The North West Company built the Spokane House in 1810, the first non-indigenous settlement in the Pacific Northwest. In 1821, the Hudson Bay Company absorbed the North West Company and took over the operations at the Spokane House. The Spokane River was not navigable, and it was expensive to move goods to the Columbia River. In 1825, the Hudson's Bay Company built Fort Colvile near Kettle, closing the Spokane House. The fort was named for Andrew Colvile, a London governor of the Hudson's Bay Company. It served as an influential trading post in the Northwest and an important part of the fur trade route to England. By 1830, the Fort planted 24 bushels of potatoes to feed the personnel at Fort Colvile. One-half of the potato crop was eaten by rodents. By 1838, the trappers at the fort would have snared over 18,000 fur-bearing animals. Fort Colville sent surplus meat and produce to Alaska. The Hudson's Bay Fort Colvile continued to operate until 1871 when it was shut down and abandoned. The remaining buildings would burn in 1910. Its location is now under Lake Roosevelt after Grand Coulee Dam was built.

A variety of languages were spoken at the trading forts: English, French, Cree, and Hawaiian. Mat was quick to understand many conversations. When ships stopped in the Hawaiian Islands, locals were transported to the United States for labor. Fort Vancouver employed 100 Hawaiians, and another 400 worked at river posts in Washington Territory. The Hawaiians were denied citizenship and land ownership. Many descendants now live north of Fort Vancouver in Kalama. Hawaii exported coffee, sugar cane, molasses, salt, and sweet potatoes. Hawaii imported lumber, furs, wheat, and smoked salmon. In 1819, three Hawaiians working for the North West Fur Company disappeared when trapping on a small river. Their camp was found, and trappers named the area Owyhee on their maps. Owyhee was the common phonetic spelling of Hawaii. A river, a stage stop, a mountain, and a county have all been named Owyhee.

The United States built Harney Depot in 1859. The barracks were made of rough-hewn logs with an unfinished interior. The sleeping quarters slept forty men and kept them dry and warm. A wood-burning stove glowed in the middle of the room, providing warmth in winter. If a man slept at the end of the barracks, he could be cold. The garrison had over 350 acres of tillable land and five square miles of pasture for cattle and horses. The troops planted wheat, oats, peas, potatoes, and barley. Mat felt at home with his compatriots in the military. They would go fishing at Kettle Falls for salmon and have wonderful fish dinners with potatoes and greens. They also purchased dried salmon from the tribe.

Mat arrived at Harney Depot in August 1860 and found himself at the fort's first Christmas dinner. The British at Hudson's Bay Fort Colvile were occasional guests at the U.S. Army Fort Colville. A British officer, Lt. Samuel Anderson, describes a Christmas feast in 1860: "The Americans at the garrison celebrated Christmas in their usual way, one man stabbed, another shot at, several heads broken, and eyes blackened, accompanied with several other incidents of a minor character, such as their military surgeon breaking his fist in some pugilistic encounter with a citizen. At dinner, they have a curious fancy of heaping all kinds of miscellaneous articles on their plate at the same time and don't seem to care for a change of plates. They all make a practice of putting their knives into their mouths, diving into the salt with their knives, for they are not aware of the existence of salt spoons and we had to drink sherry out of liqueur glasses!"[32]

Mat began to spend more time at the newly established Harney's Depot. It was renamed Fort Colville in August 1860. Mat hoped he would find better opportunities in Fort Colville. It was a fast-growing community with forty buildings that included a church, hospital, pharmacy, school, library, dairy farms, fruit orchards, gristmill, and sawmill. Mat's application for a homestead claim was accepted. He made plans to further invest in land.

In the 1860 census, Mat was listed at Harney Depot in Washington Territory. [33] The surveyors at Harney Depot established and cut the border on the 49th parallel between Canada and the United States. Brigadier General William S. Harney authorized the fort to protect settlers and miners who encroached on Indian lands, as Americans did not have a treaty with the tribes. As a young officer, Brigadier General Harney was at Jefferson Barracks in 1834 and was known to be mean, vicious, and ambitious. He had been court-martialed four times and had murdered his sister-in-law's slave, Hannah, by beating her in 1934. Harney was acquitted of the woman's death.

Indian Bush Camp at Ft. Colville by Paul Kane. The Chualpays were fishing at Kettle Falls, Washington, and hung salmon to dry. [34]

Mat learned that Abraham Lincoln was elected President of the United States in 1860. Lincoln opposed slavery, and by the time of Lincoln's inauguration on March 4, 1861, seven states had declared secession from the United States to become the Confederate States of America. Sitting on the steps of the Mercantile, the people talked about the new president and his opposition to allowing the Southern states to succeed. On the 12th of April, 1861, Fort Sumter was fired upon by South Carolina, as they wanted Federal troops removed from their state. Shortly after, four more states joined the Confederacy, and the Civil War began. Lincoln refused to accept any compromise that allowed secession. No one imagined the war would last until the spring of 1865. Lincoln led the people through the Civil War, which ended slavery and promoted economic modernization in the United States. President Lincoln was killed on April 15, 1865, when he was 52 years old.

Two hundred and sixty-six soldiers were living at Harney Depot. Most of the men were recent immigrants. In 1861, President Lincoln required officers to retake their oath of allegiance to the United States. Four of the seven officers at the Fort were discharged with tensions rising in the South. The U.S. military had eleven hundred and eight officers. Three hundred and thirty-nine officers left the military, and most joined the Confederacy. Troops of the regular Army were ordered to Fort Walla Walla in preparation for the Civil War. They were replaced by volunteers from California, including recruits from Alcatraz to the concern of the local citizens.

In 1861, the Pony Express added a relay station from Rathdrum, Idaho, to Spokane. The riders were eleven to eighteen years old, skinny, and not over 125 pounds. They were paid $50 to $100 a month. Orphans were preferred as there was a risk of death. The horses were exchanged every 20 miles. The Northern Pacific transcontinental railroad route was completed in 1883, and news moved faster. James Monaghan opened a store next to the saloon where Mat boarded near Mill Creek. James became the school superintendent and justice of the peace at Colville, and he worked to supply water from Kettle Falls to Colville. James Monaghan later helped to establish the city of Chewelah, 22 miles south of Colville.

In a tribal ceremony in 1862 at Colville, Mat married Mary (Marta) Lott, a petite Kalispel woman. Mary was 22, and Mat was 30. A disproportionate majority of the whites who had moved west were men, and it wasn't uncommon for them to marry native women. A year later, their son Louis Antoine Hayden, was born. Mat was delighted to have a child and enjoyed the companionship of his wife. Mary was gentle in disposition, industrious, and diligent. Father DeSmet said that the Kalispel possessed "virtues they learned from nature." The Kalispel had converted to Catholicism when he arrived over twenty years earlier. Father Joset said the people were in "want of everything." They would often trade for guns, knives, pans, and woolen items. In 1865, James Monaghan married Irene, a native woman, who bore them two sons. James roomed with a saloon keeper by the name of John Utz while he was building his cabin. Mat built a cabin on Mill Creek, which flowed through Pinkney City. The land was breathtaking, with the meandering creek flowing through the property providing fish, game, and a variety of timber. His

45

neighbors to the south were Joe LaPray, Leon Peone, the Hallers, Bates, Matthews, and Dennises. The settlers that were east of Mat across Mill Creek were James Lafleur, Francis Wolfe, the Charettes, Ketts, and Wyns. Like Matt, more migrants, soldiers, and trappers began to settle. They grew winter and summer grains and vegetables. It wasn't long after the farmers moved in that the area's agricultural production doubled.

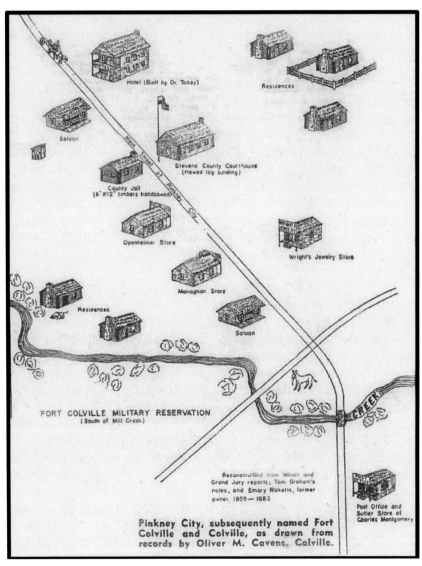

Pinkney City (Colville) was the seat of Spokane County, which was created on January 18, 1859. James Monaghan's store is on the main street.

By 1871, there were 1,000 people in Stevens County. At that time, ninety-one farms were prospering in the Colville Valley.[35] The census listed a four-year-old "half-breed" by the name of John Monaghan, but his father, James, was not listed.[36] Despite having a child with Irene, James married Margaret McCool, a white woman he had met during his travels to Walla Walla. As more women migrants moved into Western territories, the men often abandoned their native wives and married frontier women. In 1878, James moved to Walla Walla, where he negotiated a contract to supply the forts. Margaret was pleased, as it was closer to her family since James spent a lot of time traveling. They would later live in Coeur d'Alene City and eventually settle in Spokane. The Spokan Times reported on November 13, 1879, that Capt. James Monaghan made a successful trip down the Columbia River with a load of timber and freight for the new Fort that was being built on Lake Chelan. James hurriedly built two large flat-bottomed scows for carrying the timber, hay, oats, flour, and other freight. The paper stated, "Good fortune favored the brave but it remains to be seen if businessmen and farmers will embrace this golden opportunity."[37]

Fort Colville, April 1, 1879.[38]

James brought his sister Rosanna, her husband Tom Graham, and seven children from Ireland in 1878. Tom had emigrated from Scotland years earlier and married Rosanna Monaghan. James felt the family needed to leave Ireland as life was still difficult after the famine years. They sailed to Liverpool and boarded another ship to New York. Next, the family boarded the Southern Pacific Transcontinental Railroad, which would take them seven days to arrive in San Francisco at the cost of $65 for emigrants. From San Francisco to Portland, they went by ship. It is one of the cheapest and fastest modes of transportation. The next stop was to take a riverboat to The Dalles, where the family would portage around the cascades to catch a steamboat to Wallula. Their anxiety was high from trying to stay together. They needed to find a place to rest, obtain food for meals, and secure their baggage. They now boarded the Baker Railroad, which traveled from Wallua to Walla Walla. The Baker Railroad originally used rails made from wood covered in cowhide, but coyotes ate the cowhide the first year. The ties were then capped with metal straps, which occasionally came loose and went through the passenger cars, which became known as "coffin" cars. At Walla Walla, James met the family with wagons. The 200-mile trek took seven days to Chewelah, where they settled.

When at Mass, Rosanna said that she didn't know if Father Joset was "blessing them or cursing them" because she could not understand what he was saying, since he carried a thick Swiss accent. In 1883, Rosanna's husband, Thomas, passed away. James hired the Graham boys to help deliver the mail, despite being underage. When James was out of town, Antoine Paradis was in charge of his store and often took home the day's receipts stuffed in his pockets. When the Graham children reached legal age, they were able to accumulate property by filing homestead claims. The settlers dressed in their best on Sunday, and after church, they shopped at the open market in the spring and summer and enjoyed visiting with neighbors or picnicking. Foot races and potato sack games were popular, and betting prevailed among one another and local tribes. Mat became good friends with the Graham family and often stopped when he was near. He took pleasure in hearing the "gossip" of government news or the troubles in Ireland and what the country's situation was since he left home nearly thirty years before. Mat always offered a helping hand when one was needed.

Mat and James Monaghan continued to work for the military, carrying supplies between forts. He would be gone for a month or more. Marta enjoyed the camaraderie of her people and traveled with her close-knit family. She would take Antoine with her to fish and hunt with the tribe. They would dig the camas' roots in May and early June. The women would steam and dry the camas before grinding the flour and packing it into bags. In winter, they would coat the bag with deer marrow or bear grease to keep the flour from spoiling. As Mat traveled, Marta spent time away as well. The Kalispel were known to be wanderers seeking roots or game in specific areas and moving long distances in their sturgeon-nosed canoes made of pine bark and cedar ribs. The canoes were 10-14 feet long and tightly sealed with pitch, enabling them to travel long distances on the Pend Oreille River. Mat and Marta slowly drifted apart as their lifestyles were different. They never seemed to be in the same area at the same time. Antoine lived with his mother, and Mat visited when he could. When Mat was away, he missed the antics of his young son.

In the fall, the fluttering needles and leaves turned red, orange, and gold. They were a beautiful sight against the dark bark of the tamarack that would soon shed needles. The smell of the damp, musty leaves in the thick underbrush and the sharp chill in the air forewarned the families that winter would soon arrive. Miners, soldiers, and teamsters gathered outside the saloons when the weather permitted, and one usually kept the others up to date with the politics of the country and local news stories. The newspaper told who was shot over a game of cards in a saloon or when the girls from a particular saloon married. News from the Walla Walla Statesman reported in January of 1866 that the "Walla Walla territory" exported 7,000 barrels of flour, 1,166,000 pounds of hay, 459,247 pounds of oats, and barley, 581,265 pounds of onions, 42,462 pounds of potatoes, and 15,500 pounds of wool, as well as large shipments of hides and furs. They felt that they could supply Portland and reduce imports from California. The paper suggested that the people should grow tomatoes, as the soil was well adapted for them, and if they were prepared and preserved for the export market, they would "make a large return."

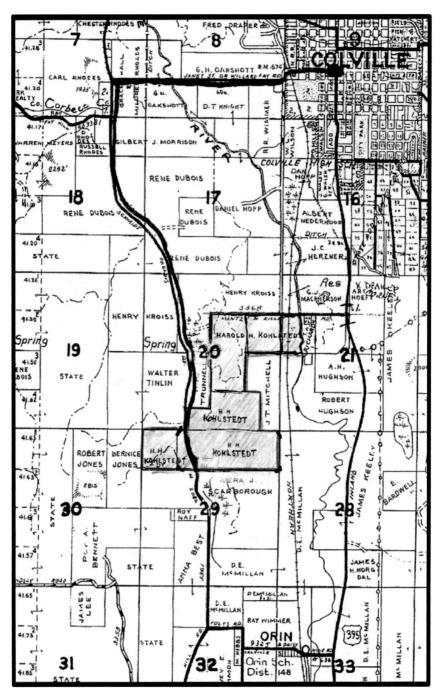

Mat's property on the map in the NE section of Sec 29, and Sec 20 and 21 is marked as Harold Kohlsteadt. Mat's Colville Ranch was sold in 1919 to Kohlstedt for $12,000.

Homestead

The settlers took advantage of the Homestead Act, which was passed by Congress on May 20, 1862. It stated that male citizens could qualify for one-quarter of a section (160 acres) of land with a nominal fee of $18 if they could provide evidence that they had improved the land and lived there for a minimum of five years. Their wives could also qualify for 160 acres. Mat paid $16.00 to a legal representative in Colville to file his application for a land claim south of Colville on January 20, 1871. Three weeks later, on February 10th, he paid the Register and Receiver another $16.00 fee to process his homestead claim for his Colville Ranch.[39] He included the non-mineral affidavit stating that, to his knowledge, "no vein or lode of quartz or other rock in place, bearing gold, silver, cinnabar, lead, tin, or copper, or any deposit of coal; is not within the limits of said land." At that time, Mathew's estate was estimated to be $1,000.

Mat's two witnesses for the Homestead claim were Fred Keiling and Joseph Lenrent, who testified that Mat was a single man over 21, and they worked with him for nine years. They said he built a house of logs 20 x 16 feet with a floor, roof, doors, and windows and he lived in the house and made it his exclusive home from 1865 until the present time. He assembled a sturdy stone fireplace for cooking and heating. He built a table and chairs and a bed with a straw and horsehair mattress. He slept on fur robes from the animals he had killed while traveling between forts. He plowed, fenced, and cultivated 80 acres including a fruit orchard. A good team of workhorses was essential and Mat knew how important it was to take good care of them. To ensure the survival of his farm. He erected a barn for his stock and hay, a horse stable, and a chicken house. His claim was approved on January 15, 1878.[40] **(A-1)**

When clearing the property of snowberry bushes and vine maple, Mat left a grove of aspen on the side near the cabin, which provided good habitat for wildlife and forage for livestock. He grew onions, carrots, and potatoes that could be stored in the winter. He produced crops of timothy hay, corn, beef, pork, and poultry. He sold his excess to Fort Colville. Six months before his homestead claim was approved, Mat rode to Colfax in Whitman County to apply for his naturalization papers. On July 1st, 1887, Mat appeared before Judge Wuiford to testify that he was a native of

Ireland. Joseph Mortin and F.W. Perkins acted as his witnesses, stating that Mat was of high moral character and that he had resided in the territory for more than a year.

In Mat's Declaration of Intention **(A-2)** to become a naturalized citizen, it is stated that he is a native of England and that he would renounce all allegiance to any foreign sovereignty, particularly to Queen Victoria of England. Ireland was a part of the United Kingdom of Great Britain from 1801 until 1914. In addition to his land claim and citizenship application, Mat applied on June 17, 1877, for a pension for his assigned duties during the Indian Wars. Eleven days later, he took advantage of another recent government program and applied for a warrant for bounty land that was issued to veterans. It was a multi-step process, and once it was approved, the government would issue a land patent to grant ownership. After 1842, veterans could redeem the patent in other states than Missouri, Arkansas, and Illinois and they could sell the land without ever living on it. Mat submitted his bounty land application but was told he must wait until his military pension is approved.[41] The government thought it would be advantageous to have war veterans act as a defense against the Indians. Most veterans elected to sell their patents to land speculators, but Mat signed an affidavit drafted by his attorney, W. K. Mendenhall, stating that he would not sell his land. Mat's application was officially rejected on July 24th, 1877, because he was not engaged in war during his time of service. In processing his claim, the Adjutant General reported Mat's service in C Company, 2nd Dragoons, from June 3, 1852, to August 1, 1856, when he was transferred to Company B.[42] He further stated that there was no record of being engaged with the Indians. **(A-3)** For $25, Mat retained Mendenhall, who was accustomed to soliciting claims in Washington, D.C. to protest the decision and to act as his power of attorney. It wasn't until 1892 that the pension was finally granted.

Chief Spokane Garry

Chief Spokane Garry was a leader of the Middle Spokane tribe. When he was a child, the Hudson's Bay Company sent him to a Winnipeg school, where he learned to speak both English and French. His father, Ileeum Spokanee, died when he was away at school, making him chief of his tribe. Brought up in both worlds, he tried to be a friend to all the whites and spent his life ensuring peaceful coexistence with the white settlers.

When a Colfax agent refused to register Chief Spokane's land, a white man commandeered the Chief's ancestral land, near Peone Prairie. Settlers claimed his farm with all of his livestock and animals. He was powerless to stop his property from being stolen. An anthropologist, David Beine discovered documents at the National Achieves in 2018 and found papers that gave Chief Garry the rights to his land. The papers revealed fraud by leading citizens in Spokane and the Chief of the Indian Division from the Department of the Interior colluded to confiscate Chief Garry's fifteen acres.

Chief Spokane Garry[43]

Chief Spokane was respected and known to be a kind and understanding man. He was progressive in his thinking and worked to help make the lives of his people and those around him better. He worked with John Mullan's team to provide guidance and assistance during the road-building through the wilderness. Chief Spokane started the first Indian school, a flour mill, and the first agricultural farm with potatoes, squash, corn, and pumpkins. Chief Spokane knew that if he didn't do something to protect his people, everything could be taken from them. He asked government officials to move 100 of his tribesmen to a reservation in 1887. Nina, his wife, and daughter Nellie were forced to move the family to a teepee at Latah Creek. When her mother, Nina, lost her eyesight, her father led Nina with great care and dignity. Nellie helped support her parents by doing laundry for the white men. Ruffians continued to bother their camp by throwing rocks and stealing from the impoverished family. A white man befriended the family, allowing them to camp on his land near Indian Canyon on the confluence of the Spokane River and Latah Creek. Chief Garry passed away in January of 1892, destitute. Nellie returned to retrieve their ten horses but found they were all stolen. Mat felt he had escaped many of the injustices in Ireland, but now he saw the same things being done to the Native Americans. Nellie moved her mother to the Coeur d'Alene reservation. She was a staunch Presbyterian on a Catholic Reservation. Nina died in 1900 and was refused burial at DeSmet. She was interred in Fairfield, Idaho.

Renting the Colville Ranch

Mat's Colville Homestead farm was producing well, and he continued to carry supplies between forts. He began spending more time at the newly established Fort Coeur d'Alene and Spokane Falls. He hired out the work on his farm in Colville and eventually leased it. A neighbor, Joe Stitzal, wrote Mat that he didn't have a chance to rent the property for cash. He concluded it would be best to leave it with John Rickey, who would be responsible for the farm and would give him half of the hay in the stack. Mat rented the Colville ranch to John Rickey. A letter Mat received from John asked:

> If you will fix the fence which I spoke to you about I can get the posts and the poles and have them set for $35.00. This is what it will cost. Besides the wier (wire) it will take about 350 lbs. of wier to make the fence this will make a good fence with the three strans of wier and two poles. I will take the ranch for five more years at $250.00 year providing you will allow me $50.00 for grubbing. This I will keep out of the first years rent and I will break up and seede the timothy. Sixty acres and fix it in good order. This $50.00 I ask is to clear the balance of the brushes of scatered willows which is on the place and you must have the railroad fence from Sulivans fence to mine along the track for if this is left open I cannot sow any grains for stalk will destroy it, pleas let me know about this at once as I wish to get everything ready for spring." J Rickey Six months later John wrote again to stay that the "I herewith send you $150.00. Hay is going to be poor on the ranch this year, but the Timothy will be good.

> *Yours Respectifuly John Rickey* [44]

Rickey leased Mat's Colville property for several years. In 1896, Rickey was sent $616.50 worth of lumber to make repairs. The invoice was paid to Father Philippe by James Monaghan. Two years later, freight, shingles, and nails were transported from Spokane for $43.50. In 1898, Rickey renewed his lease until 1901 sending a check for $1,000.

Hayden's Lake

In 1878, James told Mat of opportunities and land near Camp Coeur d'Alene after Rutherford B. Hayes had sent General Sherman to establish a fort between Fort Walla Walla and Fort Benton. Mat found himself intrigued and carried supplies for the Army to the camp. The trappers traded with the Indians near the lake for furs. The Indians called the men "small hearts which in their language meant Coeur d'Alene." [45] He was struck by a flawless lake north of Camp Coeur d'Alene, and his mind raced with the ideas he saw for the land: a ranch, and a town. He was overwhelmed by the land's astounding beauty and tranquil waters.[46] Mat stayed with Phillip Sellers, a single farmer on the Spokane Prairie, on June 14, 1878, whom he knew when they were both in the Army. He leased his Colville ranch and moved to the lake northeast of Fort Coeur d'Alene.

Boating on Hayden's Lake[47]

Mat was nearly forty-seven, and his dark, curly hair and neatly trimmed beard were beginning to gray. His body was strong from physical labor. Like most men of the frontier, he had a chiseled body and a rugged look, keeping a keen eye on what was going on around him. He occasionally smoked stogies. Mat was respected by his neighbors and acquaintances as a man who kept his word. The people who knew him often asked him for his sound advice when it came to farming.

An Act of Congress, on July 2, 1864, granted lands for the construction of railroad and telegraph lines from Lake Superior to Puget Sound on the Pacific coast. By selling some of the land granted to them, the railways could recoup some of their construction costs and pay off the stockholders who invested in them. Mat purchased from the West District of Pend d'Oreille division, 209.82 acres for $543.53 from the Northern Pacific Railroad Company, and the deed was granted on September 1, 1879.[48] The land grant did not include any mineral rights for coal or iron. The Railroad reserved the rights to a strip of land 200 feet on each side of the tracks, the right to the lake water, and the right to explore and develop coal and ore. The railroad required Mat to have a substantial fence to hold his stock. He or his heirs were to maintain the fence. He was to be free and clear of all lien charges and encumbrances, except taxes.

It didn't take Mat long to clear the land and cut a wagon trail into the ancient forest near the lake seven miles northeast of Coeur d'Alene City. Mat's cabin was cut from large fir trees. He hewed the logs and shaped them with his axe. He hired several young men from a local tribe to help him clear the underbrush and taught them how to put up the walls and shape the cedar shakes for the roof. The natives appreciated earning money that they could use for trade at the post. The first winter was cold, and Mat's cabin was not finished before the snow fell in November. He spent most of the winter in Spokane and Colville. He returned in the spring to split logs to lay foot-wide white pine for the flooring.

The water in the nearby lake was pristine, and it provided a filling meal of trout or waterfowl. The red-breasted merganser and mallards were plentiful, as were the ruffled grouse and cooing doves near his cabin. When he rode into Spokane, some 40 miles away, he purchased farming machinery from Knapp and Burrell. He planted potatoes and other root vegetables to be sold at Fort Coeur d'Alene, as well as timothy hay, wheat, and other grains. He produced three thousand pounds of potatoes to be sold in his first year. It wasn't long before he planted a fruit orchard on his property. Mat hired new migrants to the area and natives to help him work the land. He and his men spent warm summer nights on the beach of the lake, cooking trout or roasting small doves and ducks over the smoky campfire after a long workday. The men would talk of their lives, their military service, their home, and what may lie ahead for them. The only disturbance in the clear nights was the comforting sound of croaking frogs as the men slept along the sandy shore.

In the winter, the men looked forward to the warm fire with an aromatic game stew cooking and homemade liquors from the wild berries and fruit trees. The trees and brush provided prime habitats for birds, deer, and elk. The solitary brownish-yellow porcupine, with its strong short legs, would methodically climb to the treetops to eat bark on winter nights. One would see signs in spring where a porcupine ate twigs, leaves, and plants like clover or skunk cabbage. The new settlers learned to keep their dogs in at night so they wouldn't be picking out a nose full of quills the next day. In several of the large red fir and cedar trees, the scars left by the claws of a bear gave a warning to new settlers to be aware of their surroundings, Bears are good climbers with their long claws. Since they can run as fast as 30 mph and walk quietly on the soles of their feet, a settler could easily lose his life when coming upon one unexpectedly. When someone killed a bear, everyone looked forward to a fragrant stew. The hide would be tanned and provide warmth on cold winter nights. The women would boil the meat or dredge it in flour and brown it in a large pan until it crackled. Many of the settlers found the meat to be coarse, but all savored the tongue. The men enjoyed the winter days and, when they found the time, they would repair farm equipment to be ready for spring planting.

When Father DeSmet traveled between the original St. Ignatius Mission on the Pend Oreille River and the Sacred Heart Mission at Cataldo in 1846, he saw a beautiful lake south of Pend Oreille. He named it Lake DeNuf, paying tribute to a benefactor of the Sacred Heart Mission. He was the first missionary to visit and write about what would become Hayden's Lake many years later. Father DeSmet wrote of several Native American superstitions surrounding the lake. One local tribe called the lake the "swallowing monster" because tradition says a great whirlpool swallowed a chief as he fished from his canoe. The tribe feared the spirit's temper and avoided the lake. Another fable tells of two chiefs from different tribes who opposed the marriage of their children. The brave canoed from his camp near the Clark House to her camp along the west shore, near where the Bozanta Tavern

Hayden's Lake[49]

was built in 1907.[50] The young brave and the princess drowned when their canoe capsized during this trip. The father of the princess went to search for his daughter, and when he found that the young couple's canoe had capsized, he was so overcome with grief that he drowned in the whirlpool. Legend says that his body was found floating near Spokane Falls, though there is no known outlet on the lake.[51]

On December 12, 1989, the legend came to the attention of the District Court of Kootenai County in a lawsuit by Idaho Forest Industries, Inc. vs. Watershed Improvement District. The county wanted to prove where the shoreline of Hayden Lake was when Idaho became a state in July 1890. A previous suit was filed in 1911, and Pat Flood, John Clinton, and James Casey submitted affidavits stating that a whirlpool was visible at a substantial distance east of the dike in the 1880s. Pat testified that he helped Mat dynamite the whirlpool that had become clogged with silt and timber from the lake. He stated that the lake extended west and, the land was cultivated in 1884. Mat grew timothy hay, wheat oats, and potatoes on the land 600 feet west of the dike. The statements were not challenged by the Irrigation company when the dike was rebuilt in 1910. It was found that a "drainage sump or whirlpool would be consistent geologically with present-day conditions" and that a subterranean channel did exist between Hayden Lake and Post Falls on the Spokane River. John Clinton, a resident for 33 years, and James Casey, the road supervisor for the road district at the west end of the lake, stated that Mat put in the ditch and cleared the land of trees. The purpose of draining the land on either side was for cultivation. James stated that after 1888, the water gradually rose each year since the old subterranean outlet was stopped.

> Personally, I think the "Hntag'n" has reference to the whirl pool that was once at the south west end of the lake. It may mean "where" the water enters the earth. This was where the young man was swollowed by the whirl pool and finally came out at what is now Post Falls.
>
> When the young man finally came to the end of the underground stream, he found it impossible to get out. For there was a falls about the mouth of the stream.
>
> But, suddenly, he saw a bird fly under the falls and went out between the falls and a rock wall. The boy then came out.
>
> When the boy grew up and learned from Fr. Joset, S.J. and others about the Holy Spirit, who was sometimes represented by a dove, the young man exclaimed, "Oh; it was the Holy Spirit that showed me how to get out of the falls, Post Falls.
>
> Lo Lo

An affidavit attesting to the Hayden Whirlpool and underground stream on Hayden's Lake.[52]

Mat dynamited the southwest side of the lake every spring to keep the rocks loose and to prevent the mud from damming up Honeysuckle Bay. He drained the land west of the current dike. The deepest part of the lake was 178 feet, with forty miles of shoreline. It is seven miles long and three miles wide. Hayden's Lake, as it is marked on early maps, showed many inlets that were full of large trout and many nesting ducks and geese. The mountains were covered in evergreens, providing good timber for building and large game animals for hunting. He began plans for a town to be platted on the west side of the lake and south along the road to Coopers Bay, leaving the wide expanse of the beach for the people to easily access the lake for boating and fishing. Mat's plans included several stores, a saloon, and lodging where they were needed at the lake. James Monaghan planned to bring the railroad and tourists from Spokane.

Mat met John Hager, a man who had also moved to the lake north of Coeur d'Alene. John started farming on the Spokane Prairie in 1878 and later moved to the area where he took up squatter's rights, raising cattle and farming nearly 1,500 acres. He and his two sons, William and Charlie. The boys worked with their father to build a one-and-a-half-story cabin for their family. Fredericka, Mary, and Margaret, John's daughters, helped at home, and Mat often enjoyed a meal with the family. The two men spent winter evenings with a warming whiskey and reminisced about their days in the army. John felt that the lake where Mat purchased his property and built his cabin should have a name. He told Mat that whoever won the poker game would have the privilege of naming the lake. Mat won. Like Mat, John had come west with the army and had served in the 1st Dragoons, Company C, until 1858. He was born in Germany in 1830 and arrived in the States in his early 20s. He enlisted in 1860 and was involved in skirmishes and battles during the Civil War, where he lost most of his hearing. He served in the Army until 1870. John received accolades for his courage and valor in his service. Mat and John are both listed in the 1880 non-population census as living at the foot of the Coeur d'Alene Mountains. John moved to Coeur d'Alene after a hard winter when he lost his cattle in a blizzard and began working for the government. He died at 77 in 1907.

The mountainous area around Hayden's Lake was covered with an old-growth forest of ponderosa pine, cedar, tamarack, and white and red fir.[53] Mat built a second cabin at Yellow Banks Creek across the lake from his first camp and started a logging operation. He hired a group of men to cut the timber and float the logs across the lake. Mat's crew panned for gold, trapped, and sold hides.[54] Twelve beaver hides would purchase a gun, six would purchase a blanket, and four would purchase a pistol or a gallon of brandy. One hide would purchase 1¼ pound of gunpowder, twenty fish hooks, twenty flints, scissors, 1 skein of twine, 12 needles, 5 pounds of sugar, or 1 pound of tobacco. In 1880, dry or green wood was $2.90 a cord, oats were selling for 6½ to 7¼ cents per pound, timothy at $16.25 a ton, and fifty tons of straw for $12.00. [55]

Picnic at Hayden's Lake.[56] Picnics were popular and one could rent tents or cabins for $2-$5.

The Hayden Lake ranch was known to be one of the first local attempts at systemic farming, a method Mat learned in New York.[57] He rotated his crops and used composting as well as "green manure'" plowing the crop of vetch under to prevent erosion, improve the soil, and keep the weeds out. James Monaghan came to Hayden's Lake and established the first store and post office near the little mill. The area soon became known as Monaghan's Beach.[58] James platted the area southwest of Hayden's Lake and named the township Monaghan's land.[59]

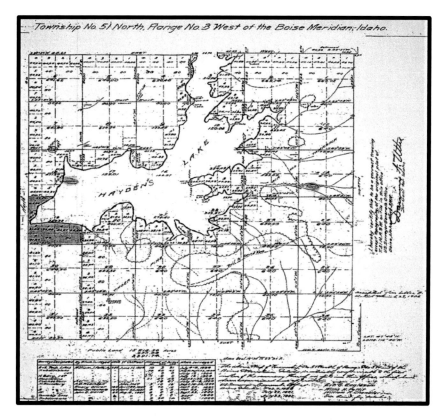

Hayden's Lake Map. Mat purchased 209 82/100's acres in Section 19 for $545.53 from the Northern Pacific Railroad on September 1, 1879. He added lots 6 and 7 and S1/2 and SE1/4 from the railroad with contract #3890. On October 1, 1883, he added 141 acres for a total of 350.90 acres. [60] The map surveyed by John B. David in 1880 showed the lake as Hayden's Lake. The 1905 map was of Hayden's Lake. The map shows Hayden's cabin on the left, circled in *red*, and Hayden's second cabin on Yellowbanks Creek east of O'Rourke Bay.

During this period, there were numerous lawsuits over contracts and land rights. In 1883, Charles (Cliff) H. Montgomery, the postmaster of Fort Colville, sued Mat, [61] alleging that Mat delivered to him a promissory note on the 12th of July, 1878. Mat admitted that 90 days after the date for the value, he received the loan and promised Cliff a value of $107.64 with interest from the date until paid in like money at the rate of 1.5% per month. He added that if a case needed to be instituted to collect the note or any portion, he would pay thirty dollars as an attorney fee. Mat was very busy building his cabin, and sawmill. Mat worked to improve his land around Hayden Lake, and as time passed, he remembered Cliff but never made the time to take a trip to Colville to pay off his debt. Cliff was a good friend of Mat's and the lawsuit came as a surprise to him. Mat paid him what he owed, and it wasn't long before Mat hired James Majors to do his bookkeeping, manage his property taxes, and keep up his life insurance policies. Margaret Montgomery, Cliff's wife, sued for divorce. She alleged that Louise River had committed adultery with Cliff. She threatened to kill them both. Between 1867 and 1907, the number of divorces rose from 10,000 to 72,000 per year in the United States. Divorce was more prevalent than most people realized[62] Cliff was involved in several other suits that involved promissory notes and foreclosures on mortgaged property.

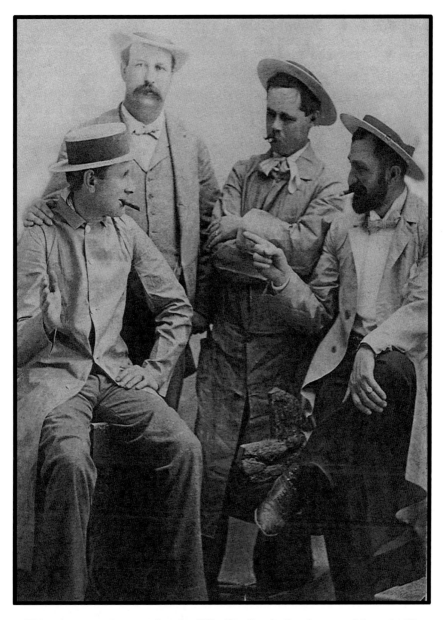

This photograph was taken by Elite Studios in Spokane and found with James Monaghan's and Mat's papers at Foley Library, Gonzaga University. The "best guess" is that Mat is seated with the cigar on the right and James is standing in the back on the left.[63]

Bananzy City to Murray

There were 44 people listed in the census in Bananzy City on June 14, 1880, and Mat was listed as a resident and a farmer, even though he spent most of his time on his ranch in Hayden Lake. Bananzy City was six miles west of Fort Coeur d'Alene.[64] The small enclave on the river grew up around George Wonacott's mercantile. George was from Canada and found his prosperity in building a store at the end of the stage line and ferry landing. The Bananzy City[65] census included General Frank Wheaton, his nurses for the children, servants, and a Chinese cook. Two of the nurses were Margaret Brinksman, 18, and Jan Robinson, 17. These women were not single for long. The town's teacher, 31-year-old Mr. Lackaberry, taught four students the rudiments of reading, writing, and arithmetic. Three other children were four, two, and six months of age. The town's saloon was owned by twenty-four-year-old Michael O'Conner and was a popular gathering place for people waiting for the ferry. They were able to buy a slab of meat with potatoes or beans. A small shingle business was kept busy making and selling supplies to the many new businesses and houses in the area. By 1898, there were only a few remaining businesses and some transit miners waiting to hear of a gold strike in the Coeur d'Alene's. It was not long before Bananzy City disappeared.[66]

Andrew J. (Andy) Prichard made his way through the pass named by John Mullan and his men, "the 4th of July", and arrived at the Fort on Coeur d'Alene Lake. Andy was originally from Ohio and had arrived in Kootenai Country at Bill Osborn's trading post. Andy left his wife and four children in Missouri and planned to send for them after he made his strike. His heavy beard, piercing blue eyes, and height of over six feet commanded a good deal of respect from other travelers. He had spent the spring and summer hoping to make a gold strike in the mountains without prospects. Andy was destitute. Mat first met Andy in the fall of 1878 at Camp Coeur d'Alene, which was being constructed. The camp was designated Fort Coeur d' Alene the next year. Mat hired Andy to work at his mill and farm on Hayden Lake. Mat and Andy talked about their days in the military. Andy had served in the Civil War in the 11th Ohio Cavalry Regiment. Later, Andy was with the Army, stationed in Idaho, to protect trappers and settlers. Andy worked for Mat for four months when he accepted a job in Spokane Falls at a mill. Andy was optimistic that the Coeur d'Alene Mountains held what he was looking for. He would return to the mountains to continue prospecting.

In the severe winter of 1879, Andy nearly lost his life. He needed work and moved to Spokane Falls for a job at the water-powered sawmill. There he met another prospector,[67] Tom Irwin, whom he told about finding quartz lead two miles west of Osburn[68] The two men decided to work together. Andy was advanced a 'grub stake', in Spokane, promising the Liberal League a share of his profits. The Liberal League was a group of utopian free thinkers who believed in the separation of church and state.

Mat ran into Andy and Tom in Bananzy City on June 14, 1880, when they were traveling to the Coeur d'Alene mountains. Mat had taken the stage to Spokane Falls and returned to pick up his horse at the livery.[69] He rode with them to Fort Coeur d'Alene. Andy and Tom picked up needed supplies from Wonmacott's mercantile before continuing on the Mullan Trail. Bananzy City was a good place for Mat to glean news that had developed in the previous week. The trip from Spokane Falls to Prichard Creek is 87 miles by road. It took Andy and Tom three and a half days to travel along the Mullan Trail to Cataldo. The men started prospecting along the South Fork of the Coeur d'Alene River and spent a year in a log shack near Osburn. The cold and hunger were more than Tom wanted to tolerate. Tom gave up his search for gold and left for Montana in the spring of 1881. In the 1900 census, Tom Irwin, 62, was found living with his wife and five children. He was working as a farm laborer in Mount, Idaho, which is three miles from Grangeville. He passed away in 1922 at 85 years old. Tom Irwin's career as a placer miner was disappointing, as it was with many men.

Andy was back at the Osborn camp in June 1882 when Bill Gelatt persuaded him to take him over the trail to prospect with three other men. He struggled over the brush-tangled mountain, following gulches and panning for gold in the creeks. Bill was a mountain man, and he relished the attention his bag of gold dust brought him. He could not keep the strike a secret. Bill later made a claim that was one of the richest in Idaho. In 1882, Andy struck a lode on the South Fork of the Coeur d'Alene River with Bill Keeler. Andy believed in Darwin's theory and named it Evolution. It was the first gold quartz mine discovered and was about three miles from Bill Osburn's store. Again, Andy found himself in a small cabin with three other men and barely survived the winter with little protection from the cold and snow and very little to eat. One man complained that the trees were as thick as match sticks and the snow was twenty feet deep in the mountains. Andy filed the "Widows Claim" in the fall of 1883 under Mary Lane's name. He had not filed earlier as he did not want anyone to know he had discovered placer gold, which could start a stampede. The Northern Pacific Railroad published a brochure that stated they were the only railroad that could carry seekers to the gold fields of Northern Idaho. A man would have to find his way through dense forest without roads for the last twenty-five miles. The Northern Pacific Railroad added fuel to the fire by passing out handbills promising gold and stating the nuggets found were worth $50, $100, or $200, which could easily cover the price of a ticket on the railroad. The pamphlets described the North Fork of the Coeur d'Alene Mountains and reported miners found quartz and placer gold at the head of Prichard Creek, claiming the veins had so much gold they sparkled in the light. Merchants saw opportunities to establish businesses in an area where the miners gravitated, Mat was one of them. He quickly made plans to build a lodge in Cataldo. Eight to ten thousand placer miners traveled to Cataldo and into Shoshone County in hopes of striking it rich. Miners died in the heavy winter snow near Murray. It became the county seat of Shoshone by 1885. Most of the major mines were established in a few weeks. There were a variety of languages and many misunderstandings. Murder was often excused and justified. Saloons were in canvas tents where gamblers set up card games to take the gold from the miners as fast as they found it. Andy wrote family, friends, and Liberal League members across the United States that the claims would employ 15-20,000 men.[70] He filed claims for his family, friends, and the Liberal League. The local courts decided how many claims one could file, dictating it was illegal to file by proxy for someone living out of the area. Andy was unsuccessful in claiming half-ownership.

Andy Prichard wrote to the Spokane Falls Review on the 9th of February, 1884. He replied to the many inquiries and addressed questions throughout the paper. He had built his cabin in 1879. Andy spoke of the difficulties he had with fourteen inches of snow on the 12th of November. He said it took him two and a half days to earn $42.00 in gold, but he left as snow drove him out. He warned prospectors of the difficulties with the amount of brush and fallen timber, the cold weather, and the danger if they were not well prepared. On the 6th of December, 1884, the Spokane Falls Review wrote that "jumpers have taken every inch of Prichard's property. Prichard toiled for months alone and is now a wanderer and others are getting rich: not a man who has found precious metal has profited by it himself." [71]

In 1884, Eagle City was the first gold mining camp in the area. Wyatt Earp and his brothers arrived, challenging Andy and others' right to tie up the land. The Earp brothers, well-known throughout America for their gunfighting, opened a loud and boisterous tent saloon three years after their infamous shootout at the O.K. Corral. Wyatt located four mines and instigated several legal entanglements. He soon became the deputy sheriff of Shoshone County. William Buzzard said, "Wyatt was the brains of real estate fraud and claim-jumping schemes. He sat in the saloon while his henchmen went out and did the dirty work." [72]

Arriving at the Mission [73]

Prostitution was brought in by the gold rush. An Irish woman, Molly Burden, joined the rush and set up a business. She let the town know that she would be taking the first tent in the row of red lantern tents. Most people couldn't understand her accent, and she became known as Molly B'Damn. She was a hard and crass woman around the miners, yet she helped those who needed a meal and nursed men through smallpox. She is celebrated every August at Molly B'Damn Days in Murray, Idaho. She died of tuberculosis at the age of 35 in 1888.

A packed steamer arrived at Mission Landing with miners and entrepreneurs looking to find a way to Kingston and further north along pack trails. It was 23 miles to Murray. Prichard Creek descended rapidly for eight miles, with the current running quickly through the canyons[74] Andy knew the river had rapids and shallow stretches. He described to Mat the earth as a rich black loam soil which was interspersed with small lakes that would be ideal and profitable for growing hay. There were several homesteaders in the area, and one could negotiate a grubstake.

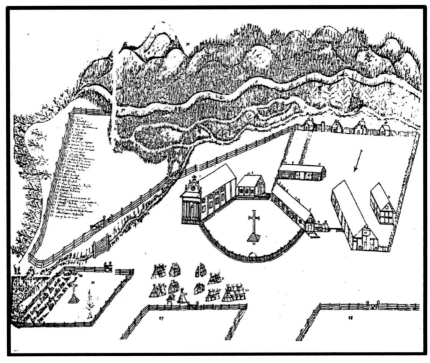

The sketch by Fr. Gilmore was printed in the Idaho Register in Boise in 1860. 1. Church 5. Rectory, a place for prayers and the kitchen 6. Refectory, where meals were served 8. Forge 9. Grain Storage 13. Carpenter Ship 14. Grist Mill and Indian dwellings are similar to a drawing made in 1860.[75]

Coeur d'Alene City

Father DeSmet described the land around Coeur d'Alene Lake as "the territory that enchants the traveler who happens to traverse it. It is so diversified with noble plains and enameled with flowers that are surrounded by magnificent forests of pine, fir, and cedar with towering mountains, ridge rising above the ridge, robed with snow, and their summits with clouds. The lake forms a striking feature in this beautiful prospect".[76] Father Point arrived on the shores of Lake Coeur d'Alene in 1842, where the lake met the Spokane River, and was a place where the tribe camped every winter. Father Point held his first service on the shores of the lake. He worked hard among the people, teaching them Christianity.

In 1877 General Sherman was surveying the land for a fort. He requested Congress build one near where Lake Coeur d'Alene flows into the Spokane River. Congress agreed and set aside 1,000 acres for the establishment of Fort Coeur d'Alene. The government was concerned because several nearby tribes were being moved onto reservations. The Coeur d'Alene tribe wanted to protect their territorial lands and natural resources but saw more and more wagons with settlers, miners, and gold seekers invading their land. They were moved to a small reservation eighty miles southwest. The government continued to take their land and allowed settlers to break the treaties. The army was sent to Southern Idaho to help quell the uprising of the Bannock tribe in 1878 and then again in 1892 during the Mining Wars at Kellogg. Soldiers were to keep the peace. They would guard the railroad and telegraph lines and any conflicts on the border with Canada.

Soldiers from the Fort Lapwai garrison were moved to help build Fort Coeur d'Alene. Colonel Henry C. Merriam brought circular saws and thirty civilians to build a mill. By 1883 the fort included *"barrack buildings and officer quarters, seven company officer's buildings, four staff buildings, an office, a guardhouse, a two-story hospital, a chapel, library, bakery, a blacksmith and carpenters' shop, a plumber's shop, a granary, a stable for pack mules, stables for one hundred horses and stock, hay sheds, ice houses, two kitchens, a recreational hall, regimental band building and storage building."*[77]

In 1884, the first official school was built on the NE corner of First and Wallace. Father Joset heard confession on Saturday and served Mass on Sundays if the Fort chapel was busy. The salary for male teachers was $53 a month, and women received $49 by 1893.[78] There were many people from the British Isles and European countries. The children would play a guessing game as to where their school friends were from.[79]

The sawmill provided lumber for the Amelia Wheaton, the lake's first steamer that Colonel Merriam built to carry supplies and patrol the shore. The post trader, Mr. Yeaton, owned a store at Fort Coeur d'Alene that was "strong and substantial" when complete, and the hospital at the Fort was the best in the territory. Coeur d'Alene City grew rapidly with the many settlers who had come west. By 1881, the 2nd Infantry Band led by Private Matteson, entertained families with a grand ball in the second story of an unoccupied barracks. The soldiers decorated the space with flowers and evergreens. The guests and soldiers ate dinner and danced to the light of sulfurous candles until 4 in the morning.[80] Coeur d'Alene City was a stopping place for people traveling to the mining districts of Prichard, Murray, and Kellogg.

In 1892, when the miners struck for more pay and shorter hours, the soldiers helped to quell disagreements. Fort Coeur d'Alene was a good assignment for the soldiers. The soldiers were sent to the Spanish-American War in 1898. John Fernan was in charge, and the fort closed two years later in 1900. The buildings were sold and Fernan stayed to homestead near the small lake east of Coeur d'Alene.

One of the early men to come to Coeur d'Alene was Tony August Tubbs.[81] In 1880, he owned a restaurant and a boarding house in Wallula, Washington. Tony married Hulda (Hilde) Knight, on October 4th, 1879. He had three civil suits pending involving promissory notes, and in early 1881, he was charged along with three other men in a criminal case for harboring deserters from Fort Walla Walla.[82] It was time to move. He sold his restaurant and boarding house and took Hulda to Coeur d'Alene City. The gregarious German immigrant staked out a homestead claim on land near the fort and worked for Mr. Yeaton.[83]

There was a large amount of timber on the hill overlooking the lake, and it could easily be transported to build the fort and Coeur d'Alene City. Tony wasted no time in seizing the opportunity and soon registered several lots on that hillside as "Tubb's Addition." He also divided the northern part of his homestead into building plats which quickly sold. By 1884 Coeur d'Alene City was growing as the gold rush was at its peak. Steamers began to appear on the lake to support the fort, logging, and mining operations. Tony saw the opportunity to sell his land to a steamer company as he had deep-water landing sites. It would be used to transport passengers and freight to Mission Landing. That spring, he planned and surveyed six lots that were 300' x 300' and located south of Coeur d'Alene City at the end of First Street. Tony planned a park near the beach where many activities were available. The Beach Bay Park was to be kept open and free for the people on the water's edge. The first hotel in the city was one of Tony's first projects. He worked as an attorney with John B. Knight, arranging property purchases in Coeur d'Alene City, and became the first Justice of the Peace, but found himself involved in several lawsuits involving a promissory note, a sale of land, a foreclosure, and the sale of his Hotel d'Landing. He was known to be flamboyant and reckless in his business dealings. Tony's pretentious air, audacity, and reputation followed him. The dashing man often traveled to Spokane Falls to promote his property by the lake in Coeur d'Alene. In January 1884, the Spokane Tribune said that Tony Tubbs, "the proprietor of the Coeur d'Alene townsite was in the city on Tuesday. Mr. Tubbs has a good thing and will make a stakeout of the property."[84] The paper went on to say that Weeks and MaGee started a stage line running three times a week, Monday, Wednesday, and Friday from Spokane Falls to Fort Coeur d'Alene, returning Tuesdays, Thursdays, and Saturdays at 7:30 a.m. On a humorous note, the paper stated that "roller skating is the rage." Many people skated over brick streets and wooden sidewalks as other modes of transportation were at a minimum. Bathing became a popular pastime in the lakes, and waterways when temperatures rose in the summer. [85]

Church picnics were popular on Tubbs Hill in the summer.[86]

Tony filed his Declaration of Intent to become a citizen on March 18, 1886, in Kootenai County. [87] He declared he would renounce his allegiance to William, the Emperor of Germany. A year later, Tony sold most of his property in Coeur d'Alene City and moved alone to Kentuck, Idaho, where he became head of the mess hall while providing meals for the miners working at the Bunker Hill Mining Company. Tony later organized the meals to feed the men in the bullpen in the mining war of 1892.

Hulda Tubbs filed a lawsuit on May 16, 1890, claiming Tony deserted and abandoned her in October 1887.[88] The sheriff of Multnomah County, Oregon, searched for Tony but could not find him. It wasn't until December 1890, that Tony claimed the complaint filed did not sufficiently state the facts for the cause of the motion. The couple's divorce was granted, and Tony remained in Kentuck. He sold all of Block 1 including 50 ft. east of the Northern Pacific Railroad dock and water frontage of 300 ft. to Jacob Sattler for $200.00 in December 1893. Tony married Versa Camp on the 9th of February, 1897 in Wallace, Idaho.[89] Versa was born in Washington Territory. She was fifteen years younger than Tony and lived with her parents in Whitman Country near Walla Walla before her marriage. Her father, Ben, was a farmer. Tony and Versa were boarders near Portland in 1900 where he is listed as a restaurant keeper. Tony died in a construction accident in 1925.

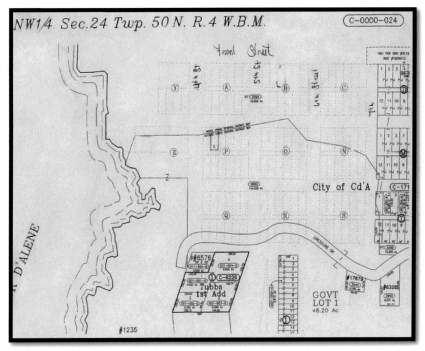

Mat purchased two lots in Coeur d'Alene City from Tony for $50.00. [90]

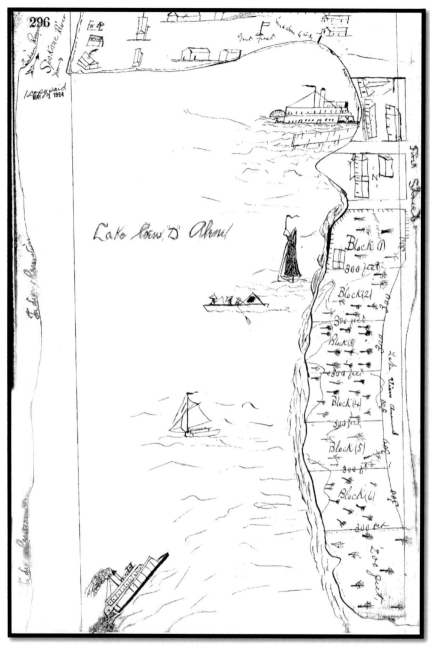

Approved by the City of Coeur d'Alene. Resurveyed Tubbs Addition D Plate Page 11. Recorded April 20, 1867, Book 50 Misc. records p. 308. Filed May 23, 1884. A line marks the Indian reservation west of the Spokane River.

Northern Idaho

The pretty Mary Maybens came from Ireland and arrived in Idaho looking for work and a husband.[91] She met Mat not long after she arrived by stage at Bananzy City in the fall of 1883. Mary agreed to work for him if he paid her transportation fee of $20.50. He agreed. He felt it was time to hire someone to do the cooking and help at his camp overlooking Hayden Lake. He needed someone he could trust to watch his property when he was away on frequent business trips. Mary would live in a tent near Mat's log cabin overlooking Honeysuckle Beach, where many men who worked for him lived. Her employment relationship with Mat soured, and in May of 1884, Mary sued him for services rendered[92] The housekeeper demanded judgment for $670.00 which was awarded to her on October 20, 1885.

Mat rented additional land from Pat Flood, who lived near him and owned 160 acres. Pat Flood was considered a wealthy man who was on the police force at Fort Sherman. One winter, Pat asked Mat to take care of two of his cows, and in the spring, Mat could take his pick between them. That winter, one of the cows died, and Mat with his good judgment, prudently chose the cow that survived. Pat passed away at the age of 80 in 1910.

Oscar F. Canfield and his wife, Ann, lived south of Mat. Oscar came to the Coeur d'Alene area as a prospector about 1878 and settled on the prairie. Mat and Oscar supplied fresh vegetables and beef to Fort Coeur d'Alene. Oscar's contract was revoked in January of 1881 when his family contracted smallpox, but it was soon reinstated on the 10th of February. His brother and a nephew succumbed to the disease.[93] Oscar's two sons later went to Montana to ranch, and his two daughters married and remained in Coeur d'Alene. Oscar would become one of the first county commissioners in Kootenai County. He passed away at age 88 and is buried at Evergreen Cemetery on Government Way.

Clement B. King and James Monaghan purchased and platted land that became Coeur d'Alene City from the Northern Pacific Railroad. In 1885. C.B. King and James bought the trade stores at Fort Coeur d'Alene and Fort Spokane,[94] from C.F. Yeaton, the post trader. James and C.B. King owned the post store, a dance hall, and a gambling parlor, "for the pleasure of the soldiers".[95] C.B. King purchased Tony Tubb's Hotel d'Landing, a two-story hotel, and renamed it "The Lakeside" in 1884. Monaghan and C.B. King had a propelled boat built to carry freight to the Mission. Captain Sanborn tried to cut them out of the business by charging only a $1.00 fare, while Monaghan and King charged $3.00. James secured a contract with the priests to be the only business that could disembark on reservation land and pay the Indians $2.50 for a cord of wood. They negotiated with Captain Sanborn to ensure that there was a sufficient amount of business for both of them. The men netted between $1,000 and $2,000 per trip.

In 1887, the Dividend Saloon had a bowling alley in the basement with a separate entrance. [96]

As Coeur d'Alene grew, saloons were added outside Fort Sherman. The Dividend Saloon and Fatty Carroll's Dance Hall were popular. The Dividend was owned by John H. Brown. He advertised 'fresh beer always on tap, and wines, liquors, and Havana cigars." They had billiards, pool tables, a bowling alley, and private club rooms with a lake view. Fatty hired forty disreputable women. The gamblers, transients, and others involved in illegal trades all followed, hoping to make easy money. Opium dens were not uncommon in the mix of saloons, gambling houses, and dance halls.[97] Guns were used freely as laws were not enforced.

Mission City

Mission City

THE KEY TO THE

~MINES !~

Commercial   Metropolis

of the

'Cœur   d'   Alene   Valley.

North   Fork,   Jackass,   and   Evolution   to

EAGLE CITY,

Through this point all need go and with the

Narrow   Guage   Railroad

Bud from

Spokne Falls

to

CŒUR D' ALENE
CITY,

Connecting with the

STEAMBOAT LINE

To the head of navigation at All stages of water landing freight and passengers at the wharf at

Mission City,

This is bound to become the popular route to the mines and over which all who consult their comfort and pocket book will go.

To all desiring to engage in business this is the place you are looking for. To this point you will have cheap freight by rail and boat and be able to supply the mining trade at a heavy discount on those who took their goods in all the way on pack trains. A large

Ferry crosses the River

at this place. A commodious hotel will be erected immediately and other business houses follow as rapidly as the lumber can be gotten to the town site.

For full information, price of lots, etc. Address,

W. ABOTT LEWIS,

PROPRIETARY,

CŒUR D'ALENE TOWN CONPANY,

Spokane Falls, W. T.

Mat registered his Mission City Homestead of 157.5 acres at the land office in Coeur d'Alene on August 30, 1882. [98] The Spokan Times Review warned, "No money, No grub, No Business" when prospectors were heading to the Coeur d'Alene Mountains. The area wasn't prepared to support the influx of migrants when gold was discovered in the fall of 1883. Many prospectors, mountain men, and migrants flocked to the hills of North Idaho in the late fall of 1883 and 1884 with rumors of gold. The men were in search of land, wealth, and freedom. The snow was more than ten feet deep on New Year's Day, 1884, and temperatures plummeted to minus forty degrees. Many animals and miners struggled with starvation or froze to death that winter. Tempers were short, and men died in gun flights. Beds made from fir boughs with a blanket covering them were known as "Idaho feathers." The beds proved to be comfortable for the hard-working gold seekers. Mat saw hundreds of poor immigrant men flooding into Idaho, searching for gold they would never find.

Mission City was advertised that winter in the Spokane Falls Review as the place businessmen were looking for. [99] They would have access to cheap freight by rail and boat, which made it easy to supply the mining trade. The advertisement referred to a "commodious hotel that was to be erected immediately" that was being built by Mat Hayden. The townsite was located at the intersection of Mullan Road and the Coeur d'Alene River on the route to new gold diggings, one mile east of the Mission of the Sacred Heart. The town grew quickly and was said to be a "prominent place and a firm location of a large and flourishing city." The telegraph line was nearly finished to Mission City in January 1884 [100] allowing people to communicate as far as Spokane. There were initially no amenities to draw people who had to pass through on their way to the mines. Enterprising parties laid out plans to build several houses, and growth was predicted to be rapid and solid. The paper encouraged people to believe that investments would be profitable.[101] The Coeur d'Alene Railway and Navigation Company line was completed in 1887 from the mining district to Mission Landing.

Thomas Slade of New Whatcom, Washington, loaned Mat $1,000 against his Colville ranch with 1.5% interest, which Mat used to construct his hotel in Cataldo. Mat contracted W.H. Hamilton,[102] the landlord of the Western Hotel in Spokane, to manage the hotel for him. Mat's Hotel Denver became a popular stopping point for many of the miners and businessmen planning to seek their fortune in the northern mining towns of Murray, Prichard, and Eagle City. With the flood of miners and migrants into the valley since gold was discovered, it was busy. The hotel was overcrowded with transients as many looked for a place to lay their packs down. Mat had twenty cots in the attic and several private rooms. The costs of grub and beds skyrocketed. Fights over drinks were not uncommon.

Father Cataldo became General Superior of the Rocky Mountains in 1877. He used the Mission as his headquarters for ten years. He had a solid working relationship with Mat as well as one of strong faith. The elder Father Joset became one of Mat's permanent boarders. Mat became a close friend and confidant of both men. The Mission had a building established for transient travelers and priests, but it was often filled. Mat was happy to help when the Mission was full, and his hotel provided warmth and shelter for the many tired people passing through. Father Cataldo had such an influence in the area that Mission City was eventually renamed Cataldo after him. It wasn't until much later, in the 1930 census, that Cataldo was permanently named an incorporated place. On May 26, 1884, Mat negotiated an agreement with

Father Cataldo, **(A-4)** "One hundred dollars of the two first installments would be remitted as pay for the board of Father Joset, that for the following installments would depend on how the business of the hotel shall succeed, and that if the hotel should be closed," the payment would cease. Father Cataldo stated that if, after the terms elapsed, "Mr. Hayden would remove the building on his grounds and they would not quarrel about it"

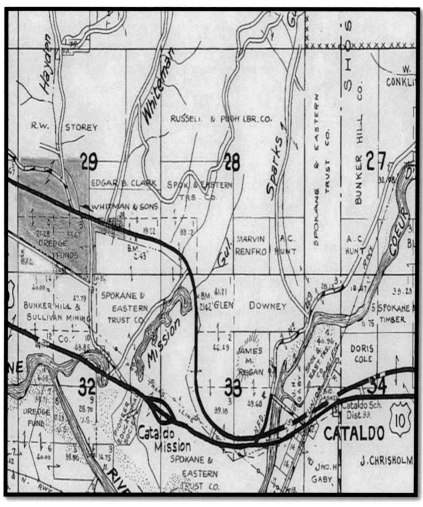

Mat's Mission property on Metsker 1959 map. Lots 2-3-4 and N ½ SW ¼ Sec 29 &Lot 1 Sec 32 Tp 49 NR 1 E.

Mat deposited and registered the Mission City Homestead of 157.5 acres, on August 30, 188, at the land office in Coeur d'Alene He received the Homestead papers on July 12, 1890, stating that he had made full payment for the land located in the Territory.[103] Mat built a cabin, cleared land, and negotiated to become a foreman for the Jesuits.[104]

Mat struck a deal with Father Cataldo that allowed him to ranch on the Mission property. The agreement was signed at Spokane Falls: "Mr. Hayden after paying $110.00 would pay $500.00 for the farm, $75.00 for one house and $100.00 as above next July, and the same on November and July after, and so on till July 1887." Mat hired several trusted confidants, which made it easier for him to run his two farms nearly thirty miles apart. The trip over the 4th of July Pass took three days, and he was glad to catch the Forts government steamer, the Amelia Wheaton. The Wheaton was used for hauling hay from the Mission for the cavalry mules and miners at Fort Sherman.

Mat purchased John Deere plows for each of his farms. In 1837, John Deere used a polished steel saw blade and shaped it into a plow blade that pulled easier than other plows. Improvements continued to make the John Deere plows productive and popular.[105] After the hay was cut, the tedder moved through lifting and fluffing the hay so it could dry evenly and reduce the mold. The hay loader would scoop the hay with the long forks to carry it to the top of the machine where it fell into the wagon, making farming more efficient. Mat's largest crops were hay, wheat, and potatoes. He hired Od-a-wah from the Coeur d'Alene tribe and paid him $140.00 for his work. Od-a-wah was hardworking and willing to learn Mat's new farming methods. He and other part-time workers would assist with feeding the livestock, baling the hay, and preparing the beef and pork to be sold. The wheat was milled into flour and large slabs of butter were prepared for sale. In November, Mat produced thirty-five tons of hay, two tons of potatoes, and five sacks of flour that he hauled from his Mission Ranch to the Landing to be sent to Coeur d'Alene City. The garden produce was used for his family and the hotel. Mat became a strong benefactor and supporter of the Gonzaga School. Mat enrolled his son, John Powers Hayden, in the first class in the fall of 1887.

Mat was always willing to take the time to help another man, and his reputation grew as a trusted friend. Charles Turner, one of the men who worked for Mat, asked both Mat and George Wonmacott to come to the Judicial District Court to act as witnesses for his record of citizenship on April 28, 1882. Pat Lucas,[106] who worked for Mat as his overseer at the Cataldo ranch, rode into Coeur d'Alene with Mat and purchased two Winchester rifles for $21.80, along with eighteen boxes of cartridges for $9.10, 4 ½ dozen steel traps for $5.10, two bear traps for $10.00, rubber boots for $6.50, and three saddles for $13.00. Mat gave Pat the traps, saddles, and boots to take back to Cataldo, Mat trusted Pat and paid him $3.00 a day with room and board. Lucy Grimes of Ellensburg loaned Mat money on February 4, 1887, to be payable on March 1st, 1892, against his property in Section 19 in Mission City.[107] He had borrowed against his ranch properties to support other investments.

Farming near Cataldo. *In* the foreground is a man plowing the field and a small carriage on the road.[108]

On June 7, 1887, the Spokane Review reported flooding in Mission City: "The whole of the narrow valley through which the Coeur d'Alene River winds its crooked, placid, way twixt banks of rush and meadows had been turned into a shallow lake from the Mission to the lake proper, by backwater, the tops of the brush and the trees standing out of the water as a careful Captain guides the boat up the only proper course amongst the waste of woods and water. At the Mission, the one lone hotel sits in the middle of a little lake and the rail cars slide around on water-covered rails. But the boat runs up close to the coach and transfer is made on a gang-plank without any inconvenience".[109]

Cataldo Flooding in 1933.[110]

Cataldo was prone to flooding, and again in 1894, unusually warm weather caused rapid snowmelt and water spilled into all low areas. The telegraph lines were down and the Pacific Hotel in Wallace was washed away. On June 2nd, the Bunker and Sullivan mines were closed for days as water covered the railroad tracks to Cataldo. When the waters broke through, basements and nearly every building in Cataldo flooded. The damage was estimated at a million dollars. The railroad bridge and the old steel frontage bridge were weakened by water and more flooding would be devastating. Troops from Fort Sherman had been sent to help, but upon returning to the Fort, they were forced to leave tentage and heavy luggage in Wallace and Wardner. The troops struggled to make their way across bridges that were washed out. The march was very difficult. When they reached the short line tracks at Cataldo, they were carried by handcar to where they boarded the Georgia Oaks. On arrival at Coeur d'Alene, the wharf was washed out and the area was like an ocean. The troops were exhausted, and wet after their march. The soldiers found the hospital, storehouses, laundry, and officers' quarters under one to six feet of water. Lake Coeur d'Alene was 21 inches above the highest level previously recorded. Two years later, raging floods returned to the Coeur d'Alene River. Lake Coeur d'Alene rose and breached the levee on the Dike Road in Coeur d'Alene. $7,000 was spent on pumps and pipes.

Flooding at the Mission of The Sacred Heart.[111]

The meadow land at the nearby Mission has been owned by the Coeur d'Alene Tribe since 2001 when it was deeded by the Diocese before being leased to Idaho Parks and Recreation.

The Garry Family

Mat's son, Louis Antoine Hayden, 21, married eighteen-year-old Annie Chittiulshe Garry on October 21st, 1884 **(A-5)**. Mat's close friend, Father Cataldo, officiated the wedding on a crisp autumn day at a chapel in Spokane Falls. [112] The marriage ceremony included a short prayer with the couple holding hands, and the family sang a hymn in the Spokane language. A feast was held with people from the Spokane and Kalispel tribes camping nearby for the fall salmon runs.

Hangman's Creek and the Spokane River provided Chinook (King) salmon for 8000 years to the tribes. Two to five thousand tribal members would gather annually to harvest 300,000 salmon known as "June Hogs." Many of the Kings were 60 to 80 pounds and some were as large as 100. The Coho (Silver) salmon migrated soon after the King. The salmon was smoked near the camp for winter storage. Fish were cooked by dropping hot stones into hand-woven baskets or over a fire. Everyone looked forward to having the fish with fresh berries the women had gathered. The festivities included children playing stick games as ceremonial dancing began to the resonating rhythms of drums.

Weddings were festive occasions. Among the gifts given were hides, horses, and baskets for storing and carrying dried food. The hides had been smoked and tanned and were supple and soft as butter. Chief Spokane's granddaughter, was beautiful with her long dark hair and eyes. She wore embellished knee-length moccasins and a light buckskin dress decorated with elk teeth, and beads made from shell, seeds, and bone. Porcupine quills, dyed with vegetables and minerals, added more ornamentation. Antoine wore a long buckskin shirt with leggings, a breechcloth, a belt, and moccasins. The breechcloth, decorated with motifs across the front and back, was made of buckskin and worn between his legs and tucked over the belt. His mother, Marta had sewn beads and quills onto his shirt in stylized patterns taken from nature. Chief Spokane felt it was a good match, as he knew that the white men were in his territory to stay. Mat had earned a distinguished reputation with the Spokane tribe as a fair and good businessman and spoke the Salish language with them.

Mat wished his son well and returned to the Coeur d'Alene Mountains. He packed the gifts of dried food the family had given him into a beautiful gathering basket. The basket was a work of art made from coiled cedar roots. The red color came from the berries and roots along the creek banks, the black was made from mixing coal or charcoal with spit or animal fat, and the white came from limestone, gypsum, or eggshells. He stopped at a mercantile in Coeur d'Alene to catch up on local news and gossip before going to the farm. Departing town, Mat enjoyed the trail as it threaded its way into the isolated forest as he headed north to the little lake that would carry his name. He would spend a day with the men that worked his farm and camp. The fruit trees he had planted were beginning to produce apples and pears. He would be able to sell the abundance of the crop at Fort Sherman. The day was magnificent in the surrounding forest as the trees were beginning to change colors with Tamarack turning a brilliant gold.

Annie and Antoine's son, Ignace Hayden was born on October 25, 1886. A daughter, Catherine, was welcomed on September 14, 1887, and baptized the following day. **(A-6)** Unfortunately, she died as an infant. Antoine took the tribal name Temsinhie, from the Kalispel language. The middle part of his name could be spoken or sung while the consonant clusters sounded like a whisper or an afterthought. It most likely meant *he didn't or doesn't*. The name wasn't transcribed and may have meant *It's not him, or He's not the one*. The Spokane tribesmen had several names in a lifetime, and they may have been given a name for a significant event, a life transition, the death of an older relative, or even because of an unfortunate or humorous event that would not be forgotten. Names reflected physical characteristics, such as *"Walks Like a Frog, Hump Back, or Fish Eye."* [113]

Four years after his marriage, Antoine died in 1888.[114] Measles and scarlet fever were prevalent and killed nearly half of the Native Americans in the area in 1888. Antoine and his infant daughter, Catherine, are assumed to have been buried near Hillyard. At that time, there were 520 members of the Coeur d'Alene tribe. Annie later married Joe Noser (Nozier) and had two daughters. She died in a car accident in 1946 near Worley, Idaho. When Ignace was a child, his grandmother Nellie and her mother took him to live in Indian Territory. He was registered in school as Ignace Hayden Garry to ensure the continuation of the Garry name. He would grow up to be the last Chief of the Coeur d'Alene people.

Four generations: 1. Annie Garry, wife of Louis Antoine Hayden. (Mat's son) 2. Joseph R. Garry, (Mat's great-grandson, and son of Ignace Hayden Garry). 3. Ignace Hayden Garry, son of Louis Antoine and Annie Garry Hayden. 4. Marta Lott Hayden Nicholas, Mat's first wife. [115]

On October 26, 1964, the Spokesman-Review reported the death of Ignace Hayden Garry. The Idaho Catholic Register wrote of Ignace's death:

A long and colorful chapter in Idaho history closed Oct. 23 with the death of the Chief of the Coeur d'Alene Indian tribe Ignace Hayden Garry. His 78 years encompassed the last of the Indian massacres, the Battle of Wounded Knee, enforced living on reservations, governmental neglect, and today's education, self-determination, and lessening discrimination.

He was born Oct. 25, 1886, near Indian Canyon, in what is now the City of Spokane, the great-grandson of the famous Chief Spokane Garry. In 1892, following the death of Chief Spokane, he moved with his widowed mother and grandmother to the Coeur d'Alene reservation in Benewah County. There his grandmother, Nellie Garry, daughter of Chief Spokane, had the youth's name changed from Ignace Hayden (his father, of French descent, is the man for whom Hayden Lake is named) to Ignace Hayden Garry.[116] This assured the continuation of the name as Chief Spokane had two daughters but no sons. As a young man, he lived on the Kalispell reservation near Cusick, Wash. In 1915 when the government opened a school there, he was one of the majority of Indians under 35 who enrolled. Most Indians were then illiterate, but Chief Garry had received four-year schooling previously. While there he helped build the church on the reservation that is still in use today. He also served as an interpreter and tribal secretary.

In 1904 he married Susette Revais in Spokane. She died in 1918. Two years later he moved to his Worley allotment and married Lucy Gates. Her death occurred in 1950. Chief Garry continued living in Worley until his death.

He served as Indian tribal judge from 1928 until 1935 and was an Indian policeman from 1935 until his retirement in 1941. He remained active in Indian affairs and was intensely interested in preserving Indian culture. He was a drummer and chanter for many Indian gatherings. Death came at Hot Springs, Mont., where he had gone to arrange a memorial for his late aunt, Mrs. Paul Charlo.

His longtime friend, Father Cornelius E. Byrne, S.J., at the Sacred Heart Mission, DeSmet, celebrated the funeral Mass. The deceased Indian Chief's funeral was the largest assemblage ever held in the DeSmet church. A rosary was recited by the Holy Name Society at the mission on Oct. 25. Sisters of Charity and Jesuit Fathers held a second Rosary service at the mission Tuesday evening.[117]

Joseph was born in 1910, the son of Ignace, the last Chief of the Coeur d'Alene. After Ignace's death, the tribe practiced a democratic form of government, ruled by a council of seven members. Joe graduated from the boy's boarding school at DeSmet, then moved to Spokane to study at Gonzaga preparatory high school, and later at the Haskell Institute in Lawrence, Kansas. Joe graduated from Butler University in Indianapolis. He was the first Native American to serve in the Idaho legislature and became President of the National Congress of American Indians (NCAI), serving six terms. Joe was eloquent, dignified, and hardworking. He was a persuasive leader and a strong advocate for Native Americans. Joe was a veteran of World War II and the Korean War. He enjoyed telling stories of his heritage and sharing the ancient dances and songs in his native dress.

The Powers and the Whalens

A few years after Mat Hayden arrived in New York, a four-year-old Irish boy, Tom Powers. arrived on the Silas Greenham in New York harbor on February 15, 1851. His parents, John and Jane Powers, found work in Haverstraw, New York. Irish migrants found unskilled jobs that were physically demanding and dangerous. They worked building canals, railroads, streets, houses, and sewers. Families worked in brick and calico factories. Wages were usually 75 cents for 10-12 hours a day. Women worked in lower-paying jobs in factories, that were crowded and dirty. As domestics, they worked sixteen hours a day: cooking, cleaning, and caring for children who were not their own. The seamstresses worked 12 hours a day. It usually took them a week to make nine shirts, and they were paid six to ten cents each, a total of 54 to 90 cents for a week's work. Newspaper cartoonists contributed to the idea that the Irish were lazy and stupid. It became acceptable for ads to state: *"No Irish Need Apply."*

Tom's father, John, eventually found work in Jersey City and worked as a farm laborer and blacksmith. A decade after their arrival, his mother, Jane, died. Tom met his wife, Elizabeth "Lizzie" Whalen when she was 18 in Haverstraw, New York. They were married in 1871. He was enamored by Lizzie. She had a lovely personality, beautiful dark curly hair, porcelain skin with large dimples, and a bright spark in her pale blue eyes that galvanized everyone around her. At that time, she was working with her father, Dennis Whalen in a calico factory. He had worked for the English gentry in County Kildare, Ireland, as a reputable veterinarian, diagnosing domestic animals and performing surgery for injuries. The Whalen family arrived in 1848 in the Irish working-class neighborhood of Haverstraw, New York. Dennis was working long hours in the factories for poor pay. He accepted a job on a plantation in North Carolina as the overseer of horses and servants, sending his wages home to Eliza, his wife, and the children. He was in North Carolina for five years when the family received news of his death in 1880. He was kicked in the head when shoeing a horse and died instantly. He was 56 years old.

Tom and Lizzie's marriage had a difficult start in the first three years of their marriage as they lost two daughters. It wasn't long until their first son, John Matthew, was born in 1875. He was followed by Mary Elizabeth "Molly" in 1877, Thomas Francis in

1879, and Patrick Michael in 1882. Tom and Lizzie both toiled long hours in the calico factory, but those were happy times at home. John grew up to be a handsome, serious boy with dark hair and eyes. He did well in elementary school. Molly was a mischievous girl. Her small frame supported her impish, knowing smile, and the musical ring of her laughter attracted everyone to her. She knew all the old Irish songs by heart and could dance many of the jigs her parents taught her. Her hair was dark and curly, and her blue eyes were the color of the Irish Sea. She knew what she wanted and let everyone know what she thought about the world around her. She was very helpful at home with her infant brother, Pat. Tom was a quiet boy, slight in build with fair hair, and often hid behind his Grandmother Eliza's skirt if someone came to the door. Birthdays were always special in the Powers household. Patrick was a charmer, built like a little leprechaun with chubby rosy cheeks and piercing blue eyes, and often bubbled over with joy. The Powers had a fourth son, Dennis, born in 1880, but he lived only a few short months.

Tom saw a gold-colored circular published by Northern Pacific stating that prospectors were taking $25 to $40 out of the gulches in the Coeur d'Alene's. Tom and his brother-in-law, Pat Whalen, were swayed by the persuasive brochure describing the land and opportunities in the Western territories. Their parents had seized a similar opportunity thirty years before when they left Ireland. Tom and Pat made plans to leave Haverstraw, New York, and the life of poverty and repression behind them. They knew they needed to move their families.

Tom decided to wait before traveling West with his family. His brother-in-law, Pat Whalen, wasted no time and set out with his family, promising he would write after he was settled.[118] Pat and his Irish-German wife, Agnes, were married in 1877. She was a serious and hardworking woman and very loyal to her family. They had two children, Dennis, four, and Catherine, two. They arrived in Rathdrum, Idaho, by train from New York City on the 15th of January, 1883 [119] They had traveled to Chicago and on to Minneapolis, then connected with the Northern Pacific on the nearly completed transcontinental route. Passengers had to transfer to a stage or wagon to continue the journey in central Montana to where the tracks began. In September of 1883, there was a golden spike ceremony near Garrison, Montana, attended by former U.S. President Ulysses S. Grant. The train took them across Minnesota, North Dakota, Montana, and finally to Idaho. Rathdrum was a bustling town and the county seat of the territory. The streets were clogged with mud, and domestic pigs were running wild searching for something to eat. The small family looked bewildered as they disembarked from the train in the morning. The town was crowded with freight wagons, frontiersmen dressed in worn leather clothing and furs, and miners pulling their burros with supplies piled high on their backs.

Rathdrum, Idaho, included wooden sidewalks and muddy streets. Power poles would not have been there when the Whalens and Powers arrived.

Four-year-old Dennis was wide-eyed seeing the Indians in their colorful clothing and hearing strange languages being spoken, unlike the ones they heard in New York. The new arrivals were searching for information and transportation to Mission City. Pat was relieved he had been able to make arrangements for a stage from Rathdrum. The ride to Bananzy City on the crowded carriage was very difficult, the passengers all bounced and bumped against one another. They grumbled and whined and were quite relieved when they were able to disembark. The crowded stage sat four or five people across, and the passengers were forced to put their feet on the luggage with their chins nearly resting on their knees. Travel could be quite cold in winter as the canvas curtains were rolled down only to keep out the rain or snow. Most of the stages delivered the mail, cash payrolls, and bank transfers. Although the trip between Rathdrum and Bananzy City was only a few miles, highwaymen were known to hold them up. At Bananzy City, the Rathdrum stage intersected with the stage from Spokane Falls. Pat's family boarded a second stage after a short respite in Coeur d'Alene City. They found lodging until the Amelia Wheaton made a trip to the Mission Landing at Cataldo after the ice thawed on the lake.

157 An Idaho Stage-Coach.

Mud Wagons are used for passengers and mail.[120]

The air was crisp upon their arrival at Mission City, and they all marveled at the surrounding snow-covered hills. Pat and his family found a place to stay with the Jesuits as he had written them months earlier when to expect him. Prospectors from all over the country were looking for lodging, and many pitched a tent or slept in their wagons. Pat seemed to be the only immigrant man in the area with a family, and the Jesuit Fathers soon put him to work. For thirty years members of the Coeur d'Alene tribe lived at the Mission. A large building on the west side of the Mission was used for the Jesuit brothers and travelers. It had kitchen space with a stove and a river rock fireplace. Other buildings contained a blacksmith forge shop and a harness repair shop. The Mission was built using timber from the nearby canyons. Saplings were laid in a crisscross to form a lattice pattern and caked with mud and grass to form the adobe walls. The interior of the Mission was beautiful. Father Ravalli hand-painted the walls, which were covered with fabric purchased from the Hudson's Bay Trading Post at Fort Walla Walla. The chandeliers were made from used tin cans and crosses were carved from pine. The wooden altars were painted to look like marble. In 1865, the exterior siding and interior paneling were added, both fashioned from logs cut nearby and milled at the Mission site. The parish house adjacent to the Mission was not built until 1888.

The priests and experienced inhabitants in the area gave Pat advice on how to get started in the Idaho wilderness so he could support his family. Pat did odd jobs that winter for Mat as well as the Jesuits. Pat acquired his property as a squatter two miles east of Mission City and cleared land for his first home. Mat shared his knowledge of planting and building, encouraging Pat to hire help from members of the Coeur d'Alene tribe. He was able to use old-growth timber with few limbs. The trees were tall and straight, which helped minimize the gaps. The children filled the spaces with mud and grass. On the advice of other early settlers, Pat located their first home on a knoll to maximize drainage and take advantage of the sun. The length of the timber designated what the size of the house would be.

Pat moved his family into a tent in the spring. The Coeur d'Alene's were inquisitive, seeing Catherine busy imitating her parents. Agnes would put a gunny sack of burlap over Catherine's flour sack dress to keep her warm in cooler weather. The common flour sack dresses were not as scratchy as the gunny sacks. The sack was too long for Agnes as she would struggle, when it became caught in the underbrush, falling. The native women, gathering berries nearby, found her to be very amusing. Agnes eventually felt more comfortable with the group watching and she slowly warmed to them. Dennis was four and he wanted friends. The family lost their fear of the natives in the area as they began to make trades and share an occasional meal. The children loved playing outdoors in the forest following and learning from native children. When the land was surveyed, Pat applied for a homestead of 160 acres. Agnes planted a garden in the spring and a root cellar was built to keep their produce. Pat built a cabin with a fireplace for warmth and cooking. A lean-to for animals and fencing were added to hold cattle and hogs.

In the fall of 1885, Pat and Agnes had a second daughter named Mary Elizabeth after her grandmother. She was one of the first white children to be born in the Coeur d'Alene Mountains, a range that stretched along the Montana border from Lake Pend Oreille to the St. Joe River and reached heights of 7,000 feet.[121] Several other babies were born to families in the Fort Coeur d'Alene area in Kootenai County.

Pat Whalen sent a letter to his brother-in-law, Tom, describing the many opportunities he found in the Northwest. Unfortunately, in New York, Tom had fallen ill. Two years had passed since Pat and his family had moved west, but Tom was growing feeble and could not muster the strength to join them. He had worked with unprocessed cotton bales in the calico mill for twenty years. After decades of breathing in the cotton dust and other fibers from the mill, he began to feel a constricted tightness in his chest as his airways narrowed.

Whalen Farm near Cataldo: Pat Whalen with his arms crossed. On October 18, 1907 a fire destroyed Pat's barn. Eight horses were lost plus farm machinery and seventy-five tons of hay went up in flames. The total loss was estimated at $6000.

Lizzie and her mother, Eliza, took turns nursing Tom while Lizzie continued work at the factory. He would wheeze heavily as he tried to catch his breath but his symptoms only worsened. The bacterial infection, byssinosis, or "cotton lung disease," took over his lungs. He passed away on July 28, 1885, at the age of 38. Tom would not see the mountains of Idaho, but Lizzie, the children, and Eliza promised they would fulfill his dream by moving west with the children. In late September, they boarded the train for the Northwest. Lizzie's younger sister Katherine and her husband Frank Reilly did not follow them. The families wept as they knew they would not see one another again. Lizzie, her mother, and her children boarded a train west. Standard Railway Time was established in the United States and Canada on November 18, 1883. Towns based their time on when the sun was at its highest point with the sundial indicating it was noon. Before the standardization of schedules, it was confusing for travelers to know the current time. Unfortunately, the multiple times resulted in train accidents, and fifty railway times would be replaced with five time zones.

Lizzie Powers, her mother, Eliza Whalen, and her four children stepped off the morning train in Rathdrum in 1885. Dust was swirling around from the wheels of wagons and horses' hoofs as a soft breeze cooled the warm air. One mercantile owner was encouraging the townspeople to start building wooden sidewalks to control the mud and filth left by wandering animals. Citizens and businessmen were advocating that all the pigs running loose in the streets ought to be penned up. At thirty-three, Lizzie's diminutive stature and pale blue eyes caught the attention of men, despite the widow's black dress and veil lying loosely around her shoulders. Molly stayed close to her mother and hung firmly onto her younger brothers, Tom and Pat. Lizzie and her mother, organized porters to help with the trunks to be taken onto the stage. Pat squirmed, trying to free himself so he could wander about with his older brother. The boys were inquisitive and in awe of everything around them. Their mouths were agape as they stared at the local tribesmen who were nearby. Their grandmother was suspicious and uncomfortable in those unfamiliar and strange surroundings. The stage to Bananzy City was the same creaking; jostling buggy that Pat Whalen had taken two and a half years before.

As they boarded the steamer to the Mission, the children were excited on that crisp fall day. Miners crowded aboard with pickaxes, mules, jackasses, and horses loaded with packs. The men looked rough, wearing shabby clothing, dirty broken fedoras, and full grizzly beards. A young man with a clean-shaven face played Irish tunes such as "Molly Malone, I'll Take You Home Again Kathleen, and Whiskey in the Jar" on his harmonica. Young Pat was enthralled and wanted to escape Molly's grip. Lizzie was apprehensive of the strange men and stranger surroundings, but the familiar music of home helped soothe her nerves. She was accustomed to the many languages she had heard in New York.

P.J. Whalen is on the front left and Patrick Dennis Whalen is on the far right holding the dog at the Wayside Inn, Cataldo. [122]

Lizzie and Eliza, still in mourning, wore long black dresses. Both were relieved that they were safely on the Spokane River and on their way to Coeur d'Alene City. The family did not disembark, and they were soon crossing Coeur d'Alene Lake to Mission Landing. Eliza was known to be a woman dedicated to her family and church. She was generous, kind, and a true humanitarian for those in need. As the sun warmed them, Lizzie, Eliza, Pat, and Tom were soon asleep despite the noise of the voices onboard. John and Molly were curious about the steamer, the placer miners, the prospectors, and the moccasin-wearing natives, wrapped in bright-colored blankets. They whispered together, barely able to hold in their excitement and fear. They were astonished at the smell of the pines, the fresh air and the lush vegetation along the river. The water was clear as glass, and one could see it was teeming with fish. The ducks, geese, herons, swans, and egrets were prolific along the river. They were all glad they were no longer in Haverstraw, New York.

When the imposing Mission of the Sacred Heart came into view, the widow and her mother both breathed a sigh of relief. The setting sun gave the Mission a welcoming glow, and behind the sky was a translucent blue with pink and orange billowy clouds draped across. Pat Whalen, with two-year-old Mary Elizabeth on his shoulders, his wife Agnes, and his children Dennis and Catherine, met his mother and sister at Mission Landing. It wasn't long before they were settled, and Lizzie began cooking and cleaning for the residents at Mat Hayden's hotel. Mat was smitten.

The Mission of The Scared Heart. Cataldo, Idaho. Gustave Sohon [123]

Gold, Rails and Silver

After Andy Prichard found placer gold traveling through tangled underbrush in a deep timbered ravine on the North Fork of the Coeur d'Alene River, he went to Spokane for the winter. Prospectors began to question him, and soon word spread that gold had been found. The 1883 gold rush mania started and spread rapidly through the ravines and forests of North Idaho.

Mat was happy to see a quicker mode of transportation provided by the completion of the transcontinental Northern Pacific Railway in August 1883. The immigrant car charged $35 to $50 from New York, half of the cost of the 2nd class. Fares were cheapest during the winter, and if one settled on land near the railroad, the fare was negotiable. Water and lunch baskets were available for a dollar. The cars were packed with travelers, and many of them bought lunch baskets with wedges of cold beef, dried venison, bread, and cheese. Mat's hotel was prospering and he quickly earned the reputation of running a creditable hotel.

Noah Kellogg's was not having luck prospecting near Murray, Idaho, with the number of prospectors and disputed claims. He set out with a grubstake from two investors[124] who sent him on his way with a burro, named Bill in the spring of 1885. The people in Murray wanted to get rid of Bill because of all the braying and problems he caused. Noah woke one morning to find Bill gone and went in search of him. He found him grazing on a hillside side of Milo Gulch near a large lode of galena ore that eventually produced over $12,000,000 in silver and lead. Old Bill lived to be 21 years old and was given credit for his role in finding the cropping of ore. When Jim Wardner heard that Kellogg had struck a good vein of silver, he immediately claimed the "water rights" that were needed to open the mines. He then contracted Noah to form a partnership. The town of Kentuck sprang up and soon Jim managed the name to Wardner. Hearing of the discovery in Idaho, Daniel Corbin, an entrepreneur from the east took the Northern Pacific Railroad to Rathdrum, Idaho. He traveled by stage to Coeur d'Alene City and by steamer to the Mission. He arrived in Kentuck by a "mud wagon stage" from the Mission landing.[125] It was April and everywhere one went there was mud. Four to six horses usually pulled the mud wagon, and a simple canvas top helped to reduce the weight. A coach typically had three rows of seating for nine passengers with an extra person could be squeezed in. Often the stage carried mail, payroll, or a valuable supply of whiskey. The roads were rough and rutted, and the trip would jostle the riders, testing the stamina of the most rugged individual. He met Jim Wardner who escorted him on a tour of the mine that became known as the Bunker and Sullivan.

Kentuck, Idaho,1886. The water barrels on the roof of the mercantile were for fire protection. Sam and Frank Poteet are standing next to Noah Kellogg's burro. Margarita Crane and Jerome Day are riding "Old Bill", a third child is facing right. Mr. George Crane is standing at the corner of the building in a black hat.[126]

Phillip O'Rourke, Noah Kellogg, and several other miners filed claims to develop the Bunker Hill property in September 1885 in the Coeur d'Alene mining district. Samuel Hauser, the governor of Montana, obtained smelter rights to process the ore from the Bunker Hill Mine. Hauser had prospered as a prospector and owned six silver mines and several silver smelters. Hauser contacted Corbin to return to the West to develop the mining railroad. On July 6, 1886, Corbin formed the Coeur d'Alene Railway and Navigation Company with Sam Hauser. Daniel Corbin capitalized on the silver, zinc, and lead by shipping the ore to a smelter in Wickes, Montana. The ore from Bunker Hill was put into burlap sacks and loaded into wagons to be transported to

Mission Landing where steamers took the ore to Coeur d'Alene City. They continued the branch of the Northern Pacific Railroad from the docks in Coeur d'Alene City in 1886 to Hauser Junction. The railroad from Mission Landing reached Wardner Junction, a distance of fourteen miles. The next year the railroad was extended to Wallace and Burke. James Monaghan and Clement King owned the steamers and sold them to Corbin in 1888. They profited by $17,300. By July 1889, they had shipped 80,000 tons of ore to Wickes and smelted $1.3 million in silver, $350,288 in gold, and $1.7 million in lead.[127]

A second rail line was proposed by the Washington and Idaho Railroad between Mullan, Idaho and Tekoa, Washington passing through Indian territory. The railroad was asking for a right-of-way from Kentuck mines through the reservation along the chain lakes to Tekoa, where it joined the Northern Pacific Chief Seltice (Saltice/ Saltese), Steve Liberty, and his brother-in-law, Pierre Wildshoe, went to Washington to meet with President Cleaveland to negotiate the rail line to cross tribal land. They also wanted to have their lands restored after being taken unfairly. The group was happy to return home away from the humidity of Washington D.C.[128]

The Coeur d'Alene Tribe, (Schitsu'umsh) signed the Treaty in 1858 including for friendship and peace. It did not protect their tribal lands and they wrote to the government asking for their lands to be returned. The railroad began hauling ore from the Kentuck junction in October of 1887, taking business away from D.C. Corbin's railroad. Unfortunately, the treaty was disputed until 1901 when the tribal lands were reduced by the American government after forty-three years. In 1924, the Supreme Court recognized five tribes in Idaho for citizenship in their own country. Chief Seltice and 500 of his tribe would go each year to Liberty Lake to have foot, canoe, and horse races on the 1st of July. Chief Seltice passed away in 1902 knowing that only part of his land had been retained. Today the trail of the Coeur d'Alene follows the route of the Washington and Idaho railroad.

Daniel Corbin stayed at Mat's hotel in Cataldo and hauled in supplies when the railroad was being built. The increase in transportation made it easier for Mat to travel and procure supplies for his hotel and farm. The first year, the rail bed collapsed during the spring thaw because it was built on frozen ground and one of Corbin's engines stuck in the mud. With only two passenger cars, many of the paying customers rode on benches nailed to the flatcars or in the caboose. The train could carry sixty people. The ferry would take them to Coeur d'Alene. Two years after forming his company, Daniel Corbin signed over his line to the Northern Pacific on October 1, 1888, giving them a 999-year lease. The line "was on a single track from Mission Landing to numerous mines and crossed the river thirty times in twenty miles."[129] Train engineers were often forced to hold their cars onto a side track until another train passed as there were no telegraph lines. The river flooded in the spring and the tracks were often washed out. Transportation and progress were slow.

A story was told that Pat Whalen helped Colonel Wallace move his household goods from Mission Landing to where Wallace, Idaho, stands today. The Colonel paid for the 80 acres of land near Burke with Sioux scrip. It was paper money issued for temporary emergency use. It was declared illegal, and Colonel Wallace and the City of Wallace had property disputes for many years. Changing occupations was nothing new to Pat, as he had worked in the brick factory, the railroad, and the boats on the Hudson. Pat began a livery stable that included hiring horses and carriages, and as the rails and transportation improved to the isolated mining areas of Prichard Creek and Murray, Pat needed to find another occupation.

Cataldo was built in a low-lying area and flooded every spring as it was near the Coeur d'Alene River. People would lose their livestock and farms would be underwater. Typhoid was a real danger after the floods. In 1895, Pat Whalen built a dance hall next to the railroad substation. Pat would organize a dance after a long log drive. He found a fiddler or two, stocked his hall with plenty of whiskey and beer to go around, and hired bouncers to get rid of anyone starting fights or having too much to drink. He eventually changed the dance hall into a boarding house which became known as the Old Whalen House. The two-story building, with its spacious porch and balcony, became a stopping-off place for travelers. He kept a large iron cooking pot over a fire and served the standard fare of moose or bear stew for hungry travelers.[130]

Building the West

Clement King, James Monaghan, Daniel Corbin, and Mathew Hayden were all well-known entrepreneurs and friends, building and reshaping Kootenai County in Idaho Territory. Many men were instrumental in developing Northern Idaho. Clement B. King was born in Iowa in 1843 and came west with his parents by the ox team when he was ten. He would become the proprietor of the Royal Duke Stables in Colfax. Clement King began operating the stage line between Colfax, Spokane Falls, and Fort Colville with James Monaghan. In August of 1879, he visited Spokane with one of his teams of horses to advertise his City Stables and was officially added to the list of business houses. He worked with James at Fort Coeur d'Alene to plat Coeur d'Alene City. Clement King and James Monaghan hired the native populations to clear the land for marketable timber. The next year, Clement King married Belle (Hannah A.) Wimpy. Two years later, Clement King and James Monaghan set up a store at Fort Spokane at the confluence of the Spokane and Columbia Rivers and a second store at Fort Sherman.[131] In 1884, the two men built a wagon road to Osborn to make it easier to transfer the ore from Murray so it could be loaded aboard the steamer and taken down the river. Clement King netted $300 a day during good weather. A local stopping place for miners on the North Fork of the Coeur d'Alene River to Prichard and Murray was named Kingston.

On December 19, 1885, the Spokane Falls Review reported that Clement King was "a rustler of Coeur d'Alene City who spent a month or two junketing on the Sound and Western Oregon, looks as though he has been living off the fat of the land with his fill of clams and oysters". In 1906, Clement King sold his property to the Hayden Improvement Co. which today is the Hayden Lake Country Club. The King family lived at a large ranch north of Coeur d'Alene City. The upper floor of the carriage barn housed the laborers and the pedigree horses were trained on a half-mile race track. The King family named a small lake near their home Avondale. They stocked the lake with trout for house guests. Their son, Guy, attended Page's Military Academy in Coeur d'Alene. He spent time with his grandfather, Major Wimpey, in Georgia after contracting tuberculosis but never fully recovered. His parents moved him each winter in search of a climate to cure him. The King family moved to Phoenix, Arizona, in 1907 and packed a fright car with their household furnishings and finest horses. The journey took them three weeks.

When several of the businessmen in the area discussed expanding the railroad from Spokane Falls to Colville and north to the mining district of British Columbia, Daniel Corbin needed to raise $100,000 from investors to begin construction. James Monaghan helped to secure property rights and money. Mat reached an agreement on March 20, 1889, for a strip of land on his Colville property 50 feet on each side of the centerline of the Spokane Falls and Northern Railway Company.[132] On May 7, 1890, Mat and Lizzie gave the railroad a warranty deed to the company[133] across their land in consideration of $1.00. Forty acres of land in the town were to be used as a railroad yard. The rail to Colvile was built for less than $8,000 a mile when $10,000 was considered cheap. Following wagon trails and limiting blasting reduced construction costs. Corbin went to New York to buy rails and told Edward J. Roberts, a chief construction engineer, to build the line as fast and inexpensively as possible.

A water system for Coeur d'Alene City was first developed by James Monaghan and C.B. King. Daniel Corbin, James Monaghan, and Clement King built an irrigation ditch thirty-four miles long, providing water to Post Falls and the Spokane prairie. The Corbin Ditch can be seen near the Post Falls dam.

Late in the fall of 1883, a family arrived at the Mission, coming over the Mullan Road by wagon from Montana. Titus Blessing was born in Dubuque, Iowa, in 1855. His parents, Frank and Helen, both of German descent, moved the family to New Elm, Minnesota, where they learned masonry. He and his brothers moved to Helena, Montana, to assist in the building of the Montana Capitol building. Titus joined up with Buffalo Bill, who was then the private scout for General Miles. Titus was part of the scouting team, in battles with the Sioux near Fort Peck. He loved telling of the time when they sat in council with Sitting Bull and smoked the peace pipe. He was caught up in the pandemonium of the mining strikes in Western Montana. His wife, Anna Hoffman, had immigrated to California with her family. She was visiting a cousin in Montana when she met Titus. They married in 1879. Drawn by the opportunity of grazing land, Titus, his three brothers, and their families set off by mule train to the plains near Spokane. The Mullan Road had been cut through the dense forest and hard rock hillsides twenty years earlier. The Mullan Trail was constructed to bring military supplies and troops across the Rockies and was later used by migrants to cross into Idaho and Washington. The government had no money to reconstruct roads or bridges during the Civil War. The road had washed out and hadn't been maintained. If Andy Prichard hadn't found gold near Murray, the forest would certainly have reclaimed the road. The fur traders, prospectors, and land seekers continued to move west, disregarding the perils they faced traveling over the road. The determination of the settlers kept the winding trail open.

The US Army arrives at the Sacred Heart Mission in Cataldo, Idaho.[134]

When Titus and his brothers headed west, it was a laborious task to carry their families and household goods over the mountains. When their mule train pulled into the Cataldo Mission, they were met by a party of Native Americans who appeared agitated by the threat of white migration. The Jesuits were trying to understand their frustrations when they realized the Indians were not familiar with white children. Anna and Titus put their daughters, Amelia, 13, and Anna Katy, 2 in the back of the wagon so the Native Americans could view them. Amelia said she was so scared it stunted her growth. She was barely five feet tall. The snow was falling when the family arrived in Spokane Falls. Titus left his family in Spokane and headed out with dreams of finding gold in the Coeur d'Alene's with 10,000 other miners and prospectors flowing to the mountains. He organized a grub steak and headed for Eagle, Idaho. Prospectors died in their tents during the winter months and were not found until the spring. Titus was optimistic and believed he would be lucky. Most of the men were not prepared for the difficult and dangerous winters, diseases such as cholera, or the starvation they would face.

One spring, Titus traveled by snowshoe fifty miles from the mines to visit his family. He returned to Spokane to build the cabin for them. When the snow melted, he realized he had built a cabin in the middle of a street in the frontier town. He tore it down and moved his family closer to his brothers, who had settled in Trent, Washington, and helped them concentrate on the cattle business. Titus returned to Eagle and sold his claims when he heard that occupied land had been opened to squatters that was owned by the tribe in the lake's region near Medimont, Idaho. Titus obtained placer ground and continued to work a claim near his home on the St. Joe River. As Justice of the Peace, Titus could perform criminal and civic duties, and provide certified documents. He was instrumental in passing a bill banning the Chinese from Coeur d'Alene County and from owning land.

In 1891, the Coeur d'Alene Reservation was opened to settlers. Titus sold his claims in Eagle. Titus then claimed 140 acres between Medicine Mountain and Cave Lake. Medicine Mountain later became Medimont. After his first cabin burned in 1903, he built a "rock house" with a foundation and walls four feet thick. The house stands today. Tragedy befell the family when the youngest three of their seven children set off to go ice skating on Thanksgiving Day of 1906. John, 10, Katie, 13, and Phillip Robert, 16, joined two friends on a nearby lake. The five children skated onto thin ice and fell through. Frantic rescue efforts were made, but only one of the two friends survived and three of the Blessing children died. When their bodies had been retrieved, the children were laid out in the family parlor to await the arrival of the undertaker. The front porch was never finished and the piano was never played again. Today, there are many descendants of the Blessing living in Idaho and Washington.[135]

The notion of cheap labor was prevalent, and many migrants to the area typically fulfilled that role. By the 1880s, one could often see signs stating: "Chinamen need not apply." Before that time, a Chinese immigrant could be hired for $100 a year. In some areas, there were more Chinese laborers than European laborers. Chinese laborers made up 80 percent of the Northern Pacific workforce that built the railroad east of Seattle.[136] Many earned $30.00 a month and their housing. They proved to be very efficient workers, with better diets, hygiene, and less sickness. After the railway jobs ended, the Chinese established businesses: restaurants, dispensaries, laundries, stores, and gambling clubs. By the 1880s, over 10,000 Chinese were residing in the Boise area. The average age of the Chinese immigrant was thirty-two years. They were exploited in the mines earning 75 cents to a dollar a day.[137] The prejudice against the Chinese persisted with the newspapers referring to them as "rice eaters" and adding "the music of the Chinese is deliciously horrible, like cats trying to sing base with sore throats".[138]

Chinese reworked the claims after the Europeans were finished. They were industrious yet they were shown a lack of respect by many who were jealous of their success. They dug the ditches to bring water to the mines and worked in other support services at hotels, restaurants, laundries, and railroads. The Chinese were paid less than the Irish. They would wear a heavy, wooden yoke over their shoulders, balancing two large baskets used for carrying food to the mining population. Some of the Chinese migrants worked more favorable jobs at Camp Coeur d'Alene for the officers or soldiers, doing laundry and cooking. In the mines, the Chinese worked some of the most dangerous jobs, including setting explosives. The Chinese who grew fruit and vegetables for the mining camps were referred to as "celestials." Celestials believed that goodness came from the sky. Mat realized how fortunate he was with the care and help he had found in the West, far from the prejudices he felt in New York and the East Coast of the United States. He respected the work and the people without prejudice.

In 1882, the Chinese Exclusion Act, the first major law that restricted immigration, was signed by President Chester Arthur. State laws restricted the Chinese from establishing mining claims or owning land. When Andy Prichard found gold the next year, many immigrant miners felt the Chinese might make a gold strike and they would miss out. Prejudices began to grow and in 1883, residents of the Coeur d'Alene Mountains passed a law that said the Chinese would be expelled or killed if they came into the camp. In May 1877, a group of Chinese from San Francisco were working near Lewiston, Idaho, when they were attacked and killed by seven men. They stole several thousand dollars in gold from them. All the men were found innocent by an all-white jury, though details were given at the trial. By 1890, the Idaho legislature barred Chinese or Mongolians from holding mining lands and in 1897 they were restricted from any mining activity. Many of the Chinese left Idaho, moving to coastal communities where they were granted rights of land ownership and other freedoms. The census showed that 4000 people, or 28.5 percent, were Chinese in 1870 in Idaho Territory. The acts were not repealed until 1943, and in 1980, only 625 people claimed Chinese ancestry. Dozens of Chinese miners were killed in prejudicial violence, and many suffered cruel attacks under the wrath of other migrants who didn't like their religion, clothing, language, or mannerisms.

Chinese miners worked sluice boxes by washing the ore and tailings. Many Chinese arrived after the Northern Pacific railroad was completed in 1869. By 1870, there were 4,000 Chinese in Idaho. The Chinese Exclusion Act prevented men from marrying, attending schools, owning homes, and entering professions. By 1900, only 859 Chinese people remained.[139]

Mat Ventures into Mining

Mat was not immune to gold fever, and he began to try his hand at investing in mining. Mat was spending more and more time in Idaho and never seemed to have the chance to get back to Colville to check in on his ranch. On June 14, 1886, Mat mortgaged the land for $1000 to G.M. Todd, a teacher from Sing Sing, New York.[140] He would pay 10% interest for three years. In April of the following year, Mat temporarily transferred ownership of the property to James Monaghan for $1500.[141] Mat was glad to have a close friend he could trust to manage the property and happier still to be able to spend more time in Idaho. There were so many opportunities at hand. $2500 afforded him the possibility of investing in mining or property.

Three years after Andy Prichard first struck gold along the Coeur d'Alene River; Mat's peers were also investing in mines. A few laborers working the placer creeks achieved financial success. The prospering migrants would gladly help their fellow man with a grubstake when they achieved the means to take a chance. Seeing the opportunity, Mat signed a notification of location for the Tuff Nut Mine on May 25, 1886, near the Metaline Falls mining district. Six weeks later, on July 6th, 1886, he further invested with a fellow entrepreneur, George. W. Forester. Forester lived in Conconully, six miles northwest of Ruby, Washington. He paid $1000.00 for a one-eighth interest in the lode that was located on the east side of Sullivan Creek in Stevens County, Washington [142] The Mining Act of 1872 granted patents to individuals to prospect on public land and stake claims. Once a patent was filed, the receiver owned the mineral and surface rights forever. The owner was required to register with the county auditor. If he did not have proof that he put $100 worth of labor on the claim every year, he would lose the title, and the mine would be up for grabs. Mat and George would hire laborers to work the site. Using a 150-foot ore chute, they could easily load the ore that was extracted into wagons. The ore was sold for $50 per ton for the gold, silver, and lead they extracted from the mine. Mat garnered $1875.00 on his initial investment. The Tuff Nut Mine was reported to contain 47 to 86 ounces of silver and 640 to 860 lbs. of lead per ton. It produced $9000 before 1901.[143]

Wasting no time, Matt signed a second mining deed with John Gobar with a stake of $150.00 for an undivided one-quarter interest in the Salmon River Chief in Stevens County. [144] The Salmon River Chief, near the Tuff Nut mine, was the principal producer of a group of mines in the region. The ore was richer at the Chief, and they averaged $75.00 a ton in gold and silver with 200 pounds of lead. [145] A ledger showed that Mat was billed for $33.33 for his portion of assessment work on the US Grant and Silver Crown Mines, in the Metaline Mining District.

Spokane Falls and Coeur d'Alene lodgings were crowded with prospectors and gamblers looking for ways to the Coeur d'Alene Mountains. Mat's hotel in Mission City was busy. In the winter months, navigation on the waterway became impossible for skiffs working to provide supplies to the mines. Pack trains were leaving Spokane at a regular pace, and the snow in the mountains could be five feet deep. Toboggans and sleds were used to transport supplies to the mines. In the winter of 1884, the Evolution Trail was blocked by snow slides, and it took Marian Davis and the party nine days to clear twenty feet of snow. [146] Flour prices jumped to $60.00 a barrel, bacon $.65 a pound, beef $.50, and venison $.25. Men on their way to Eagle City were told that it would cost them $4.00 a day to live, with drinks a quarter and meals a dollar. Carpenters could earn $5 a day building cabins. Five thousand miners arrived in the Coeur d'Alene Mountains in the winter months. On November 4th, 1885 the Spokan Times reported that there had been an unusual amount of activity as M. Jacob Frost had paid several uninvited visits. He was ferocious and many people disliked him. He bites everything, and it is impossible to get any medicine to cure the bite. He bit the potatoes, pumpkins, onions, and everything he could. A sergeant digging one hill of potatoes found 13 on one plant, and all together they weighed 18 lbs. He took them to Mr. Yeaton's store and the largest was 2.5 lbs. They will be distributed to the 21st Infantry in the spring.

Mat hired D.E. Coulson on the 10th of May, 1887 to run a twenty-five-foot tunnel on the *Ore Or No Ore Quartz Claim*. The claim was two and a half miles upstream from the mouth of Moon Creek, east of Kellogg and McAuley. It was an extension of the Charles Dickenson Quartz Claim and ran northwest of Osburn, Idaho. Coulson was to do all the work and furnish the powder, fuse, time, and tools necessary to complete the tunnel. When the work was completed, Mat would give Coulson one-quarter interest in *Ore Or No Ore Claim* of which Mat owned one-half.

Nine claims covered one hundred and eighty acres at Moon Creek. The mines were developed with a boiler, hoist, drills, air compressors, and a four-foot Pelton water wheel. The Pelton wheel designed in the 1870s was the most efficient of water turbines, extracting energy from a jet of water. In 188, a small electric plant was installed. The silver found in the Coeur d'Alene Mountains made it one of the most successful regions in the world. The Lucky Friday mine in Mullan is the deepest in the United States. The Bunker Hill mine was the largest and the Sunshine was the richest.[147] During the exploration of mining, the surrounding hills were striped on trees that were needed for support in the tunnels and building cabins for the miners. Many men were pleased to find work at a lumber mill after spending a winter in a mining camp. In February of 1890, twenty-five lucky men at the Custer mine on Nine Mile Creek in Shoshone County

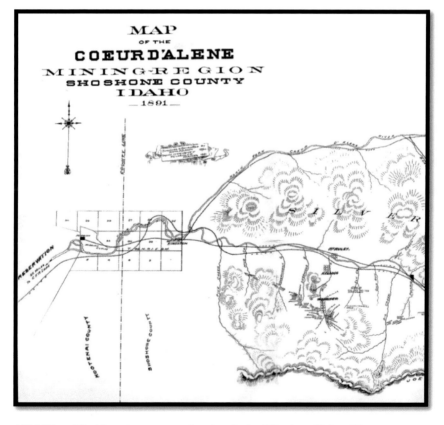

1891 Map: Marking the reservation land, the Mission Claim, Kingston, the North Fork of the Coeur d'Alene River, Pine Creek, and Milo Creek. McAudly is North of Kellogg, and Wardner is east. Moon Creek is north.

were laid off from work. The fifteen workers remaining were at dinner when an avalanche struck the building and sent a cascade of broken timbers and the men down into the gulch. Three were killed instantly. After fifteen hours of digging, six men were found alive, and another six friends were killed. Those lost were John Galbraith, the foreman; Thomas Sturgeon, a miner; J. Gillbright, a miner; Mike Flynn, the cook; Tom Malloy, assistant cook; and Ole Olson, waiter. Numerous slides occurred that winter in the Coeur d'Alenes costing many lives. Murray's gold production began to decline after three good years. In 1884, gold mined was $258,375; in 1885, it was $376,607; in 1886, $182,371; and in 1887, $152,276. As gold production collapsed, the mountains drew prospectors who were able to secure other precious metals. Silver production began in 1886 with a value of $115,664 and by 1887 the amount had doubled. The first silver hard rock mine was the Tiger Mine on Canyon Creek in Burke in 1884.

Local Moonshiners[148]

With the prospectors and the military came the saloons and the girls that entertained them. The saloons were a place where a man could get the news, a loan, or cash a payroll check. Stills were found throughout the backcountry and the moonshine produced was often sold to the saloon keepers. The oak barrels were charred for the production of bourbon to give the liquor a caramel or vanilla flavor. The alcohol was often made with at least 70% corn and aged for two to four years. With the ramshackle distilleries came lead poisoning and illnesses from unsanitary conditions. In the early days, the illegal distilleries were generally left alone, but as the territories grew, new laws were made and enforced. The excise tax on a bottle of whiskey was $2.15 a gallon and a nickel for a beer. One man was fined $500 for selling whiskey to Native Americans. Many operators produced between one to two hundred gallons of whiskey a month. **(A-7)** "Boomtowns, gambling, saloons, and substandard beds - Life in a mining camp." *New York Times.* **(A-8)**

What's Seldom is Wonderful

The Hayden home in Mission City was full of music, laughter, and dancing. Mat taught the children string tricks, guessing games, and cards on snowy days. The game of fox and geese was played when the snow was deep enough to make a good ring for running. In the summer, they played marbles, shooting into a dirty ring. Pat won a lot of marbles, but his brothers favored him to win. Mat taught the children a good work ethic and the importance of being part of a family, showing respect to everyone they met, and offering to help others in need. The boys would often tease their grandmother about her heavy Gaelic accent, as she shooed them out of the kitchen with her broom. They loved the warm peppered soda bread and a heavy broth of venison or beef-barley stew their mother and grandmother prepared for them. Their grandmother, Eliza continued to wear the heavy black clothing of mourning since her husband died. Lizzie had given up her mourning clothes since arriving in Idaho two years earlier when she began cooking and serving at the hotel Mat owned.

During the summer and fall, the family preserved food for the winter. A root cellar stored onions, potatoes, beans, beets, and carrots. They made jam from the wild berries and preserved the dried trout and venison. Mat grew several acres of timothy for the horses and livestock. The cattle, pigs, and chickens were raised not only for the family but for the hotel, and other boarding houses as far as Wardner. The children loved it when the hay was cut so they could climb into the rafters of the barn, daring one another to dive into the hay from the highest beam. Mat would bring home a poor man for dinner and a night in the barn if there was someone in need. Some would stay a few days and work before heading north into the mountains in search of their lode. Molly preferred to help her grandmother and let the boys do the weeding in the garden and chores in the barn. Molly and her mother prepared many meals and baked bread, pies, and cakes for the hired hands and the hotel. Molly did not like the geese as an old gander would chase the children in the barnyard. Several of the ducks imprinted on the boys and followed them on their way to do chores. One particular female bonded with Pat and greeted him every morning. Pat was three. He loved his duck and would carry it or pull her in a little wagon. When they were hoeing the garden, the ducks would lunge in to snatch a worm or bug. Pat was also assigned to feed the kitchen scraps to the pigs and chickens, with Tom or John. Mat warned them that the pigs could be dangerous and not to go into the pen. John and Tom helped the hired men with the timothy grown along the river below the Mission as well as taking responsibility for feeding the livestock and mucking out the barn.

The Hayden Homestead near Cataldo.

Mat would marry Elizabeth "Lizzie" Whalen Powers, a widow with four children, on March 27, 1887, at the Mission of the Sacred Heart. Father Joseph Joset officiated. Lizzie and Mat shopped in Spokane Falls where she had purchased a deep burgundy brocade dress for the ceremony. The dress had large velvet-covered buttons, a pleated bodice, and prominent cuffs on the sleeves. Most women during the Victorian period wore wedding dresses that could be worn again. Lizzie's children, John, Tom, Molly, and Pat, were very excited that their mother and Mat would be married. John was going to be a witness. With news of a wedding, people from Kingston and the surrounding area traveled to attend. It meant good 'pickings' and drinks. Mat's good friend Pat Lucas spent two days preparing the pit to roast a large hog. He dug the pit three feet deep and seven feet long behind the hotel. Pat and the boys gathered river rocks to line the pit. A fire started to heat the rocks. The hog was rubbed with sage, thyme, and juniper berries. When the rocks were hot, some were added to the abdominal cavity, and the hog was wrapped in chicken wire and lowered into the pit. It was covered with corn stalks and wet burlap bags. The hog was covered with a layer of soil and left to steam for 12 hours. Pat told them the temperature in the pit would stay between 200 and 250 degrees. The roasting of a deer is easier. Trout would be served and their grandmother had planned on roasted potatoes, sauerkraut, and greens. The hotel dining room would be cleared out for dancing that evening. Friends played their fiddles and they would clog and dance until everyone fell asleep in the early morning hours. Molly loved to dance, and she had learned several polkas and reels. Lizzie had taught her children to dance by tying hay on their right shoe and having them start on their hay foot. Molly knew all the dances flawlessly. One of Molly's favorite dances was the Irish 'handkerchief" dance. She would move her feet with her arms straight to her sides, where she held a handkerchief between her and her partner. Molly remembered dancing with her grandfather, Dennis Whalen when they were in Haverstraw. Her brothers were quite skilled dancers as Lizzie often danced with the boys. Pat, the youngest, loved the dances and was quite adept for a boy of four and a half. Lizzie laughed watching young Pat do a jig and tap to the music. He looked like a puppet on a string. The family often called him "fast feet Patty" as if it were his name. He would often take his younger cousin, Mary Whalen, by the hand and take her out on the floor. Molly was delighted her mother had married at the Mission.

Two Friesian horses, with their long silky manes and tails, pulled the carriage to bring the couple luck. Father Joset's white robes contrasted with the slate-dark horses. The Sacred Heart Mission was the beautiful church sitting up on the grassy knoll overlooking the Coeur d'Alene River and their home. The ceremony in the church was a crowded affair with Pat Dunnigan and John Powers as witnesses. Members of the Coeur d'Alene Tribe and numerous guests crowded into the church.

The guests would stop by after the ceremony at the hotel to give their best wishes. Her mother, Eliza, had begun preparations for the wedding guests a few days earlier. She was anxious to go back to the hotel to finalize the preparations. Mat built a large two-story house for the family the previous year below the Mission. Molly felt comfortable and safe at the house. Mat added a large river rock fireplace and they had a good iron stove for cooking. Several friends and tribal members helped him with the construction. A second wood stove kept the upstairs rooms warm. Molly was very happy to be living in Idaho where there was so much space, food, and good people. Her Uncle Pat's daughter, Mary, was four years younger and she was the only other white girl that lived nearby. Molly enjoyed her time with the cousins and children that lived near the Mission where she learned many ways of the Coeur d'Alene's.

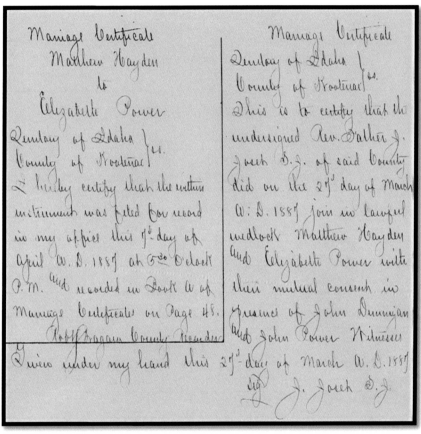

Mat and Lizzie's marriage certificate, signed by Fr. Joset, March 27, 1887.

Kathleen

Mat and Lizzie's daughter, Kathleen, arrived quietly. She was so small that Lizzie worried that she would not live long. The winter that year was particularly cold, and tiny Kathleen's lungs were not very strong. Her eyes were as pale as a light winter sky, a sharp contrast to her black curly hair. Molly was amazed at how noisy a baby could be making little grunting sounds, burping, sneezing, stretching, and squirming while trying to make herself comfortable. The boys were fascinated and roared with laughter when she displayed noisy antics. Their grandmother tried to hush them, but it would make them laugh all the more. Mat smiled to himself. He was very pleased to have a growing family and realized how much he enjoyed the sounds of the children. Molly loved staying home with Kathleen while the others worked either at the hotel or the farm.

The cold snow squeaked as they walked out to the sleigh. The sky was white and clear as the family made their way along the wagon trail to the Mission. The family wrapped the children with blankets and Mat's old buffalo robe lined the bottom of the sleigh to keep out the cold. Mat told the old stories of how the robe saved his life more than once, and it was good luck to keep it. The sleigh, painted dark forest green with flowers and birds painted on the back, glided effortlessly over the snow. It didn't get stuck like the wagons would every spring in the mud and dirt. Mat recently brought home a new harness with large nickel bells attached. The children loved the bells and would flip the reins so everyone could hear them arriving. Lizzie wore the fox cap and muff Mat had given her for Christmas. He had traded several beaver pelts with a trapper for the hide of the fox which he took to a millinery shop in Spokane to have the hat and muff made for Lizzie. The muff, with its champagne satin lining and a hidden pocket, was finished with the white tip of the fox's tail, which contrasted beautifully against the red-orange fur. Kathleen slept soundly in the luxury of the fox mitt covering her. The soft noises that came from her sounded as if a kitten was mewing. Lizzie's worries began to wane in the next few weeks as Kathleen was getting stronger daily with a feisty personality and alert twinkling eyes. All welcomed the petite little girl with a gregarious personality.

The snow was melting fast as the weather warmed. The family arrived at the Mission one sunny afternoon in the fall when Kathleen was nearly ten months old and would be baptized by Father Joset. Mat and Lizzie were happy and excited to show off their beautiful daughter. Several of their friends from the tribal community and neighbors stood with them. There were smiles and a few snickers as many realized Mat's son Antoine had a daughter also named Catherine in Spokane Falls. The family often joked about Mat's fast horse[149] as they teased that Catherine was Mat's daughter. Father Joset led the ceremony, and Lizzie's eldest son, John, and her mother stood as witnesses. Father Joset moved discreetly in his long dark robe across the floor of the Old Mission to greet them. He was thin and pale, but there was always a playful smile and loving words for the children.

Father Joset had been boarding at Mat's hotel for three years and had become a close family friend. He was quite proud of being the only priest to have a horse and buggy. He would pick up Mat's children when he was living at the hotel and take them to the Mission for mass. He kept busy making linguistic studies of the Coeur d'Alene and Kalispel tribes, helping to translate between the tribe and the settlers. He advised the local natives on what to plant at the Mission and helped the people learn to communicate with one another. He traveled between the Mission and Spokane as he was asked to supervise and manage the construction of the Gonzaga Preparatory School. He passed away in 1900 at the age of 90.

Molly

Molly Powers Hayden

Molly walked along the banks of the river, singing softly. It was early spring and there were still patches of soft, slushy snow along the embankment. The clear sky gave one the impression that it was much warmer. It was a wonderful spring day and Molly looked forward to summer. She wore the heavy wool sweater that her grandmother knitted for her at Christmas. The speckled gray and brown nubby wool was a stark contrast to her curly dark hair and blue eyes. Molly was ten years old. She was very happy thinking about her mother's marriage and skipped along the banks of the river. Molly could see the Old Mission church and signs of activity among the teepees and small log cabins on the hill. The family all spoke the Salish language. Her brothers spent time in the woods hunting and tracking with friends who lived at the Mission. They quickly learned the ways of the wilderness.

The hemlock and cottonwood trees along the bank were budding and one could see the ferns and wild ginger beginning to push their sleeping heads up from the forest floor after the long winter. Molly was on a special mission to find as many flowers and grasses as she could. She loved to find the small bright flowers full of sun. One of her favorite flowers was the delicate fairy slipper. She could find them hiding in shaded areas near rotting tree stumps. The prolific grass widows were blooming, and the meadow was a lavender sea floating over the green stalks of the lacy ferns. The bright Glacier Lilies (dog's tooth violets) with their bright yellow petals curled under were a good addition to a bouquet. Molly found several leggy buttercups to go alongside them. Molly knew her grandmother would want to put them on the table in the lovely blue China vase Mat brought from Coeur d'Alene City. Mat told her the buttercups were poisonous and not to be tempted to eat them.

Molly was wandering in the fields while her brothers John and Tom were successfully fishing and displaying the trout on the bank nearby. The river was very clear and one could see the smooth river rocks below the surface. The boys were casting their poles far out into the water and Molly could hear them laughing. They were also excited that Mat and their mother had married. He was the father they would remember best. It seemed like a long time since they were in New York. The boys were bantering back and forth as to who caught the largest fish. She would help clean them before heading home.

Mission Landing[150]

Mat kept busy expanding his investments. While he was in Spokane Falls in January of 1887, he purchased lots 6 and 7 in block 1 of the Sanders addition. He was to pay Jacob Hoover

$375.00 with 1.25 percent interest per month. A handwritten note dated February 24, 1887, showed that Mat borrowed $500 against his property at Hayden Lake. Lizzie signed the indenture as "Louise Hayden". She and Mat were married four weeks later.

Catching the wind. Soldiers from Fort Sherman would build boats with runners like ice skates and a three-point suspension, allowing the ice sailor to tack.[151]

Mat agreed that he would keep the Spokane Falls buildings insured for four hundred dollars. Three fires that year in Spokane caused $80,000 in damage in four weeks, and when the city was slowly beginning to recover, six more buildings burned. The fire started on the second floor of the Rising Sun Lodging House, but without any water or ladders for the volunteers to put it out, it quickly spread into Sires' Saloon, the new Occidental Hotel, a millinery store, and grocery stores causing damage to both sides of the street. Mat was surprised at how much destruction the fire caused, and how fast the city was growing with new migrants arriving daily. Thirty new residences were built that summer.

Two years later In August of 1889, 32 city blocks of Spokane burned. The commercial buildings were rebuilt in stone, brick and terra cotta. The "sporting people" lost their established way of earning a living when the saloons burned. [152]

Legal Disputes and Property Claims

Father Joseph Cataldo was very popular with the Spokane tribe. They called him S'Chuisse, which means dried salmon. He studied over twenty languages and became proficient in Salish, Nez Perce, and other native languages. He eventually wrote one of the first books in the Nez Perce Language. Several members of the Coeur d'Alene tribe complained to Father Cataldo and Mat about the number of settlers that were moving onto the Mission land. Mat's homestead property was half a mile north of the Mission and he had contracted with the Jesuits to grow timothy along the river. He knew that the settlers would keep coming.

Less than a week before his marriage to Eliza, Mat filed a lawsuit at the Kootenai County Court House on the 22nd of March, 1887, in Coeur d'Alene against Arthur Frost and fourteen others.[153] The defendants, who resided on the land in dispute, hired attorney Mr. J.S. Allen of Spokane Falls. They were served the next day. Mat received $400 from Father Cataldo for the case. The cost for filing the complaint was $7.50. Three days later, Mat paid Reverend Father Diamedo $10.00 for reporting and transcribing the case of M. Hayden vs. A. Frost et al.

Looking north on Railroad Avenue, Cataldo, Idaho. Mission City's name was changed to Cataldo.[154]

The settlers claimed land surrounding the Mission and said Mat and the Jesuits were not entitled to possession of the land. The defendants claimed that Mat and the Jesuits had not claimed the land before March 2, 1853, and had not received the title from the United States. They argued the land was in the public domain and subject to settlement under the Homestead laws of the United States. The defendants claimed they did not injure any crops, trees, grasses, buildings, or fences that were previously erected. They built valuable and permanent improvements. The group filed their defenses on April 2, 1887, with the plaintiff and his attorney. Mat's attorney questioned why they did not hire an Idaho attorney and why they did not know the land was occupied.

On August 13, 1883, Mat stated that the religious association known as the Society of Jesus bought the land mentioned in the complaint from the Coeur d'Alene tribe in 1846. He sent a telegram from Coeur d 'Alene City asking for the Rev. Joseph M. Cataldo to come to court as a witness to testify. Father Cataldo confirmed that he was a member of the Catholic Religious Association known as the "Society of Jesus" and their objective was to civilize and convert the native tribes of the earth. He added that as early as 1846, missionaries were sent into territories inhabited solely by native tribes. He felt that it was the duty and object of said missionaries to establish missionary stations so that the indigenous peoples might have an opportunity to avail themselves of religious teaching. Furthermore, the Society of Jesus paid the native tribes the price offered for possession and occupancy within the laws that were established at that time. Louis Brown of Missoula County in Montana Territory testified that these statements were true and he acted as the interpreter between the Jesuits and the natives. Mat realized how fortunate he was with the care and help he had found in the West, far from the prejudices he felt in New York and the East Coast of the United States.

The judgment called for the defendants to vacate the land. Mat agreed with William Lane to "rent a tract of land covered by certain buildings known as Mrs. Madden Log House." The rent would be $2.00 monthly, paid in advance. Upon forfeiture of the lease, he would quietly and peaceably deliver up the possession of the premises and all buildings and improvements which he may have added.

Not long after the judgment, Mat went by the steamer into Coeur d'Alene City on the 11th of June of 1887. He paid the three dollars, to Robert E. McFarland, the Register, and Receiver of the Land Office, to file his homestead claim for his ranch near Mission City. Receipt, No. 62 acknowledged that the land of 157.45 acres was settled on June 1st, 1884. On March 3, 1879, a law was passed stating that a notice of intention to file a land claim must be given by publication in a newspaper for thirty days in five consecutive issues of the paper. The notice was to include the names of the witnesses by whom the facts of the claim could be established. On the testimony of the claimant, it is written that evasive answers will be fatal to the proof. Mat answered the questions about his claim by stating:

June 1, 1884: That he used the land for farming and haying. He said the timber amounted to nothing with a few scrubby pine and fir trees on the land and that he had only taken enough for fencing or firewood. He added that he did own a house and lot at the lake. He swore that he did not have any other housing or boarding place and that his family moved there in the fall of 1886 and has lived there since. He described "our house as 20x30 log, hewed, lined and sealed with three rooms and an upstairs worth $300.00 with a 14x20 addition. And another house, log, hewed 14x18, $100. Smokehouse, chicken house, and woodshed worth $200.00, bunkhouse, barn, and stable 60 x18 worth $300.00. All worth at least $800. I have also $300 worth of ditching. I have 2 ploughs, one rolling harrow, one mowing machine 2 wagons, 2 axes, spade, shovel and hoes, 50 head of cows and steers, 30 head of hogs, 4 horses, eight mules, bedsteads, chairs and washstand, tables, kitchen furniture, 4 beds. I have had such things ever since I have been there. I have a few head of stock around Coeur d'Alene, they are cows. I have raised crops 8 seasons. They are vegetables, hay, grain and corn. About 50 acres each year. I can't tell how much I raise because the crops are different. It is in crops this year. I carry on no business there but farming. I work for myself only and have done so since I went there. I have been assessed at the Mission for personal taxes alone and paid there in Kootenai County. They are assessed for taxes. I don't know what valuation my stock is and all but the amounts to over $7. I use it exclusively for farming no one else uses it. I have not sold or done anything of the kind.

Mat's land claim for his Mission Ranch was filed on July 30th, 1887.

The official signature of the claimant, Mathew Hayden.

Octave Quay, Richard Wilson, Ben Nason, Joe Wimpy, and Pat Whalen gave testimonies to Robert McFarland as witnesses for Mat.[155] The men testified "they were not related or interested in Mat's claim and that he had built and paid for all the structures. They stated that Mat raised and sold crops, like timothy, oats, hay, and vegetables, and that he worked for himself and was never absent more than a day or two at a time to some town not far away on business. They swore he lived on the property for three years, breaking the land and farming. They stated that his family resides on the property and had moved in the previous autumn and became married. They added that Mat built the second house for them, stating both houses were good and habitable for all seasons with windows and doors. They agreed the land is mostly prairie and has little timber. Richard Wilson said he lived a half-mile from Mat and had worked for him in the past plowing. He said he, Richard, now sells whiskey." After his claim was approved for the land near the Mission, Mat paid the Receiver's office $2.50 per acre for the land.[156]

Kentuck / Wardner

When he was in Coeur d'Alene, Mat would stop at J.P. Healy's, a grocer and merchant, to pick up supplies for his Hayden Lake camp. Mat typically stayed at his cabin on the west side of the lake and built a second cabin for his men on the east side of the lake on Yellow Banks Creek. Since he was often gone, Mat negotiated with Clement King to keep an eye on his Hayden Lake ranch while he was out of town. Mat collected a good supply of hides to trade, and local merchants purchased most of the timber the workers provided. The timber was disappearing as fast as the ax man could fall it.[157]

1887 receipt from J.P. Healy's for goods for the Hayden Lake Camp.

After stopping by Healy's, Mat visited with Tony Tubbs and James Monaghan and discussed the booming economy of the small towns being built in the wilderness, particularly the town of Kentuck. Mat decided to purchase land in Kentuck. Mat purchased

Lot 14 in Block 12 on Main Street in the town of Kentuck on March 3, 1886, for $75.00. He purchased a second lot for future commercial buildings. In the fall of 1887, he built the post office and was busy constructing two twin cottages to be used as rental properties. The Morning Oregonian reported: "Improvements in Kentuck were rushing along right into winter. Among them, we note in the course of erection a large store by W.A. Haskins, a two-story frame by Mat Hayden, two dwellings by Parter and Comer, one by Block, two dwellings by A.L. Bradford, and one dwelling by C. Bill." [158] On April 4, 1886, a group of men met to rename Kentuck to Wardner. Sixteen years later in 1902, a charter was granted to change the name of Kentuck to Wardner.

Kentuck was a "rip-roaring western mining camp. Its log and rough board buildings sprawled along both sides of the narrow Milo Gulch with a rough dirt street down the middle. It ran from below the site of the Bunker Hill discovery, northeastward to Kellogg. Its structures consisted of log dwellings, and false-fronted business establishments like restaurants, saloons, gambling casinos, dancehalls, a bank, mercantile stores, mining supply shops, and of course, the inescapable red-light district." By April 1886, the population of Kentuck was 500 people.

The people of Kentuck wanted a school and by December they had raised enough money to hire a teacher for a few months. Most of the miners in Kentuck were from Wales or e Scandinavian countries. In the spring, they looked forward to the folk tradition of May Day with bonfires and speeches, followed by the Maypole dance and feast. The children picked flowers for filled May baskets and placed them on the steps of homes. If they were caught, they were often given a kiss and invited in for something to eat. Among the many migrants that flooded into North Idaho in the late 1880s were the Finnish. Despite finding English difficult to learn, the Finns were politically active in the area. They constructed six workers' halls within a forty-mile radius of each other but never built a church. Enaville was the center where they held workers' meetings and performed amateur plays, sometimes infiltrated with socialist doctrine. Finnish-style saunas were popular and men were given the privilege of going first. Switches made from willow branches were used to make the bather tingle.[159] The men were praised for their woodworking and log construction in their homes and farms. Finnish women were known for their luscious cardamom bread twisted into rings. They grew productive vegetable gardens and braided colorful rag rugs. Many of them worked as the area's midwives. On the 24th of June, a midsummer festival was celebrated with picnics, music, footraces, and speeches. Skis were carved from red pine and straps were made from old leather harnesses.

One transplant, Sarah Krogue, an energetic young brunette, arrived alone in the turbulent roaring town of Kentuck after leaving her family behind in Spangle, Washington. Sarah found work in a boarding house to earn her keep and started taking in laundry in a shed behind the house. When Al Page was going to close his seedy and dilapidated restaurant, "The Mint," Sarah told him she would clean it and do the cooking. The restaurant was such a success that Al purchased clothing and a buggy to go "courtin" with some of the local widows. Sarah told Al they needed fresh produce for the restaurant and that he better plant a garden. The Mint later burned and Sarah talked Al into leasing a hotel that was about to close. She soon hired two cooks, four waitresses, three bartenders, and maids to clean the rooms. With the success of her business, she was buying beef, hogs, and chickens from Mat and giving out tokens stamped with Page Hotel to trade for a drink or a cigar. Many of the businessmen would bring their wives to the Page Hotel for dinner. Al started courting local women, Sarah decided to gussied up and, went to Spokane and ordered a chic wardrobe. Sarah convinced Al that it was time to marry her. She was 28, industrious, and smart. Dances at the Page Hotel were popular for many years and people from neighboring towns would pole up the river from as far away as Kingston to attend.[160]

This Indenture, Made the *3rd* day of *March* in the year of our Lord, eighteen hundred and eighty *six*.

WITNESSETH: That *Lloyd Beall*

of *Town of Kentucky* part *y* of the first part,

for and in consideration of the sum of *Seventy Five* Dollars, *lawful Money* of the United States of America,

to *Him* in hand paid by *Matthew Hayden*

of *Town of Kentucky* part *y* of the second part, the receipt of which is hereby acknowledged, do *es* by these presents, remise, release and forever quit claim unto the said part *y* ot the second part, and to *His* heirs and assigns forever, all of the following described real estate, situated in *Shoshone* County, *Idaho Territory* to-wit:

Lot Number 14 Block 12

Main Street Town of Kentucky

Said Lot being on the Town Records

Together with all and singular the tenements, hereditaments and appurtenances belonging or appertaining thereto, and also all *His* estate, right, title, interest, possession, claim of dower and homestead; and the rents, issues and profits of, in and to said real estate; TO HAVE AND TO HOLD the same to the said part *y* of the second part, and to *His* heirs and assigns forever.

IN WITNESS WHEREOF, The said part *y* of the first part ha *s* hereunto set *His* hand and seal the day and year first above written.

Signed in presence of

James H. Kelly

L. Beall (Seal)

(Seal)

Mat purchased Lot 14, Block 12 in Kentuck, on March 3, 1886, and built two twin homes on the property he rented. The city of Kentuck assessed the property at $2,000. He also owned Lot 12 Block 11.

Kentuck's name was changed to Wardner in 1887. The United States census of 1890 gives the population of Shoshone County by precincts: Burke, 482; Carbon, 157; Delta, 106; Eagle, 56; Elk, 339; Kellogg, 324; Kingston, 158; Mullan, 818; Murray, 450; Osburn, 269; Pierce, 238; Wallace, 913; Wardner, 858; Weippe, 156. Totaling: 5,882.[161]

Sarah and Al rented one of Mat's Kentuck homes and he insisted on including a clause in the lease agreement that the "lessee would prohibit subletting." The Goddard sisters were planning to move out and they recommended a "reliable gentleman" as a good tenant. The postmaster, J.C. Feahan, agreed to pay Mat the rent through 1891 at which time he said he would vacate the premises. Mrs. Tilly rented the other half of the house from Mat. Mrs. Tilly asked him to put an awning over the front doors to keep the "snow from the doors." A local carpenter offered to build it for $40.00. It was known as Tilly's Lodging on Lot 12, Block 14, which had two twin cottages. Mrs. L. Tilly agreed to purchase the lots on October 15, 1891, for $1,650.00. The rate of taxation would be $1.55 per $100. **(A-9)**

After Jim Wardner's many successes in Idaho, he went looking for a new challenge. Wardner met Nelson Bennett, a railroad conductor in Spokane, who convinced him to get involved in the building boom in Puget Sound. Bennett built the first standard gauge railroad in Fairhaven, Washington, north of Seattle. Within a few months after moving, Jim Wardner organized the Fairhaven Water Works Company. He became president of the Electric Light Company and vice president of the National Bank. He started the Samish Lake Lumber and Mill Company, and the Blue Canyon Coal Company. He purchased 135 lots and sold them making $60,000 in profit in two months. He hired Kirtland Cutter to build him a twenty-three-room house overlooking the bay of Fairhaven. The home included six fireplaces and beautifully groomed landscaping. His wife, Mary, and seven children were quite surprised at the large home after living in small cottages in Idaho.

When a reporter asked Jim Wardner what was new out on Bellingham Bay, he told him that he was establishing the Consolidated Black Cat Company. He planned to buy the 2000-acre Eliza Island, put up a few shelters, and raise black cats for their pelts. The pelts would be harvested for muffs and capes and then sold to consumers in the east as made from seal. The company was never started. His interest began to diminish in Fairhaven. Jim sold his coal company, logging business, and home, at the right time. Two years later the country was in a depression. Jim Wardner died in El Paso, Texas, in 1905.

Gonzaga Prep

Father Cataldo began a day school at Peone Prairie, twelve miles northeast of Spokane Falls in 1880 at St. Michael's Mission. He was concerned that if he didn't start a school the Native American children would lose their spiritual education or be coaxed to join the Protestants. The school proved to be a success and plans were made to build a second school. In 1881, he purchased an old carpenter shop and held the first Catholic mass in Spokane Falls. The next year, he added 320 acres on the north side of the river. Father Cataldo envisioned the school would be for Native American children. When Father Joset arrived and tried to register two Native Americans, he was turned away by Father Rehmann. The school needed the financial support of the Catholic settlers and only white students were admitted.

Mat and Lizzie felt that education was important for their children but there were no schools in the Mission precinct at Cataldo. Traveling to the Wardner School would be difficult in the winter. John, Lizzie's son, had attended school for five years in New York and enjoyed reading in the winter months when there was less work to do on the farm, although there was always plenty to do repairing equipment and getting ready for spring. He often read papers for the prospectors who stayed at the hotel and would earn an extra penny or two. Molly spent her time teaching her two younger brothers and Mat to read during the long winters.

The Spokane Printing Company announced the opening of the Jesuit school and explained the requirements for admission. The young men were to be ten years of age or older and must know how to read and write. A list of clothing to be supplied by the family included "two suits, one for daily wear and the second for Sundays, six shirts and collars, six pairs of socks, six handkerchiefs, four pairs of drawers, four undershirts, six towels, six napkins, two or three neckties, two or three pairs of boots or shoes, a pair of rubbers, an overcoat, brushes, combs, and other toilet articles." The attic of the school was divided into two dormitories which would sleep forty students. There were eight rooms on the second floor, two large classrooms, a library, a bathroom, a toilet room, and rooms for the professors.

John Powers

Mat and Lizzie made plans to send John to Spokane to attend the Gonzaga Preparatory School which would open on September 17, 1887. The 12-year-old boy was proud to be going off to school to prove to the family how independent and mature he was. The couple took John shopping at Culbertson's department store in Spokane Falls. John enjoyed watching the livery footman assist his mother from the carriage. He gained self-confidence with his new dapper clothing and was excited to be going to school to meet other boys his age. He loved the outdoor lifestyle that Idaho offered him, yet he welcomed the change of being in Spokane City. Tuition, room, and board for the ten months at the school were $250. Library fees were $1.00 and music lessons with an instrument were $6.00. There were no extra fees for laundry. The prospectus was mailed out before the final faculty selection and before the school was furnished. A Jesuit college in Wisconsin closed and offered its furnishings to Gonzaga. The first student to register was from Helena, Montana, and others enrolled from San Francisco, Fort Sherman, and Spokane Falls. The boys planted a vegetable garden, grew grain, raised chickens, milked cows, and boarded horses. The empty prairie lands gave them space to play and explore.

The students' day began at 5:45 each morning, followed by morning prayers at 6:20. Breakfast was served at 7:30, and on recreation days, the boys went on regular walks under the supervision of the prefects. Classes began at 8:45 with a recess break from 10:30 until 10:45. The elective classes continued until noon. Following lunch, they had classes or work schedules to fulfill. A light snack was provided before a recreation period at 4:30. A light supper was served at 6:15 with studying required until

8:45. Night prayers were recited and lights were off by 9:00. On Tuesday and Thursday afternoons were set aside for chores. Students were required to pass a difficult test to advance to the next grade level. Out of 35 boys, registered 27 passed their first year. As restrictive as the school was, John enjoyed it but missed home. John's father was listed as Mathew Hayden from Old Mission.

John is seated on the step next to the Father on the left with his hands folder. Gonzaga Preparatory School, 1887.[162]

Special classes were given to those students who lacked knowledge of the rudiments or prevented them from following regular courses. Students were examined and placed according to their abilities. The curriculum was designed for the students to attain proficiency in Latin, Greek, English, Christian Doctrine, History, Geography, Arithmetic, Mathematics, Penmanship, Bookkeeping, German, and French. Music classes were optional. Arithmetic is a branch of mathematics dealing with numbers and properties, whereas mathematics is the study of measurements of quantities of numbers and symbols, including the proofs of theorems.

By 1892 Gonzaga had electric power in the classrooms. Eight professors and forty students had their sleeping quarters in the attic. Poetry, rhetoric, and philosophy were added to the curriculum. Baseball was a welcome break and the boys enjoyed competition against local teams. Football was introduced but banned after several years for being too dangerous. Tom was given new skates in his second year at Gonzaga. Skating was very popular with adults and children.

Molly missed her serious and chivalrous older brother. Mat knew John was well taken care of by Father Cataldo. John was popular with the other boys. In his fourth year, 1890-91, his report showed his classes with Distinction were Christian Doctrine, English, Arithmetic, and Geography. Latin and History were 1st Premium and Penmanship was 2nd Premium. A premium award was given to Robert Monaghan, James' son, by the vote of his peers. John came next in merit with five other boys. Mat was proud of John's achievements.

Cataldo Grizzly

Life in Northern Idaho

The Hoydens were looking forward to spring. The snow was nearly all melted and the grasses were beginning to sprout. Mat and Lizzie took the steamer to Coeur d'Alene and then into Spokane by stage to celebrate their first wedding anniversary and visit John. Lizzie was pregnant and due in the summer.[163] Kate (Kathleen) was over a year old and beginning to walk on her wobbly legs. She jabbered constantly and wanted everyone to know she was the boss. She looked like a miniature adult.

Lizzie had learned about many plants that had medicinal purposes from the women at the Mission. Camus was used to induce labor or stop bleeding. It was an important food plant for the tribes of the Pacific Northwest. Lizzie learned to make a poultice from the roots of the sticky geranium to dry up sores or for aching arthritic backs and sore feet. The bluebells and camas provided a sea of blue as they floated over the hillsides above the grasses. The periwinkle blue and purple lupines were in bloom. Daisies appeared as a soft comforter suspended over the fields. Lizzie cut bouquets of white and fragrant lilacs for the house. The women at the Mission used branches for digging sticks or shaped them into pipes, harpoons, bows, arrows, and snowshoes. Lizzie loved the scents of each of the seasons. The fall would bring the clusters of red-orange berries of the mountain ash, the gold needles of the tamarack reaching to the sky, and the colors of the red and orange leaves. She cut bouquets of colorful deciduous leaves and dark Oregon grape berries and brought them into the house. In winter, she cut evergreen boughs and snowberries along with rose hips and holly.

On June 13, 1888, Mat and Lizza welcomed Anna Elizabeth into their growing family. Like Kathleen, Anna was baptized at the Old Mission in Cataldo with the seventy-eight-year-old Father Joset officiating. Mat loved taking the family by steamer into Coeur d'Alene on a summer day. It was a special occasion when they took Anna that summer and spent the night. They had dinner in town at one of the hotels. There were pleasure boats on Lake Coeur d'Alene when, ten years before, there were few families in North Idaho. In five years, the trains would bring tourists for weekends or day excursions from Moscow, Colfax, Walla Walla, and Spokane. Barges offered dancing with live music trips on the St. Joe River. The women wore large summer hats to keep the sun from their faces and carried parasols on visits to the Old Mission on the Coeur d'Alene River at Cataldo. Tourists appreciated the dramatic landscapes of forested mountains dropping to the blue of the lake. Occasionally, Mat and Lizzie would travel to Coeur d'Alene City for a weekend of shopping, dining, and dancing. They would attend mass on Sunday mornings at the little red Fort Chapel. Mat and Lizzie would enjoy a picnic when the Fort Sherman band played in the park before taking the steamer back to the Mission. They always had a lot of fun together and were happy. The boys were excited to see a baseball game when the local club "The Boys in the Blue" challenged Camp Spokane to a game. The secretary-treasurer of the club, Albert Wedemeyer, arranged for the 2nd Infantry Band to play.

Another year passed, and winter turned into summer. Mat traveled to Hayden Lake where he talked to his foreman, Chas Zetting to ensure everything was running smoothly. Chas made charges at V.W. Sander's Mercantile, and the bill needed to be paid. Nine charges totaling $124.68 were made between April 22 and June 10, 1889. He stopped at the mercantile on the 19th of June to pay $80.00 and said he would have to catch up when he had more cash. He stopped on July 21, 1889, and overpaid, leaving a credit at the store as he knew his men would need more supplies.

Mat and Lizzie were busy with their bustling family and his growing businesses. With each day busier than the last, time was passing quickly. The following spring, Mathew was in fine spirits when he placed an order with Tom Meherin's to buy trees and shears for pruning. The shears were good ones at $2.50. Tom's nursery carried a large variety and supply of trees that could be grown in the cold country of Idaho. He purchased 300 Monterey cypress trees, two Lauson cypress, five Italian cypress, and two Bovitas **(A-10)**. He was ready to go to work planting and he knew his children would help him. He would also hire members of the Coeur d'Alene tribe to help.

On April 25, 1890, Mat went into Coeur d'Alene City by steamer and picked up fabrics and thread for Lizzie, shoes for the children, and supplies for his camp at Hayden Lake. He ordered one hundred pounds of sugar, seventy pounds of coffee, tea, syrup, oatmeal and other essentials. The total at V.W. Sanders was $43.74 which he paid for in cash.[164] Oats were to be delivered to the Hayden Ranch on Monday for the calves, cows, and horses. He picked up a horse at the livery to ride over to the Hayden Camp. It was a warm day, and Mat removed his jacket as he listened, to the squeaking of the saddle. He was relaxed but was thinking of a problem in Wardner. Mrs. Tilly had complained of a leaking roof in the twin cottages, she rented. He would need a few more supplies. The rain in the spring often brought mudslides. A full stream could wash out bridges and make travel perilous. He would spend two nights at his camp giving his foreman, Chas, and his men guidance.

Mat began making plans for the proposed new businesses on Hayden Lake. He placed an order for 156 fruit trees and bushes from a nursery at The Dalles in Oregon to be delivered to Coeur d'Alene He ordered yellow prunes, Russian apricots, quinces, currants, and several varieties of pears and apples. He included a dozen English gooseberry bushes for his favorite pie, as Lizzie made the best in town. **(A-11)**

It was difficult for the United States Postal Service to deliver mail to the settlers and frontiersmen in the Western territories since they were not in one place and did not have permanent addresses. Mat's naturalization papers were deemed undeliverable and held at the dead letter office until they eventually reached him in late March 1890. **(A-12)** When Mat received his citizenship papers, he sang an old Irish pub song and did a little tap dance. Mat would now be able to continue his endeavor to become a successful landowner and entrepreneur in America. Twenty-nine years after initially signing his Declaration of Intention to become naturalized, he became an American citizen. A few months later, on July 12, 1890, he received his Homestead Certificate for his Mission property.[165] He had settled on the 160 acres near Mission City eight years prior. He was content reflecting on the life he had left behind. He had escaped the famine that struck his homeland. In New York, he toiled in indentured servitude and was persecuted for being an Irish immigrant. He combated the hardships of an enlisted soldier, often without proper nourishment or supplies. He thought about the poker game where he won his old buffalo robe, not realizing then that it would save his life and knowing some of his compatriots didn't make it through the freezing winters on the Plains. He laughed, recalling the night he beat John Hager in a card game for the right to name the lake north of Coeur d'Alene, Hayden's Lake. He was very happy and in love with Lizzie and their children. He was a lucky man, having achieved the independence and freedom he so desired when he stepped onto that ship bound for America as a thin, malnourished lad forty years ago. Mat was a profoundly happy man. He took a deep breath. He was 58 years old and felt he needed to slow down.

A cold glass of beer is a welcome break for Coeur d'Alene City bakers and restaurant employees. [166]

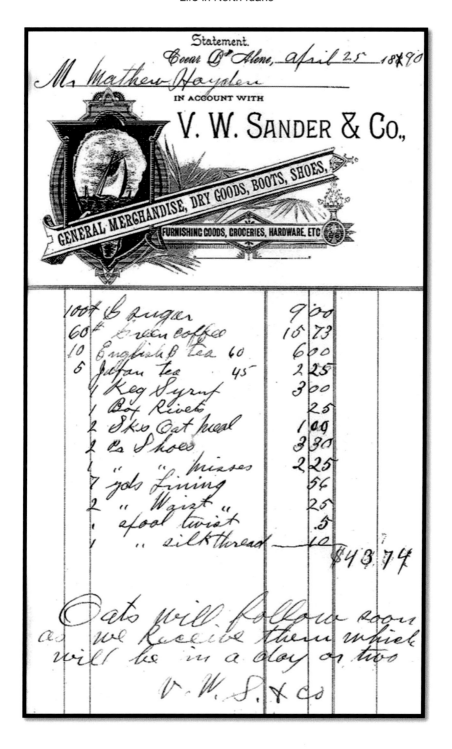

Statement.

Coeur D'Alene, April 25 1890

Mr Mathew Hayden

IN ACCOUNT WITH

V. W. SANDER & Co.,

GENERAL MERCHANDISE, DRY GOODS, BOOTS, SHOES,

FURNISHING GOODS, GROCERIES, HARDWARE, ETC

100#	Sugar	9	00
60#	Green coffee	15	73
10	English B tea 60	6	00
5	Julian tea 45	2	25
1	Keg Syrup	3	00
1	Box Rivets		25
2	Sks Oat meal	1	00
2	Prs Shoes	3	30
1	" " misses	2	25
7	yds Lining		56
2	" Waist "		25
1	spool twist		5
1	" silk thread		10
		$43	74

Oats will follow soon
as we Receive them which
will be in a day or two

V. W. S. & Co

Electric train meeting the steamer Idaho for a summer excursion on the lake.[167] *The Idaho* was first launched in 1903.

The Merriam building was completed in 1889 on the corner of 4th and Sherman. It is believed that Mat is standing (fifth from the left) on the corner with the light fedora and bag, facing east.[168]

Changes

Lizzie told Mat that they would be expecting another baby in June. He was ecstatic, and his laughter brought the children running. He loved his growing family. That spring Lizzie became concerned when Mat could not shake a bad cough. As it became chronic and worsened, he would get chest pains and chills. His sputum was often tinged with blood. The family was devastated as they knew what the symptoms could mean. Mat and Lizzie went to Coeur d'Alene City to seek the help of Dr. Colson, the physician at Fort Sherman. While in Coeur d'Alene, Mat began to make plans for the future of his family. He went to see Robert McFarland and hired him to pay his bills for the next few months.

Mat, to ensure the security of his family, began to get his affairs in order. He contacted his old acquaintance, August J. Morritz at Fort Vancouver to enlist his help in selling the merchantable timber and land he owned. He spoke with James and Margaret Monaghan and arranged to sell them the property he had recently purchased in Spokane. James purchased the two lots in Spokane for $1,100. Mat had originally purchased them six months prior for $1,250.[169]

A register at the U.S. Land Office that summer testifies to Mat's poor health:

U.S. Land Office, Coeur d'Alene, Idaho
July 5, 1890, Pre-Cash Entry No. 14 of Mathew Hayden.

The territory of Idaho County of Kootenai R.E. McFarland being duly sworn and says that he is personally well acquainted with Mathew Hayden who made Pre-cash Entry No 14 at Coeur D'Alene Land Office; that he knows the condition of said Hayden's health, and that the same is very poor and critical; that he is confined to his bed and has been for some months prior to the date hereof on account of consumption and liver disease; that affiant has been informed by said Hayden and his physician that he is apt to die of his disease at any time and that he cannot and is not expected to live longer than one month; affiant further says that Hayden is over fifty-eight years old and aside from his disease is a frail and weak man; that it is a common rumor in the neighborhood in which said Hayden lives that he cannot live longer than one month. That Dr. Colson who has attended upon said Hayden is now prostrated with grief over the death of a daughter who was lately killed in a railway accident and refuses to receive anyone by reason of which affiant is unable to procure his certificate as to said Hayden's condition; that it is said Hayden's desire to settle all of his business and dispose of all his property by will before his death and that he has so expressed himself to this affiant. R.E. McFarland. Subscribed and sworn to be before me this 5th day of July 1890. James E. Russell Register.

This is to certify that we have read the forgoing affidavit of R.E. McFarland and know the contents thereof; that his statement of Mathew Hayden's condition and the misfortune and prostrations of Dr. Corson of this city is also true and that we believe that everything stated in said affiant is true. WM. Mellure, Receiver. James E. Russell, Register.

A news article included with the affidavit titled "A Sad Accident."

Monday afternoon about six o'clock the westbound passenger train on the Northern Pacific, had its two rear sleepers derail near Drummond, Montana and thrown down a small embankment. Among the passengers were Miss Mary C. Colson, the 14-year-old daughter of Dr. J.K. Colson, at Ft. Sherman, who was killed by being thrown partially through a window and crushed under the car as it turned over. Miss Colson lived about an hour. Her father had started to meet her at Spokane Falls when a telegram announced the sad news was handed him. His grief knew no bounds. For the past four weeks, Mr. and Mrs. Colson have lived in a state of expectancy making every arrangement for the daughter's happiness when she should arrive from the east. Beloved by all who had the pleasure of her acquaintance, bright, generous and extremely courteous, there is not a single heart in the town but what is sad and full of sadness for the bereaved parents.

In 1890, consumption was blamed on spending time indoors consuming alcohol, the direct consequences of the outrageous violations of the physical laws of God, or the lymph. The Spokane Falls Review advertised several apothecary shops making promises to diminish the symptoms of consumption with a mixture of oils or a bottle of elixir from Dr. King. Free samples were available. Another article suggested if men could endure the temperature of an oven between 300-350 degrees, the hot air would attack and cauterize the diseased parts. The writer suggested that the plague was stopped by the Great Fire in London and heat would cure consumption. He suggested that someone other than himself should volunteer, and the idea could be tested in a baker's oven.[170]

At home, Mat wore a handkerchief over his face so he would not spread the disease to the children or Lizzie. A bed was made for him in the parlor downstairs. He was weak. Lizzie's mother took over Mat's care by feeding him nourishing broths and bathing him. The children stood in the doorway telling him about the pigs and chickens or problems they were having with farm equipment. Mat could still solve the problems. They listened silently with tears running down their faces. The family knew they could lose him at any time, but they also knew what a fighter he was with a strong mind. Mat always felt stronger when he was with his family. John and Tom did not want to start school in Spokane until after the baby was born. Lizzie and Mat agreed, and it was decided that the boys would not begin school until later that fall so they could help on the farm while Mat and Lizzie were unable.

With Mat's condition becoming critical and there being no signs of improvement, he and Lizzie took the train to Portland in August. They felt the urgent need to appeal to Dr. Cole at the Surgical and Medical Institute for help. Mat and Lizzie did not see any improvement from Dr. Cole's medical cure and disappointed, they continued by train to visit Dr. Stoddart at the Liebig World Dispensary in San Francisco. They spent three days at their mineral spring. The healing warm springs and mineral baths vitalized and arrested the ravages of the disease. Mat enjoyed the tranquility of the heat penetrating his muscles and the acrid smell of sulfur clearing his lungs.

On their way back to Idaho, Mat and Lizzie revisited Dr. Cole in Portland to discuss Mat's unsuccessful treatment. The men disputed the terms of the payment.

Lizzie went into labor on October 1, 1890. Tom, 11, took the buckboard wagon to the Whalens to pick up his Aunt Agnes to help with the birth. Eliza was there to assist and had been present for all the children's births. John, for his part, went to the Mission to send a message to Dr. L.M. Sims at the railroad hospital in Osburn.[171] The doctor was expected to arrive on the train. Frank Quinn,[172] (Quinny) the overseer and handyman at the ranch, was very close to the family. He spent a lot of time at the house when Mat had fallen ill, helping with meals and taking care of the children. Once everyone was home, their grandmother sent John, Tom, and Pat to wait on the porch with Anna and Katie. Frank Quinn loved the children and stayed outside entertaining the girls with string tricks and songs. Young Pat practiced spinning his yoyo. Mat's foreman, Pat Lucas, chatted with John and Tom about chores that needed to be done on the farm and plans for the months ahead. Molly stayed inside, warming towels and preparing a tepid bath for the baby.

Shortly after Dr. Sims arrived, the family could hear loud voices and screams coming from the bedroom. Eliza was yelling at Dr. Sims to get out. Agnes appeared in the doorway near the parlor with her face ashen and frozen in a state of shock. Her apron was covered in blood. Mat stood at the doorway and fell to the floor when he realized Lizzie and the baby had died. Weeping, his sorrow was immeasurable. Dr. Sims could not turn the baby with his forceps when she presented a hand and a foot in the birth canal. Lizzie pleaded with him to help her. He was too late for a cesarean. In the end, Lizzie's last words were, "You are murdering me." Lizzie and her daughter were buried at the Mission of the Sacred Heart overlooking the family farm. Father Joset officiated. The family planted a white lilac bush on the grave.[173]

Pat Lucas (William or Bill), Mats supervisor in Cataldo, wrote James regarding Dr. Sims.

Hayden Lake December 2, 1891
Mr Monaghan
You wish to know something about Dr. Simms he come to me about the middle of November a year ago when I was at the Mission and presented me a bill fifty dollars. he said he went to hospital to see Mr. Hayden. Matt told him to come to me. I told him I had no money and if I had I would not pay him. I told him he had murdered the woman and her child. Mrs. Hayden told him a dozen times you are murdering me. Pat Whalen's wife was there at the time...if she was my wife I would not pay him a cent—twenty five dollars would be enough if she lived. The logs are all roted they are not fit for woods or lumber.

Yours Respectfully WM Lucas

> Hayden Lake Dec 2. 1891
> Mr Monaghan
> You wish to know some thing about
> Dr. Simms. he come to me about the
> Midle of November A year ago. when I was
> at the Mission and presented me a bill
> fifty dollars. he said he went to Hospital
> to see Mr Hayden. Matt told him to
> come to me. I told him I had no money
> and if I had I would not pay him.
> I told him he had Murdered the woman
> and her child, Mrs Hayden told him
> A dozen Hot times Dr you are Murdering
> me Pat Whalan Wife was there at the
> Time, if she was my wife I would not
> pay him A cent. Twenty five dollars would
> be anough if she lived, The logs are all
> roted the are not fit for wood or lumber
>
> Yours Respectfully Wm Lucas

Cemetery records at the Cataldo Mission have not recorded the burial of Elizabeth Whalen Powers (Lizzie) Hayden or her baby. Family history concludes that she was buried there on the 9th of October 1890. She was 38 years old. A bill verifies that Mat purchased a coffin for Lizzie and sent it to the Mission **(A-15)**. James attended the mass for Lizzie, and upon seeing Mat's condition, he wired Sacred Heart Hospital to have him admitted. James told Mat he would order a stone for Lizzie. [174] Lizzie's mother passed away five years later and was buried next to her. Eliza's stone is within the white fence where the "good Catholics" were buried. It reads: "Eliza Whalen, Age 73, June 8, 1895, the wife of Dennis."[175] Lizzie's friend, midwife, and sister-in-law, Agnes Whalen, died in childbirth with her ninth child in 1904 at forty-four years of age.

On the 8th of November, 1890, Dr. Cole wrote: **(A-13)**

Replying to your favor of November 4, I have to say that I took your case for $125.00. You paid me $50, leaving a balance of $75. If you had continued my treatment your improvement would have been satisfactory, but instead you abandoned it in a few days and went to some California springs, then on your return, you again took treatment and abandoned that in a few days, so I am not to blame for your present condition. You violated our contract so I expect you to pay. Also I examined and treated your wife once for which you have not paid me. I will have the Dunn collecting agency hold some bill for a few days and will allow you to make me a proposition for settlement. Respectfully yours, A.S. Cole. M.D.

Mat responded from his bed to Dr. Cole's letter.

you did not treat my wife. She would not allow you to do so and told you so on my return. You said you would cure me if I remained under your care two days. I did so and at the end of that time I could not get upstairs and you advised me to go home as I was getting worse all the time. The understanding was $100 not $125, and your letter to my wife asked for $25.00 now you want 75.00 and you also told me to send you 25.00 when I was leaving and that would be satisfactory.

A better relationship was kept with Dr. Stoddart of San Francisco. The Haydens continued to purchase medicines from him, which he shipped to Idaho every month.

A letter dated Nov. 6th, 1890. **(A-14)**

Mr. M. Hayden,
Dear Sir, Yours of Nov 1st enclosing $10.00 has been received and same placed to your credit in books. Thanks for remittance. I have forwarded a full month's supply for your complaint. Persevere for a few months and you will be restored to health and strength. You have functional debility of several internal organs that can only be cured by preserving with the remedies for a few months. I will forward another supply in one month from now. Write in three weeks and give me all symptoms of cure.

Yours confidentially, Dr. Stoddart

The Old Pioneer

An article appeared in the *Spokane Falls Review* by Wm. Varker on Thursday, November 27, 1890.

A Dying Pathfinder

Mathew Hayden for Whom Hayden Lake was named is Nearing the Grave.
Noble, Hospitable Pioneer Whose Many Good Qualities Will Long Be Remembered.

Mathew Hayden, an old pioneer of the great Northwest, is lying at death's door at the hospital of the Sacred Heart.

Others there are who, in various institutions, where the suffering are tenderly cared for, are nearing life's extremity. Each short hour, marked by the hands of a million clocks, besides adding sixty minutes to the age of the universe, adds hundreds of names to the list of the world's great majority. During all these, there is not one sorrowful event that is surrounded by such an atmosphere of pathos as the story suggested by the lamentable illness of one of the sturdiest pathfinders that Idaho and Washington ever knew.

Three motherless and almost fatherless children are now being taken care of at St. Joseph's Orphanage, near Spokane Falls. At the Old Mission, on the CDA river, are three others, sons of the same father, to whom the Mission's sheltering walls are a home, and the love of the Jesuit fathers the only parental sympathy they are conscience of. Seven members of the same family, separated by unkind fate, the father dying and the youngest children unconscious of their impending bereavement, form the characters of a story that all of the Northwest's pioneers are deeply interested in.

Mathew Hayden, the father, was one of the earliest settlers of the beautiful valley of the Kootenai. Nearly forty years ago he entered British Columbia, and opened a roadside Inn. He established terms of amity with the Indians, and became a firm friend of all the early settlers. Travelers in those regions found in him a genial host, and the unfortunate an ever ready friend and sympathizer. "His latch–string was always on the outside of the door and the good cheer of his hospitable home was everybody's," said an old friend, in speaking of their early days of boon companionship. "Although he kept an Inn, it was more of the nature of a home, where everyone might find shelter and a welcome. It was for this reason, perhaps, that, after a few years spent in that locality, he was forced to seek a better paying location. Others, whom he once had fed and clothed, were in affluent circumstances when he shouldered the few remnants of his shattered fortune and made his way into the Coeur d'Alene valley."

His early education, through circumstances controlled by others than himself, was neglected. Thrown into contact with all that was rude and uncouth, and buffeted by the not too gentle zephyrs of adversity, he still maintained the peculiar integrity that characterized him in all his transactions with other people. In the beginning of his life, the principles of the Catholic faith, to which he was a strong adherent, were taught him by a loving mother, and intensified by a nature in which inherent honesty was a leading characteristic. To this same early training, is one of many of those pleasant features of character that have conspired to win him a host of friends. To the strong faith in human nature that he held, and his own principles of righteousness, perhaps is due the fact that with his opportunities he had not retained the half dozen princely fortunes that he accumulated in the course of an eventful career.

The State of Washington, even as a Territory, was little known in the days of Mr. Hayden's youth. The great wealth of Okanogan country hardly contributed subject matter for the dream of the wildest enthusiasts. There were cold winters and Indians in plenty. A few trading posts formed the foundation to fortunes since erected. The blue coated boys that worked for Uncle Sam for $14.00 per month were as few and far between as Angel visitations. It was upon the pioneer residents that the task of preserving their own interests devolved. There was the talent, in rude form, of statesman, and the physical abilities of armies in the little band that then inhabited and paved the way for the development of the country. Even under the most adverse circumstances the way was built over which the boom has subsequently traveled, and the country was open that since has borne that charming child named Spokane Falls.

The Jesuit fathers in the early days owned large and valuable tracks of bottom land these were leased to Mr. Hayden during the latter part of the 60's, and were sown with timothy. Hay was a staple commodity in the days when horses filled the place now taken by the steam engines and brought a high price. A government contract of lordly dimensions was taken by the lessee of the property. Fortunate smiled again and for a time the record of events in Mr. Hayden's life was as unvaried as Mark Twain's celebrated diary.

The financial weather remained as clear as the summer's morning on Pike's Peak. The pioneer farmer, in his own palmy days, did not forget the troubles of others, and succeeded, by his efforts in contributing materially to the success of others. He *subsequently fluctuated between the Colville and the Coeur d'Alene valleys. In 1881 he cultivated the Seltise farm. Later, in prospecting for a still better location, he settled upon railroad land near Hayden Lake and broke the first chunk of the soil of which he is now the owner. A townsite on the property was one of his pet projects and was about to be laid out when Mr. Hayden failed.*

The virulent malady, precipitated by sorrow over the death of his wife, attacked the husband and father shortly after the misfortunate that was felt alike by the children and their surviving parent. A short time ago he was brought to the hospital of the Sacred Heart for treatment. The physician said that he would never recover. Since then he has gradually declined. There are days when he seems almost to be in a way to recover, but they are followed by times when hope cannot find standing room.

He is fully conscious, but may not live more than a short time. A few days at most will witness the final scenes of the life of one who has been a singular example of unselfishness. There are many who, while they are powerless to aid, can say, when the end shall have come, "We have done all that we could." None can do more.

The Old Pioneer Passed Peacefully Away.
Anaconda Standard on the 28 November, 1890.

Matthew Hayden died last night at 12 o'clock at the hospital of the Sacred Heart. The deathbed scene was a pathetic one. Three of his little ones, who are being cared for by the sisters of St. Francis, were sent for early in the night, as it became evident that the hour of death was not far distant. The old man sank into a gentle sleep at 10 o'clock for which he never awoke. The group at the bedside watched the feeble trace of color that ebbed and flowed in his fevered cheeks. His breathing grew fainter as the clock ticked off the successive seconds of the night. A few minutes after midnight his breathing ceased, and the spirit passes unseen into the great hereafter. No sign of pain or recognition of his friends marked his last hours. Death came as the awakening from refreshing sleep.

Seventy-two years ago, (Mat was 58) Mr. Hayden was born near Galway, Ireland.[176] In his teens he immigrated to the United States and learned the secrets of American farming near Utica, N.Y. He came west thirty-eight years ago. He is known to all the oldest settlers of Washington, Idaho and British Columbia, to whom he was a firm friend. He owned large farms in the Coeur d'Alene Valley in Idaho. He leaves six children, three of whom

153

are at the Old Mission near Coeur d'Alene City. He leaves considerable property, which when apportioned among them will amply provide for their wants.

Mat passed away nearly two months after Lizzie on Thanksgiving Day, November 27, 1890. His obituary appeared in the Spokane Falls Review on Saturday, November 29. John, Molly, and Tom were with Mat during the long night when he died. They were taken to the sisters to spend the remainder of the night. The next afternoon, James' wife, Margaret Monoghan, picked up Molly to take her to Weil and Sawyers advertising "Dry Goods, Fancy Goods and Millinery" in Spokane Falls to purchase new clothing for Mat's services. They purchased a pair of black shoes, a heavy wool dress with satin lining, a felted hat with a dark purple plume, and gloves.

Catholic Mass was held outside in Coeur d'Alene during the summer months of 1887. Note the electric power lines. [177]

Mat's funeral took place at the Catholic church in Coeur d'Alene on 4th and Indiana.[178] November 30, 1890. The Catholic congregation had celebrated its first mass the week before. Mat wanted to be buried next to his beloved Lizzie, but it had snowed for days leaving Northern Idaho blanketed with several feet of waist-deep snow. It was impossible to return Mat to the Mission at

Cataldo. Mat's children, John, Molly, Tom, Pat, Katie, and Anna were picked up at the orphanage and taken to Coeur d'Alene City. They were accompanied by Frank Quinn and Pat Lucas. Quinny carried Anna who was a year and a half. Molly held tightly onto Kathleen, three. James Monaghan and his family arrived. James had made arrangements for two sleighs to meet them at the stage in Coeur d'Alene. The sleighs slid effortlessly over the snow which sparkled in the bright sunlight. Lizza's mother Eliza, Uncle Pat Whalen, and his family arrived from Cataldo.

Grey-speckled horses pulled the hearse fitted with sleigh rails. The carriage's beveled glass glistened in the sunlight. The hand-crafted oak and cedar funerary was urged on by George Winter.[179] Mat touched many lives in the thirty-three years he lived in the Northwest. People came from miles around to honor a man who was respected and loved. The church was crowded with men in knee-length topcoats, military uniforms, or heavy work clothes and women in fur-lined cloaks, plumed hats, and muffs. They came to say their goodbyes to a man who was always willing to help or loan a dollar. After the mass, a somber line followed the black-shrouded hearse, followed by Fr. Joset, Fr. Cataldo, and Fr. Mackin.[180] The casket was covered with an American flag. The procession of sleighs and people on foot proceeded south on Fourth Street, where Matt was laid to rest on his property at the foot of Tubbs Hill. His military friends fired three volleys after Father Mackin finished the prayers. The setting sun over the majestic Coeur d'Alene Lake brought comfort as ceremonial bugles played taps. The people quietly sang along: "Day is done, Gone the sun." The American flag from Mat's coffin was handed to his eldest stepson, John Powers. Large boughs of cedar, pine, and fir tied with colorful green ribbons were laid to mark the grave. Mat was one of Northern Idaho's most prominent citizens. James had arranged for the children to join his family on the return trip to Spokane.

Father Joset and James planned to move Mat to the Old Mission in Cataldo in the spring. His grave was not moved from his property at the base of Tubbs Hill until 1900 when St. Thomas Cemetery was opened by the parish on the eastern edge of Coeur d'Alene on 23rd and Sherman. John J. Costello, the county sheriff, donated the property to the church for the cemetery.[181] When you enter St. Thomas Cemetery from the east, one can see a tall white monument on the left where Mat lies. He is surrounded by all six of his children. His beloved Lizzie and her mother, Eliza Whalen, lie on the hillside below the Church of the Sacred Heart, known today as the Old Mission in Cataldo. No one in the family contracted Mat's consumption.

George Winter is driving the hearse for Thomas E. Hedel, Mortuary.[182]

On Saturday, December 6, 1890, the death of Mat appeared in the Wardner newspaper.

Matthew Hayden, a well-known pioneer of the northwest, died on Thursday, November 27, at the hospital of the Sacred Heart, Spokane. About forty years ago he settled in British Columbia where he kept a roadside Inn for some years. He subsequently fluctuated between the Colville and Coeur d'Alene valleys and in 1881 he cultivated the Seltise farm. later he settled upon railroad land near Hayden Lake, of which he was the owner when he died. A town site on that property was one of his favorite projects and was about to be laid out when he was taken ill. He leaves six children to mourn his loss.

Adapting

Molly, Pat, Kathleen, and Anna moved into the recently opened St. Joseph's Orphanage on the 26th of November. The children stayed close as they adjusted to the drastic change in their lives. They had lost their mother and father in eight weeks. Molly spent her time caring for Kate and Anna. Patrick played the harmonica to cope with his grief. According to Mat's will, James Monaghan became the ward of the children and executor of Mat's estate. He paid for the children's room and board, clothing, and necessities from Mat's accounts. The children spent their school holidays with the Monaghan's.

Spokane was a booming city with a population of 20,000, a railroad, and three parishes when St Joseph's Orphanage opened on July 25, 1890. Sister Barbara, the Mother Superior from the Franciscan Motherhouse in Philadelphia, arrived on August 22, 1890, with Sister Mary Neri. Sister Mary Onuphria's train reached Spokane on September 1, 1890. In two weeks, Sister Oswalda and Sister Rhabana joined the Orphanage staff. The following year, on November 2, 1891, the home was blessed by Rev. Charles Mackin S.J. with 70 children in residence. At Christmas, the younger children were given a toy or book. They had parties on special holidays and were given treats. On the second Sunday of each month, all girls between four and fourteen walked to Holy Names Academy to attend mass. On Sunday afternoons catechism was taught.

When Tom was twelve, he joined his older brother, John, at Gonzaga Prep. Tom missed his siblings and spent his free time at the orphanage with his sisters and brother, Pat. Tom was watchful, and quiet, with a fair complexion and slight build. He had followed Mat around the ranch and had learned to care for the farm equipment and tackle any job. School records showed Thomas Francis Hayden was born on September 14, 1879, when he was registered at Gonzaga Prep. Tuition was $250 per semester. The school organized a symphony and a military corps for the children to participate in. Tom slowly adjusted to the school and the new circumstances in which found himself. He had the security of his older brother John who told him about other students, priests, and nuns. The basement held two additional classrooms, a recreational area, a kitchen, and a refectory or dining room. The main floor had a chapel, an infirmary, and the president's room.

On Tom's record under remarks, it stated: "Remained at college during the vacation.

Tom Powers, with bow tie, 3rd row, third from the right of the 2nd Priest.[183]

The orphanage received no public financial aid and volunteers from the community came in to tutor the children. Being spirited, Molly got into trouble for sliding down the banister. The nuns were reminded that such behavior was not ladylike and set a bad example for other children. Although her room and board were paid, Molly had chores at the orphanage. Sister Mary Oswalde owned a white horse and buggy, which she used to travel through Spokane with the children to help collect funds for the Orphanage.[184] Molly was not happy to go with the begging bowl to ask for donations. Sister Barbara reminded the children that the vegetable patch needed to be carefully cultivated. Each fall the garden produced grapes, watermelons, peaches, apples, pears, and vegetables. The children canned fruit and made jellies, bread, cakes, and pies. By 1893, the orphanage had expanded to 115 children.[185]

St. Joseph's Orphanage. Mat's stepdaughter, Molly Powers Hayden, was thirteen when her parents died. Molly is in a long dark dress holding a baby in the center. Her brother Patrick, 8 is to her left. Anna, 2 and Kate, 4 are believed to be 4th and 5th from the left in the first row. In January 1891, forty children were living at St. Joseph's.

At meals, tablecloths and napkins were used. The children were expected to behave and display proper table manners. The orphanage had a bakery, kitchen, chapel, and parlor for 200 children. The infirmary was located on the second floor. The boys wore ties with white shirts and dark pants. The girls wore cotton dresses, dark hose, and a bonnet (which Molly detested) when serving meals. The children helped to cook, serve, and clean the kitchen. They made their beds and assisted the younger children.

One of the nuns was often heard saying, "Sweep the corners of the house and the rest of the floor will take care of itself." Once, when tired of sweeping, Molly threw her broom down and said, "OK, Sweep yourself." Her punishment was to do ten Hail Marys in the church with her arms outstretched. Many years later she gave similar sweeping advice to her granddaughters when teaching them how to clean.

It was not uncommon for babies and young children to be left on the doorstep of the orphanage. As the home became crowded with children, a large four-story building was completed in May of 1899. In 1901, Charles Sweeney, a capitalist and mining man, paid off the $28,000 orphanage debt and spent $10,000 to build a beautiful gothic chapel for the school.[186] A staff of physicians and nurses was on duty for the children. The orphanage building burned on February 11, 1911. Years later, the original frame building of St. Joseph's was used as the laundry on the first floor and then housed as an infirmary for contagious diseases on the second floor.[187]

Boys and girls were taught separately. The girls were taught domestic science, needlework, and millinery. Sewing, cross-stitching, and drawing with crayons and pencils were popular in the winter months. The girls made many useful articles for the home and became expert tailors and seamstresses. The boys remained in the orphanage until they were 12 and were adopted by farm families to work. Girls stayed at the orphanage until they were 16 and were then hired as domestics into private families or trained in an occupation. Outdoor recreation was encouraged for the prevention of sickness. They practiced dance steps for exercise. Kate and Anna both loved to dance. The nuns would take the children on the newly established rail line to Coeur d'Alene for school picnics. The boys carried the lunch baskets and the teenage girls kept the younger children together.

DECEMBER 9 1890.

A VALUABLE ESTATE

Consisting of Rich Farms, Town
Property and Mining Interests,
to Be Divided.

Matthew Hayden's Children Lib-
erally Provided For—Last Will
and Testament.

Mathew Hayden's last will and
testament was filed yestesday in the
probate court. The bulk of his property is bequeathed to his daughters,
Ann and Catherine. The estate
consists of a large hay ranch in
Kootenai county, Idaho, a farm in
Stevens county, Washington, four
houses and lots in Wardner, a hotel
at the De Smet mission, two lots in
Cœur d'Alene City, eighty acres of
pasturage six miles north of Vancouver, Wash., four lots in Spokane
Falls and several interests in mines
in Washington and Idaho. A
former friend of Mr. Hayden's
stated that the estate will in all
probability approximate in value
$120,000.

The legatee further desires that an
annuity of $12 per month shall be
paid to his mother-in-law, Eliza
Whalen.

To his stepson, John Powers, he
bequeated $500.

The proceeds of the Hayden Lake
farm are to be divided between his
stepchildren, Patrick, Thomas, and
Mary Powers, for their maintenance
until they attain their majorities. In
the event of the death of the daughters before they attain their majority, the entire estate will revert
to the Jesuit fathers.

James Monaghan is appointed
administrator and guardian of the
children without bond and with
absolute authority to dispose of the
estate and its income without order
of the court.

The will of James Glispin, filed
yesterday, provides "that all property, whenever and wherever found,"
shall go to his wife, who is appointed
executrix.

The Spokesman-Review [188]

The Estate

James Monaghan was executor of Mat's large estate comprising three ranches in two states, mining assets, rental property, and a hotel.[189] His main concern was to take care of the children as promised. At the time of Mat's passing, Anna was two years old and Kate would be four in January. James dictated jobs to people he knew he could rely upon regarding Mat's business affairs.

Frank Quinn and William (Bill) Lucas worked for Mat at the Mission Ranch and knew the family well. They helped James out by collecting bills owed to Mat in December of 1890. [190] Frank spent a lot of time with the children by escorting John, Molly, Tom, and Pat on a shopping trip at Sanders in Coeur d'Alene City after the Christmas holidays in Cataldo.[191] The children were thrilled to have new clothes, school supplies, and treats to take back to Spokane. James gave Frank Quinn $846.16 on the 29th of December, which included payment for railway tickets, store receipts, and labor. [192] When Bill tried to collect $95.00 from Pat Whalen, Pat said it wasn't owed. Bill and Pat appeared to not get along. A letter from one of Pat's children to James accuses Bill of being "drunk every day". (A-16) Pat Whalen wrote James to tell him he had paid the $95.00 owed Mat but had failed to take a receipt. James wrote him back and told him to pay or there would be repercussions. Pat then agreed he would pay $50.00 in 10 days. (A-17)

> *And if you will pay the balance I will remit to you at my very earliest convenience I have money standing out that I can not lay my hands on at present but expect to be able to straighten the bill within the next two months. I will allow you a reasonable interest. Please let me know if this will be satisfactory to early reply will oblige. Yours truly, Pat Whalen*

James replied: *Due Sept 1, 1890. Interest at the rate of 1% per month after maturity. Recd. $50.00 Oct 17, 1891.*

On December 2nd, 1891, Pat wrote again saying that he could not comply with the request as he was expecting money every day but hadn't come into it yet. He promised to send it as soon as he could.

Bill Lucas and Frank Quinn stayed and lived at the mission ranch to take care of the property and sell as much of the livestock as they could. [193] Follet and Harris, local butchers, purchased all but three calves that were in the brush and couldn't be found because of the fog.[194] The calves came in on their own a few days later. Follett came over the next day so he could slaughter them.

Charles Zetting, foreman of the Hayden Lake ranch, was given $695.00 on January 25, 1891, for operating expenses from June 1889 through December 1890[195] The livestock at that ranch was sold to Clement King, who rented the Hayden ranch from 1891 through 1893. He also purchased $656.20 for farming tools from the Hayden Estate. James Monaghan and Clement King worked together to transport and sell the potatoes and other goods produced at the Hayden farm.[196]

James paid several bills, including the orphanage, from Mat's accounts and gave the sisters an additional check of $100.00 for small expenditures.[197] (A-18) James hired D.K. Butler to manage Mat's business dealings and properties in Mission City. Butler paid $4.50 to ship 19 chickens that were not sold at the mission farm to the orphanage. James organized all the taxes due across the various counties on Mat's properties.[198] He knew he'd have to keep the farms running and profitable to care for the children until they reached sixteen. He tallied the value of Mat's assets in Stevens County, Washington, to be $23,225.75. A list from Mat's Estate Records[199] showed he had a personal property value of $5,000.75, which included cattle, mules, horses, and a variety of other goods and equipment. (A-19) Butler rented the Mission ranch at Hayden Gulch beginning in 1891 and paid a year's rent of $500.00. [200] He corresponded often with James about the happenings at Mission Ranch, and many of those letters have been preserved. (A-20) Frank Quinn organized the rentals of all four properties in Wardner.[201]

James renewed the Colville Ranch lease with John Rickey for five years from January 1, 1891, for a yearly rent of $200.00. The contract stipulated that he was to break the ground, put in thirty-five acres of timothy that year, keep up the fences, and pay the taxes. At the end of the lease, he was to turn the farm over to the representative of the estate in good condition with the cultivation complete and taxes paid. John Rickey was a well-known civic and business leader in Colville who, along with James, helped raise money for the Spokane Falls and Northern Railway to come through town. Rickey had arrived in the Colville Valley in 1866 and began work on his homestead. He built the first steamboat on the Columbia River and owned a general merchandise store in Colville. When a large fire spread in town, Mr. Rickey blew up his building to stop the fire. He replaced his original building in 1892 with a large three-story building.

Mat's Hotel Denver, was rented to Joe Wimpy for $25.00 a month. Not long after, he wrote to James to tell him that the rent was too high. The cost of the saloon licenses had tripled from $16.00 to $51.00 per quarter. He wrote on June 29th, 1891, that it was necessary "to cut the rent of Hotel Denver" as there was no business and that he "cannot make expenses."[202]

Receiving no reply, Joe Wimpy sent a follow-up:

> *Mission Oct 9th 1891*
> *Mr. Mauaghan   Dear Sir I wrote you several months ago in regard to cutting down the rent of Hotel to $10.00 per mo and not having received any answer concluded you had accepted my terms until yesterday Mr. Butler gave me your letter to him. I have been keeping the house in the hope Times might improve some, Licince has increased so much that it is impossible for anyone to make expenses unless times improve. I am willing to pay the above price and wait awhile longer to see what turns up. Please write me at once so I can make arrangements accordingly.*
> *Yours respectfully J.A. Wimpy*

Dr. Sims, the man who was present during Anna's birth and Lizzie's death, exchanged several letters with James in 1891. He intended to charge Mat's estate for "treating his wife in her last illness." He sent many letters demanding payment for his services. James initially ignored his requests and later refused to pay. A year after Mat's death, Dr. Sims went to the Mission Ranch and delivered his bill to Bill Lucas. Bill also refused to pay. **(A-21)**

Over time, James was able to sell off most of Mat's property. In November 1891, James asked William Appelquist to act as executor of Mat's estate and to dispose of real estate "contiguous and fronting upon Hayden Lake."[203] Throughout the following decade, Appelquist continued to sell off assets on behalf of the estate. James kept meticulous records of all the expenses compiled by the girls. By 1905, the Hayden girls, Kate 18, and Anna 16, leased the southern tract of Mat's land, where he had his sawmill for ten years, for $550 a year to F.A. Blackwell[204] **(A-22)** The Hayden girls relinquished the water rights when the ditch was constructed along the line of the customary outlet of Hayden Lake. Lot 1, was sold to John A. Finch for $2200, giving a right of way to Frederick Blackwell's electric railroad to operate train cars over his land in June 1906.[205]

The electric railroad from Spokane to Coeur d'Alene was started in 1903 and enhanced the development of Coeur d'Alene as men arrived to develop and add businesses.[206] The population rose from 508 in 1900 to 7,391 in 1910. Mr. Blackwell would have the option to lease for another five to ten years. It was agreed that he would not deposit, timber, refuse, or debris in the lake. The Granite Investment Company, owned by James with his daughter Ellen and Fredrick A. Blackwell, built the Coeur d'Alene and Spokane Railway between Spokane and Coeur d'Alene and extended to Hayden Lake in 1906 for passengers and freight.[207] Hayden Lake was a popular place to picnic and vacation. James and his heirs would have the privilege at all times to use the trains.

James continued to grow his business and investment interests in the area. He had moved to Spokane in 1886 after speculating in many business ventures and went into banking. In 1893, he was nearly wiped out by a financial panic. He reorganized and purchased a mine in British Columbia.

James lost his wife, Margaret, in April 1895. She was only 43 years old. She never recovered from the birth of her last child, Charles. John Robert was twenty-two and a cadet at the Naval Academy in Annapolis when his mother died. Margaret was nineteen, Ellen ten, James seven, and Agnes four. James's wife was known for her lovable qualities and a "kindly disposition".[208] Margaret maintained her own house and the money she saved was donated to the orphanage. James provided for the family and advised them of the importance of living honest and productive lives. Ensign John R. Monaghan was the first Washington state graduate of the US Naval Academy in 1895. In 1899 he was assigned to the Pacific station flagship, USS Philadelphia. His ship was sent to the troubled Samoan Islands during their civil war. He was killed on April 1, 1899, while serving on shore with joint British, American, and Samoan forces.[209]

On February 9, 1907, George Steele was appointed administrator and told to distribute Mat's estate without interference from the court. The amount remaining was noted as $3,140.87.[210] On February 6, 1907, James sent a courier to Mat's daughters to deliver a lease to be signed by M.D. Wright of Rathdrum for Lot 2 of Section 19 on Hayden Lake, ending at the south boundary of the land they leased to Fredrick Blackwell[211] The land was agreed to be leased for five years, paid in advance at $300 a year. The railway intersected the land and was extended to the mill at Hayden Lake to carry timber.

Anna was curiously delighted and thought it was amusing to receive a summons on the 10 of August 1909, delivered by Sheriff P.K. Pugh from the Superior Court of the Washington Drainage District 2, in Stevens County. She and Kate were being sued for water drainage rights on their property. Anna felt a special pride in the action and loved telling people at St. Joseph where she was studying nursing that she was a landowner with a large farm. It gave her a sense of importance and pride. She was 21 and could rely on James to take care of the property issues.

Kate was living in Pendleton, Oregon, and her feelings were the opposite of Anna's. She worried about being included in a suit naming her, Anna, and other families in Stevens County. She didn't want to appear in court in Colville. The decision was settled in their favor and the two young women received a sum of $6,664.01 in damages and costs.[212] Records show the girls' expenditures were paid by the estate. (A-23).

James passed away in 1916 at the age of 77. He had been a close family friend of the Hayden's for over fifty years. James had taken care of Mat and Lizzie's six children as well as his own five.[213] He was a man with high principles, notable for his business practices, ethics, and prominence in the community. In 1902, he built a stately home at E. 217 Boone in Spokane on the edge of the Gonzaga campus near St. Aloysius Church.[214] He was listed as one of Spokane's first millionaires.

Once Kate and Anna married, their husbands took over the management of the Hayden estate from James. On March 9, 1915, Kate's husband, Jim McCool, wrote to James:

City of Portland Oregon Department of Public Utilities

Dear Uncle,
In looking over the tax receipt on the girls ranch for last year I noticed that the statement had written across it 120 acres. I was under the impression there was more than that. If so than we haven't been paying any taxes at all on the rest of it.

Will you please write to me and if it isn't too much trouble give me a full description of the ranch so I can get a correct statement from the assessor and I supposed that George Ryan had gotten the figures all right and didn't pay any more attention to the statements. The girls ought to have said something but they are too careless to do anything but spend money. Hoping this finds you in the best of health and with love to Nell, Mary, Agnes and Charley.

I am your affectionate nephew, Jim McCool

Anna and her husband, George Ryan, lived in Cataldo. In 1919, they filed an action of partition against Kate and Jim, who were living in Portland. They requested that the Hayden Farm in Stevens County. Washington, be divided. The legal complaint stated that the plaintiffs "pay that judgment to be rendered," finding that they are entitled to a partition of the land.[215] The court decided that the property could not be partitioned because it affected the right of way of the Spokane Falls and Northern Railway, now the Great Northern Railway Co. The cause was dismissed on July 16, 1919.[216] The two sisters sold the land to Harold Kohlstedt for $12,000 and shared the proceeds.

Mat's Legacy

Mat left behind numerous properties and land to help support the six growing children. The Powers children used the last name Hayden after their mother had married Mat, but as adults, they began using Powers. Mat's kindness and patience were instilled in the children, as well as his keen interest in learning. Hayden's Lake in North Idaho became a popular recreation site though his planned townsite never came to fruition. He left each of the children with the desire to help others in need and to have the education to be able to deal effectively in business. James helped them wisely manage their inheritance until they came of age.

John Mathew Powers Hayden

John left school in 1892, at 17, after attending Gonzaga for nearly five years. The estate records show John listed under liabilities: $306.15. Eight months before Mat died, he had placed a

George Ryan (Anna's son) John and son Pat.

public notice in the Spokane Falls paper on April 14, 1890, saying "he would not be accountable or pay the debts of his step-son, Johnnie Powers." Tom is listed under assets: $356.90. John had the choice of attending school for two more years or receiving $500.00 to start a career. He opted for the money. One of John's grandsons said he purchased a horse and buggy "to go a courtin'." Accepting a job with R.J. Head in Spokane, John was given a check from James for $11.85 to purchase clothing. John was nineteen, he rented from James. Records show John paid rent in January 1896 for $88.88 and $55.15. Pat Lucas told James that John was at the Mission Ranch and took a saddle claiming' it belonged to him, and he let him take it. On July 11, when John was attempting to ford the river near Mission Bridge he was thrown by his horse. He floated more than half a mile, down the river going under several times when he held onto some bushes and was rescued by R.L. Nothingham and Dick Sharpely.

John worked on Mat's Colville ranch for several years where he met the beautiful Clara E. Korling. She was 21 and he was 33 when they married in 1908 in Greenwood, Washington.[217] John was known for his schooling, intelligence, and gift for writing. In 1910 John and Clara moved back to Idaho and he worked in the abstract office in Coeur d'Alene. He and Clara ran a busy restaurant in Wardner between 1914 and 1916. As a logger and a construction worker, he moved to where he found work. Clara worked at the Clark House on Hayden Lake. Clara was 37 when

Clara E. Korling

she died unexpectedly in 1924, leaving him with four children. Pat was 14, Bill 13, Clara 9 and John 4. Pat and Bill helped take charge of the younger children when their father was working.

Pat and Bill worked in Harrison cleaning boats as teenagers to earn money to help the family. Their father was logging at Fernan Lake when his son John, now 8, scratched his leg, and gangrene set in. John did everything humanly possible to fight the infection with the help of the local physician, but it was impossible to save his son. The family was emotionally shattered.

John continued logging and rented a home in Cataldo. He later moved to Coeur d'Alene and lived in a boarding house. His daughter, Clara, was working and going to school in Spokane and later joined her father in moving to Seattle, where she worked as a school nurse. John said that Idaho brought too many painful memories after losing his parents, wife, and son.

John's children knew of a major political scandal that erupted during the Spanish-American War when Brigadier General Charles Egan, a penny-pinching member of McKinley's cabinet, ordered improperly processed beef shipped to U.S. troops fighting in Cuba. The children would tease their older cousin Theodore (Ted) Egan Snyder calling him "Rotten beef Snyder" having heard the story of spoiled canned beef from Chicago that was shipped to Army troops. Military personnel wanted local beef purchased, but this was not authorized. The canned beef was known as 'embalmed beef' with its putrid smell that killed twice as many soldiers from food poisoning as were killed in battle in 1898. The Pure Food and Drug Act was eventually passed in 1906 when Ted was five years old. The Powers were known for their wit and teasing though they were ten years younger than Ted. Egan was also the name of a carpenter in Wheeling, West Virginia, who helped Ted's father, Peter Snyder, when he emigrated. Peter said he "learned a lot of the building trade" from Egan though he had worked as a carpenter in Alsace Lorraine. On June 21, 1944, John showed his inquisitive nature when he wrote a letter to a niece answering questions about his family.

> I know a lot about my folks. I was always interested in such matters, not that I thought that there was anything remarkable about any of my ancestors, but just that I was curious. When I was very young I thought it was wonderful to be Irish. Well, it is all right to be Irish but now I'm sure there is nothing special about the Irish except that conditions, environment, etc, have made so far as blood is concerned, we know very well there is no difference. Any differences in the peoples of the earth are not due to nationality or tribal origin but mainly to their method of making a living. Out of their method of making a living, there is the economic set up spring all their culture and institutions. The people of the U.S. differ greatly in their social make up depending upon the parts of the country they come from, and the economic set up there. Most often one can't tell when meeting a person from let us say Georgia, whether the person is of Irish, German or any other stock. But we'll find a person from there strongly in favor of the Democrat Party, a Negro hater, perhaps a K.K.K. or sympathizer, a Baptist or Methodist, etc. I've met people with all the above characteristics that said they were Irish decent. I know I cannot (perhaps) make this all clear to you, my object is to try to get you to see that it makes little difference what clan or tribe we descended from. The main thing is environment. I mean the environment, customs, and economic set up. all three are related "economic set up" is the parent. After a few days I'll send you another letter in which I'll tell you what I know about my ancestry. I know something about it back to the time my grandfather (your great grandfather) John

Powers was born, also another gg grandfather of yours Dennis Whalen. They were born in Ireland. Very best wishes to everyone. I'm tired now else I'd go ahead with the family information. I surely hope this letter will not disappoint you, perhaps I should not have bothered about "economic set up" etc. Uncle John

John lived at Hotel Reynolds, 41 Fourth Avenue, City Hall Park, Seattle, Washington. He wrote his nephew, Ted Snyder, about his impressionable memories of his arrival in Idaho when he was ten years old.

March 10, 1962

Dear Ted,
I received your letter, saw Leo, he read it. There is a lot I could say about things that impressed me when I first saw Idaho. We came from the village of Haverstraw N.Y. where the people were as thick as flies, to Old Mission Idaho Territory. where the people lived miles apart, and I was glad I was not in Haverstraw. We came via the N.P.Rway from St Paul, left the train at Rathdrum, then to C.D.A via horse drawn stage, then steam boat to the Old Mission. The water in the river was as clear as the water from your water tap, and thousands of ducks, geese and few swans were scattered along the river. Very few whites lived in the vicinity of the Mission, perhaps two. There was plenty of Indians. A narrow gauge railroad was built as far as Wallace about 1887. There was plenty of game edible birds, pheasant, grouse etc. I had gone to school five years in Haverstraw, I was one of the few that had any education, illiterate or near illiterate was the rule. At the time we came there Kootenai Co. then embraced what is now practically all of Idaho North of the Clearwater except Shoshone Co. I could write a lot more about it, a book in fact, but no one would read the book however accurate. With best wishes to you and Cleo.
Uncle John

I wrote this in my room, a very poor place to write...I have always interested myself in things, I was quite an observer. Will be pleased to write more about Idaho if you are interested.
Cleo, Haverstraw is near the spot where Major Andre and Benedict Arnold met.[218]

Mary Elizabeth (Molly) Powers Hayden Snyder

Molly was officially discharged from St. Joseph's orphanage on January 3, 1893, but continued to reside at the orphanage. She studied at the Holy Names Academy and helped the nuns. She was sixteen in April. The older girls who lived at St. Joseph's were placed in private homes as nannies when they were sixteen. James thought Molly should stay close to Anna and Kate, as Tom and Pat had transferred to DeSmet. In the fall Mary Hayden was given new shoes and a $30.00 fee was paid for classes.

Molly Powers Snyder

At the orphanage, the sisters insisted on calling her Mary Elizabeth, her given name. For Christmas of 1894, Molly was given two new blankets and a quilt. In the spring she was called into the Mother Superior's office and given three choices: 1) to be placed with a family to work and tend their children, 2) to stay and take the oath to serve God and become a sister, or 3) to meet and consider marriage with a young Frenchman, Peter Snyder. He recently immigrated to be near his stepsister, Sister Barbara Horas, at the convent. Peter had gone to the Mother Superior at the Sisters of Providence for help in finding a wife. After a brief meeting in the convent parlor, Molly decided to take her chances on the good-looking man. They were immediately married after the bans were read on June 11, 1895. Their eldest son, Charles, was born in Spokane a year later, followed by Leo, Roselle, and Clarence. They moved to the house and 80-acre property she had inherited in Cataldo, where Ted, Tom, Elizabeth, and George were born. Peter and Molly's family of six boys and two girls spent their early years in Cataldo. Peter wasn't a farmer but worked carpentry jobs and kept a vegetable garden. Molly would not allow her youngest son, George, to go hunting and fishing with his brothers. George had lost an eye when he was five in 1910 while he was watching one of his brothers split wood and a splinter blinded him. The Snyder's only transportation was a horse and wagon.

In 1901, Fort Sherman's land and buildings were transferred to the Department of Interior. Many buildings were auctioned on June 6, 1905, along with 1,000 acres of land. Peter helped to move the hospital and opera house on rollers from the Fort Grounds to the property on 9th and Indiana for a Catholic school and residence. John Costello, the county sheriff, donated the land at 23rd and Sherman for the St. Thomas Cemetery. Peter later worked as a carpenter and bricklayer at St. Thomas Catholic Church from 1909 to 1911. He built several homes in Coeur d'Alene, including one for his family on the SW corner of Mullan and Dollar in 1909. Peter and Molly divorced after fourteen years of marriage. Peter lived with Charles, Leo, Clarence, and Ted in Coeur d'Alene. His sons worked as newsboys on the streets of Coeur 'Alene and Spokane. Roselle, Tom, Elizabeth and George lived in Cataldo with their mother. Mine tailings polluted the Mission slough so the family couldn't raise a garden. Molly married John Nourse. They had one son, Kenneth, in 1913. The marriage was brief and Molly began working at a mining camp near Cataldo to support herself and the children.

Clarence Snyder 1st on the right. The picture was taken in front of the original opera house from the Fort. It was later moved and the words Academy IHM were over the door.

On February 9, 1913, the Spokane Chronicle reported that F.A. Blackwell planned to operate the Panhandle Lumber Co. at Ross Station. A township was laid out and the property was rapidly developed and sold to new emigrants. Another township, Ross Station was developed and Peter took the train there to begin work on new homes.

Molly and Peter's son Clarence was squirrel hunting when he fell out of a tree and was killed in the summer of 1913. Clarence was living on Mullan and Dollar in Coeur d'Alene when he died. The family was deeply affected by Clarence's death. Molly was so distraught at the funeral that she was held back so the coffin could be lowered into the ground.

Coeur d'Alene Evening News: Vol. 8. No. 20. Friday, August 29, 1913.

YOUNG BOY ACCIDENTALLY KILLED WHILE OUT HUNTING

Clyde Snyder the victim -- Small Caliber Bullet Penetrated Abdomen. Clyde Snyder, 13 years, a son of Peter Snyder, a carpenter residing in the 1300 block on Mullan Ave., was accidentally killed today when a bullet from his .22 caliber rifle entered his abdomen while hunting squirrels in the woods opposite the Catholic cemetery. The accident occurred when the boy lost his hold and fell out of a tree which he had climbed evidently to secure a squirrel he had killed. When he was found by Mr. Butterfield, who works for the Woodlawn dairy, the lad was suffering greatly. Calling another man in the neighborhood, they made the boy as comfortable as possible until the arrival of Dr. Dwyer who was telephoned. The boy died a few minutes after the doctor arrived and from the time he was first found he was unable to give a very connected account of the accident. The rifle broke at the breach, doubtless by the boys' weight when he fell on it and was found under the tree. A dead squirrel and several rifle cartridges were found in the pockets of the boy's clothing afterward. Butterfield was walking through the woods looking for strayed cows when the boy's groans and feeble cries for help were heard. The body was brought to the Coeur d'Alene undertaking parlors where it will be held until funeral arrangements are completed. It was with difficulty that the boy was identified. Acting Police Chief Steele rounded up all the young boys he could find and had them view the body in an effort to learn the boy's identity. He was too weak to give his full name when he was found. Identification finally was made by neighbors of the boy's father who is working at present at Ross station, coming home at night. Efforts are being made to notify him at Ross this afternoon. It is understood that the boy's parents separated some time ago and that his mother is now residing in the Coeur d'Alene Indian reservation.

Peter and Molly's children: Charles, Leo, Roselle, and Clarence in the back Ted, Tom, Elizabeth, and George seated.

In 1915, Molly married Billie Adams, a bookkeeper from Iowa. Molly worked as a cook in several different mining and logging camps and was well-known for being able to make a meal out of a dishrag. She and her sister Anna were busy baking bread at a camp when they decided to add a handful of salt per loaf of bread. The crew thought Anna and Molly had too much to drink and were not happy with their daily bread. The girls laughed and laughed. Molly and Anna loved dancing and would be seen clogging on a table or at a New Year's celebration. On St. Patrick's Day, Molly and Anna wore green dresses, green shoes, and green bows in their hair. Molly often left George and Kenny in the care of her sister, Anna. Molly's children walked the two miles to school from the Hayden farm in warm weather. In the early hours, they would hear the cooing of the doves in the trees and the flow of the river that brought comforting sounds to them in the morning darkness. In bad weather, their dear, reliable Uncle Pat arrived to take them to school with the horse-drawn wagon packed with woolen blankets and an old buffalo hide covering the wooden slats. Two of Molly's sons, Tom and George, later built their mother a home on Hayden Loop off Canyon Road in Cataldo.

Peter Snyder and his son Tom at home on Dollar St. in Coeur d'Alene. In 2007, the house was painted for the first time in 100 years. The Alsatian influence remains on the decorative siding.

Thomas Francis Powers Hayden

On July 1, 1892, board and tuition of $256.25 were paid for Pat and Tom at the DeSmet Indian School. Tom and Pat were transferred sixty miles to DeSmet. The boys spoke Salish from their years in Cataldo and were 13 and 10 that fall. There were nearly 200 students at DeSmet and half of them lived at the school. Tom attended school for two years at Gonzaga Prep before being transferred to DeSmet with his younger brother Pat, who had been in trouble. Pat had led a group of children from the orphanage to the river for a swim, but none owned a bathing suit. The nuns were aghast. He was immediately transferred to DeSmet, far away from a waterway. James felt it was best to keep the two boys together since John left the prep school at 16. Tom and Pat were trained in shoemaking, blacksmithing, baking, dairy, printing, sewing, cooking, and laundering. Father Charles Mackin was the superintendent. A teacher's pay was $150.00 a school year, whereas a farmer averaged $300 or a carpenter $500. The school was subsidized by a government contract.[219] Tom and Pat knew several boys from the Mission and they quickly settled into the school.

Camp McKinney, British Columbia, 1894, where Tom Powers worked.[220]

In 1894, James Monaghan, in partnership with George McAuley, owned the Cariboo Amelia mine at Camp McKinney north of the Washington State border in British Columbia.[221] For the summer, Tom 14, boarded the train to Marcus, Washington, and then traveled two days by wagon to work at Camp McKinney.[222] The camp consisted of six hotels with saloons, three general stores, a butcher shop, a school, and a church for the 250 inhabitants of miners, conmen, and outlaws. Tom helped with the paperwork. He quickly learned the mining business and was often sent down inside the dark and damp shaft to help other miners. He did not care for it.

During Tom's third summer at the camp, George McAuley was heading to Spokane to deposit three gold bars worth $12,000 when his wagon was held up. The company posted rewards and received a letter from a man who had met Matthew Roderick in a saloon and had worked with him at Camp McKinney. He told of Roderick's plan to rob the mining company. James hired the Pinkerton Detective Company and they found Matthew Roderick and his wife living in Seattle and spending more money than the couple was reputed to have. The Rodericks had recently paid their back taxes, purchased a building lot, gone shopping, and taken out an insurance policy of $3000. The detectives learned that Mrs. Roderick's neighbors said her husband was going on a business trip that would make them rich. When Roderick arrived near the camp to retrieve secretly buried gold, Superintendent Keane and two constables went out to meet him. Roderick was shot and killed that dark evening of October 26, 1896. The bullion was never found.[223] The gold carried to Spokane was secretly roped and wired into a broken section of the wagon.

After the bullion disappeared, James retired Tom from the mining business. Tom, 17, returned to Cataldo to work in the timber industry.[224] He and his brother Pat often worked together and were living in Enaville in 1910 with sixteen other boarders at a logging camp.

Tom married Christina LaSarte on April 1, 1925, a year after her husband, Henry Miller, died. She had two sons, Harry and John, and two daughters, Henri (Henrietta) and Katherine, from her previous marriage. She passed away eight years after she and Tom were married. Tom missed her, the children, and the music.

Christine LaSart Miller and son Harry 1917

Henry Miller and Christina's youngest daughter, Katherine Proctor, the stepdaughter of Tom Powers, wrote:

Our dad wasn't a very loving father. I was four when he died. So I am sure mom married the next year to Tom Powers (on April 1st). Don't remember who took care of us when that happened. They stayed on Mission Hill until I finished third grade (summer of 1928). Then moved up the little North fork of the Coeur d'Alene River. They lived there 1928-1929 in Alec Inne's house and a bunkhouse. His house had one long kitchen and eating place, one front room and one bedroom. Henri and I slept on a couch that opened up. The boys stayed in the bunkhouse when they were home. Mom always had a garden, corn, chickens and rabbits. I remember once she was out picking strawberries and her wedding band slipped off. She went into her bedroom and prayed and went out again to the garden and immediately found it. She canned fruit and vegetables and meat, using copper boilers. She pickled white fish, and made head cheese, and pickled pig's feet for Tom. She was an excellent cook. She made pies, bread and the cinnamon rolls were delicious. She never had a recipe book that I know of. 1928-1929 was the year Henrietta and I were sent to the Catholic school at DeSmet, on the Coeur d'Alene Indian Reservation because there was no school way up the river. I was in 4th grade then.

In the fall of 1929 we moved to Rose Lake, (across from the grade school, later included high school), where we lived until I graduated from high school in 1937. Our mother died 1933 when I was 13 and a freshman.

I'm sure her philosophy was to intermarry with whites and blend in. She didn't wish to live on the reservation and didn't keep in touch much with her brothers when they married Indian women and moved on the Coeur d'Alene Indian Reservation. Mom taught herself to play the mandolin, accordion, Jew's harp and Harmonica.[225]

Love, Aunt Kay [226]

Aunt Kay added:

Larry said his dad told of living up the Coeur d' Alene River and he and Johnny would go out and shoot grouse and get burlap bags full and take them home. You sure couldn't do that today. He also said his dad told of his mom almost drowning in the river close to where they were living. After Kristine died Harry and Johnny worked to keep the family together until the girls were old enough to be on their own. They moved to Desmet to continue their schooling. Tom Powers drank a lot and often did not get along with the boys. He and Kristine had purchased a house and if the Miller boys wanted to have a place to live they would have to purchase it from him. The Miller boys did stay close to the Powers and Snyder families for many years.

Harry eventually lived up LaTour Creek, in sight of the Old Cataldo Mission and Johnny lived down river. They both had nice farms and were loggers. Katherine became a teacher and taught in the Olympia, Washington area for many years. Henrietta lived in her later years in Houston, Texas and married a man who was in the oil business. Harry canned venison when he was raising his sisters and it was the envy of all the ladies round about. He roasted it first then canned it and it was unbeatable.

Tom lived in a cabin near the Bennett Bay Motel in his later years where his nephews often stopped by with groceries for him. He amazed some of the younger Powers boys with his ability to spit Copenhagen tobacco on the ceiling and have it stick!

Patrick Michael Powers Hayden

Pat Powers

When visiting the Old Mission at Cataldo, one can see where Pat left his mark high on the left wall near the altar, where he scratched his name in 1889. He must have stood on a ladder or someone's shoulders to leave graffiti illicitly when he was seven. James purchased new clothing for Pat from Mat's estate when Pat entered St. Joseph's orphanage in November of 1890. Later, he transferred to the Sisters of Charity of Providence School at DeSmet. The nuns were strict in telling the children they must speak and write English. Pat and Tom found comfort in speaking Salish with their friends, reminding them of their home at Mission City where they were free to wander. When a disparaging remark was made to friends in Salish, it was Pat who spoke up in Salish and found himself on extra kitchen duty cleaning the pans. Pat and his brother Tom were sent by train to Chewelah one summer to work on James Monaghan's ranch with their brother John. Pat, left the DeSmet orphanage in 1898 when he was 16 to live with his sister Molly and her husband, Peter, in Spokane. Molly's household was busy as Charles was two and a half and Leo was a year old. Molly was expecting a third child in January 1899. While living in Cataldo and DeSmet, Pat learned tracking skills from his older brothers. He worked as a translator and bounty[227] hunter as a young man as a means of support as well as a hobby. Bounties were paid for mountain lions, considered vermin, as they preyed on cattle herds. Pat shot many cougars and made one into a rug for the room he shared with Tom. He trapped beavers along the North Fork of the Coeur d'Alene River and commissioned a beaver coat for Anna.

Pat worked in the mines, on log drives, and eventually on the dredge on the Coeur d'Alene River at Cataldo Flats. The dredging was seasonal to avoid conflicts between dredging and the spawning of fish populations.[228] When he became the custodian of the Cataldo Grade School, he lived across the pond from the main road, and to visit him, one needed to go by boat. Pat would come across the pond to pick up his guests when one called out to him. He kept the school spotless and never tolerated vandalism. One of his nieces told him not to work too hard and to leave a few papers on the floor for the children to pick up. He never married, although a lot of the women wished he would.

Pat moved to a small house with a big porch in Dudley. He had a candy tree" grew. In the summer colorful suckers and lifesavers were suspended. Pat's nieces and nephews who visited loved to pick candy from his magical tree and listen to his music. Pat carried his harmonica in his pocket and played many Irish tunes including *I'll Take You Home Again, Kathleen,* and *The Big Rock Candy Mountain.* He entertained family or guests for hours by playing *My Gal, She's a High-Born Lady, My Sweethearts a Mule in the Mine, Golden Slippers* and one he called *Forty Thousand Bulldogs and they all had Bushy tails.* Pat was a favorite uncle and friend. He passed away in 1959 at 77.

Kathleen Hayden McCool

Kate Hayden McCool

Kate and Anna remained at Saint Joseph's Orphanage in Spokane until January 1907, when they enrolled at St. Joseph's Academy in Pendleton, Oregon. James felt it was best they were moved from the orphanage as a few months earlier, four boys had died at Gonzaga from typhoid, having been infected by a popular plunge pool. Kate was now 20, and the academy prepared the students for teacher examinations. They studied music and elocution, learning to speak precisely and clearly. James continued to pay the girls' monthly bills from Mat's estate. (A23) Kate's report cards in June 1908 and June 1909 showed she had two years in the commercial track and academics. Her grades averaged 91.5%. It was noted her Attendance was 100%, Her Conduct 90%, and her Neatness and Polite Deportment 93%. She had classes in Christian Doctrine, Bible History, Penmanship, instrumental Music and Algebra.[229] Anna's classes were similar but she only stayed for one year before moving to Tacoma to begin nurse's training. Her year included piano, violin, and watercolors. Her report cards averaged 83.5%. Nuns would yell at the girl's "corkscrew" as they pointed at their crossed legs. The girls had fifteen minutes to be up in the morning and to be downstairs in the chapel for prayers. If one wanted to chew gum, they were told it was a bovine habit to chew their cud and were told to go to their room, plug the keyhole, and draw the blinds. The school burned in 1956.

Katie wrote James Monaghan while she was at St. Joseph's in Oregon, typing on Coffman's Chocolates-Bonbon paper for Christmas,1908:

Dear Friend

Just received a letter from Mr. O'Shea in regard to the lease of our ranch, yes, you may sign my name to the lease, if you will and send it to them for me. We are having some snow here. I have been sick with the grip three days. I think it's an awful thing to get, hope I don't have it again very soon. Now I have a bad cold it seems funny for me to get anything, as I had not any for so long. I am feeling very good this morning in spite of it. I am sending the girls a nice box of Coffman fresh chocolate. Send you much love. I will close wishing you a Happy New Year.

Yours Katie.

January 18, 1909 Post Card from Pendleton, Oregon.
Mr. Monaghan, Granite Block. Spokane, Wash.
Dear Guardian.

I am back again at school and will be in so studying in earnest next week. I had a very nice time and Anna is looking fine. I received the pretty present that Nell sent me. I think it fine. Give all my love and also yourself.

Your obedient Katie

January 24, 1909
Dear Guardian

Your welcome letter was received and very glad you are well. I certainly had an enjoyable time while in Tacoma. Anna is quite well again and looking fine. The Doctor said she would be much stronger now than she was before her operation. Anna gave me the pretty present Nell sent me. I was delighted with it and thank her very much.

I helped the nurses carry trays to their patients at dinner. I do like it at the Hospital and believe I will be a nurse. Dr. Delong said I would make a fine practitioner. Now I think that was quite encouraging for a start. I did not see Fr. Driver. He has gone to live in Olympia.

We were going over one Sunday to see him but it rained so hard that we postponed it another day as it nearly always happens we never went. We had quite a lot of snow here but it has all melted now. Our refectory was flooded with water from the melting of the snow and we ate in the studio had quite a picnic.[230]

I hope you received the Tankard alright I was afraid it might have been broken.

I helped a girl make a waist or rather I taught her how to do it. It was her first experience with one and it looked fine when I had it completed.[231] I will close now with love to you all. I remain Your obedient Katie

Mr. J. Monaghan Granite Block Spokane Wa.
The Beverly, Portland Oregon
Dearest Friend
Received a letter from you which you know is always very welcome in regard to the interesting news. I think it will be all right but I should like to have some on hand for use should something turn up.

Dr. Smeall and I will be married around April. He has started to build a nice home which will be finished by then. Anna has left for Spokane as she did not like it in Portland very well. I should like to go to Tacoma for Christmas if I can and see Dr. Smeall. He wrote me to be sure and come over as he has lots to talk about. Do you think it will be nice to spend Christmas with him? I would stay with Mr. and Mrs. Gibbons whilst I am there and besides I should like to visit them. Write and let me know what you think about it. I hope sincerely that you are in the best of health. Oh, you have been more of a friend to Anna and I and we love you so much for it. I shall never try to thank you but dear friend you can always know that we feel and respect you oh so much. I am wishing to hear from you soon. Sending you lots of Love I beg to remain always your Katie

Kathleen Lavelle Hayden married James Hugh McCool, the nephew of James Monaghan and Margaret McCool Monaghan, on May 11, 1911. Perhaps James did not approve of her engagement to Dr. J. Smeall, or he thought his nephew was a better match for Mat's daughter. Jim McCool attended the U.S. Naval Academy in Annapolis and returned to Oregon in 1908. He worked for the Oregonian in Portland, writing two columns for the newspapers: *Wildlife Times* and *Fore Maybe More,* a golf column. He was known throughout the Pacific Northwest to write the best hunting and fishing columns using colorful descriptions. Molly's daughter, Roselle, left Cataldo when she was 13 to live with her Aunt Kate and Uncle Jim McCool in Portland to attend 8th grade. Jim received theater and concert tickets from the paper and shared them with Roselle and her sister Elizabeth. Roselle attended high school and two years of secretarial school in Portland. In 1927, she married Bob Collins. The readers of the Oregonian would contact Roselle, and her husband, Bob, to ask permission to hunt pheasants on their large wheat ranch.

Kate had an upright piano and skillfully played many Irish songs. Jim and their son, Kelly, would sing *When Irish Eyes Are Smiling, Mother McGhee,* and their favorite *K-E-Double L-Y*. Kate always offered a toast at parties and weddings with, "Here's to ourselves, Good People are Few." She was known to spend her money freely and was generous to those around her. She was tiny, energetic, and could sew like a couturier.[232] Her eyesight was so good that she could thread tiny-eyed needles without glasses. After returning to Portland, Jim and Kate drifted apart when their son, Kelly, was a teenager. Kate earned her living as a seamstress, tailor, and artist.

Kelly McCool and Bob Rohe

Kate traveled to Coeur d'Alene from Portland when Anna unexpectedly passed away in April of 1952 at the age of 63. At St. Thomas Cemetery, Kate noted that Frank Quinn was interned next to her father and she cried loudly, "What's Quinny doing in my spot? I want to be buried next to Daddy!" That lightened a somber day. Kate was 77 when she passed away. She rests behind her father next to a large tree. Surrounding Mat are his children: Anna Hayden Ryan; John Powers with his wife Clara Korling and their son John: Tom Powers and his wife Christina LaSarte Miller; Patrick M. Powers; and Molly, whose stone reads MJ Nourse. Molly's sons, Charles, Clarence, Leo, and Tom along with his wife Violet and daughter Joyce, are to the west near the caretakers' buildings and canopy. Molly's grandson, Theodore K. Snyder, and her first husband, Joseph Peter Snyder are nearby. The Haydens, Powers, and Snyders all contributed to developing North Idaho.

Kelly, Kate's only son, lived with his grandparents near Walla Walla, Washington after his parents divorced. He recalled taking a boat out from Honeysuckle Beach in Hayden, Idaho, in the early 1920s with his cousins, the Ryan boys. When the boat started sinking, his mother, Kate, swam out and rescued them. Kelly grew up playing golf and won many caddy tournaments. He said he won a lot of golf championships due to the summer he spent on Collin's wheat ranch near Waitsburg. He rode horseback using his golf clubs to chop down the weeds, which developed his great swing. Kelly joined the Navy before his eighteenth birthday in 1930 and became a diver in the Construction Battalion (Seabee). and retired after 28 years as a Lt. Commander. Kelly was one of the smallest sailors and was able to go into tight spaces, working with rescue operations and underwater disposal teams. He was attached to the Mine Squadron during World War II in Hawaii for four years. He transferred to Panama, and for six years, worked as a demolition expert with underwater explosives. He was on the USS Hale in Ecuador and helped rescue a sick man in the hold of the ship. After retirement, he worked as a technical writer for Boeing in Seattle and the Seattle Police as a consultant and explosive expert. Kelly returned to school and received an associate degree in accounting. While in the Navy he married Rose Marie Doerr and had six children. Kelly had twinkling blue eyes and a great memory. He passed away in Seattle in January 2005 at age 92.

Anna Elizabeth Hayden Ryan

Anna Hayden Ryan

Anna wrote to Molly: "Everyone said this is a bum picture of me." Anna trained to be a nurse between 1908 and 1910 at St. Joseph Hospital in Tacoma, Washington. The Hayden girls always stayed in close contact with James Monaghan and he faithfully wrote checks to the girls from their estate. Anna often wrote colorful postcards to James while she was in training:

September 4, 1908
Tacoma
I would love to write you a long letter if I had time, but my work takes much of my time. I am getting along fine. I will write soon. Annie (written on the front of the card) There is nothing going on here to write about. So I shall close. Hoping this will find you all enjoying the best of health
I remain with love to all. Annie

September 27, 1908 Tacoma
Dear Mr. Monaghan.
I received a letter from Katie today and she is getting along nicely. Rev. Father Dyer Sisler is here he came last Monday. I am getting along fine. Love from Annie.

(No Date). St. Joseph's Hospital Tacoma Washington
James Monoghan Granite Block
My dear Guardian
With much pleasure I will write a few lines, which I hope, will find you all enjoying good health. I am good getting along nicely with my work and I like it very much. I work Arithmetic and study an hour every day. The rest of the time I help the sister in the drug room. I can give some of the medicines alone. Don't you

think I am getting along nicely? I have many books and other things to get and I would be very thankful if you would send me some money. I received a letter from Katie today she is getting along nicely in school also in music. We are having lovely weather here and I hope you are having the same in Spokane. Last Sunday we all went out for a ride in South Tacoma and had a jolly good time. Hoping this will find you all well. I will close. Love to all I remain Yours affectionate Love Annie

February 6, 1909, Tacoma Wa. Mermaid Room Tacoma Hotel…to let you know I am getting along fine and I hope this will find you all. Hoping that Jim has fully recovered. Love to all Annie

February 8 1909 Getting along nicely in the Drug Room helping sister and like it fine. Much love from Annie

June 8 1909 Postcard of Alaskan and Siberian Eskimos: Dear Mr. Monaghan Received your most welcomed letter I was so glad to hear that you are enjoying good health. I also thank you very very much for the checks and I was more than glad to hear that you will soon be up. Love from Annie

June 16, 1909 Postcard from Seattle Alaska-Yukon-Pacific Exposition: I am having a jolly time. We are so? All the wards and rooms are full. Rec'd letter from Katie. She will come up on the 20th. Love to all. From your loving Annie

September 2, 1909, My dear Guardian I am going to Seattle Sunday and stay until Monday Annie

October 20, 09 My dear Mr. Monaghan Just a few lines which I trust will find you enjoying the best of Health. But I did not receive an answer yet. Sister Eugenia, and Sister Eugcina Ladislous were here. I was glad to see someone from Spokane.[233] Annie

February 10, 1910 My dear Mr. Monaghan. Just a little note trusting it will find you enjoying good health. I am well and getting along nicely. love from Katie and myself, Annie Hayden

January 12, 1911
Dear Mr. Monaghan In answering to the note received from Mr. O'Shea in regards to the lease of the farm to the Dupine wount to lease It for five years instead of three. Am I right? But I would rather lease it for three if possible. If not you have my consent to sign my name to the lease if you will be so kind. I do not know what Katie thinks about it. My only reason Mr. Monaghan not wanted to lease it for five years, at lease I dont But do not let this stop you. do as you think best. We are having lovely weather just a present. It snows most every day so we have plenty of it. But it is far better than mud. All the men are working in the woods so there are very few people here. Dwyers, Carrys, Havers and ourselves. Also Armdhold who have the Mission ranch. Hoping this will find you enjoying good health. With much love to all. Annie Hayden
(*Anna was 23 and living in Cataldo.*)

Anna's personality was always full of spark and enthusiasm. She chuckled for days at the thought of having painted the neighbor's children's faces every color of the rainbow. Her nephews loved it when she teased and played outdoor games with them, such as *Kick the Can* or helped them accomplish a new string trick as *Cat's Cradle* or *Jacobs' Ladder*. She was known for her infectious, melodious laughter. Once she started. it was quite hard for her to stop. She could talk her nephews and their friends into almost anything that she thought of at the moment. She convinced her nephew, George, and a group of men to put on dresses and hats in preparation for a dance. She never needed a drink to achieve a state of euphoria. When doing her laundry with a wringer washing machine, the drain hose slipped out of the kitchen sink and sprayed water over the room. Anna was never one to get upset. She couldn't stop the spraying hose, nor could she stop laughing as she and the kitchen became soaking wet.

Anna met George Ryan through his sister, Mrs. Dwyer, who was living in Cataldo. They married in 1912 and had three sons: George in 1913, Robert in 1915, and James (Duffy) in 1917. George Ryan was eight years older and from a large Irish family that lived in Nebraska before immigrating to Spokane. The couple lived in Coeur d'Alene for several years, where all three of their sons attended and graduated from the Catholic Academy. George was a farmer and cattle buyer. The family later moved to Cataldo. One of Anna's nephews once quipped, "George was an accountant when he wasn't drinking Anna's inheritance." She didn't seem to mind when her husband, George Ryan, disappeared from her life. She enjoyed her freedom. She moved into the empty one-room schoolhouse across the street from The Owl Tavern in Cataldo. [234]

Mat's grandsons, the children of Anna Hayden Ryan: George, born in 1913; James 1917; and Robert 1915.

Anna nursed and cared for Frank Quinn in his later years. He lived in Hardy Gulch near Molly and later moved across from Dwyer's store located on Highway 10. Dwyer's sold groceries, snacks, pop, and gas. The Dwyer's kept a bear chained to a tree as a tourist attraction. The bear loved to drink strawberry pop and would dance by rearing back on his hind legs and shuffling. Then he would sit back on his haunches, holding the pop bottle in his giant paws, and guzzle it down. Many people stopped by the store in the early 1950s but didn't have a dime to spend on a bottle of 'pop' for the popular bear.

Frank Quinn worked for Mat when he first arrived in Cataldo. When leveling lumber with a planer, Quinny lost his right hand. He wore a heavy leather patch over the stub. He later sold fishing licenses and worked as the Constable and Justice of the Peace on the flat below the old Mission Church. He was director of the school for five years.

Pat Powers, Joy Snyder, Violet Otton Snyder (Tom Snyder's wife), Frank Quinn, and Anna's son James (Duffy Ryan)

A story was told that Quinny saw an advertisement in a magazine that one could mail order a garage. He let everyone know he was "gonna buy a new car and get one of them gorages for his saydon." Quinny told Molly's children that his cows came home dry every day and that he didn't have any milk to drink. He said he had gone out in the field to investigate and found that the *snaakes* were nursing from his cows. He made himself look worn out and tired from chasing the snakes around and around. He was nearly falling over from dizziness because he had to stop them from hiding in the ground. When he caught and killed the snakes, he opened them up and sure enough, they were full of butter. Quinny lived on the hill above Hayden Gulch. He didn't get along much with Newt Garres, a neighbor who lived by the creek at the bottom of the gulch. Quinny said he was gonna sue Newt because he figured they were Newt's snakes and "the snaakes were comin' up out of the creek and over his fence gettin' the milk."[235]

George Hayden Ryan, Anna's oldest son, joined the Army in 1943. He was stationed at Grand Island Air Base in Alaska and served in India and the Philippines. When he enlisted, he stated he was single with dependents. His dependent was his mother, Anna. Young soldiers listed their mothers as dependents and sent

Anna's Boys: George   **Bobby**   **Duffy (James)**

all or part of their paychecks home. George worked for a time after the war at the Nu Laid Egg Company in Portland. George loved to dance and took Elizabeth Snyder Rohe's daughter to hear the Stan Keaton Orchestra in Portland when she was a teen. George began to have problems with acute posttraumatic stress and moved to be near the Veterans' Hospital in Roseburg, Oregon. After he felt stronger, he worked at the hospital. He moved to Missoula Montana and spent seven years at the veteran's home in New Columbia, Montana. He passed away in 1979.

Robert "Bobby" Edward Ryan worked at Ted Snyder's grocery in Cataldo and joined the Army in March of 1942. He was very charismatic. He lived in Spokane with his wife, Miyako Shiga Nozaki, and worked at Alaska Junk in Spokane. He and Miyiko are buried north of his mother and grandfather at St. Thomas in Coeur d'Alene. He was 62.

James "Duffy" Mathew Ryan joined the National Guard in 1940 and served in the infantry. He was the smallest of Anna's sons at 5'4". He was an actor and entertainer and died in San Francisco at age 54. Anna's sons are not known to have dependents.

Mat, like many pioneers, saw a chance to overcome the lack of opportunity he witnessed. He was willing to take the risk of leaving Ireland as a young man and having to learn a new language and gain marketable skills. In spite of this dire situation, he grew up with parents who encouraged him to leave to try to attain a better life. They instilled in him strong principles. Mat became a mentor and friend to many. He had the personality to encourage others when times were challenging and believed families should send their children to school and church. At the end of his life, he had accumulated large land holdings and several properties in Coeur d'Alene and Spokane. All families have a story and Mats is a story to be remembered.

Appendix

(A-1) Mats's homestead claim was approved on January 15, 1878.
Walla Walla, W.T. Homestead Claim 218

(4—485.)

THE UNITED STATES OF AMERICA,

To all to whom these presents shall come, Greeting:

Homestead Certificate No. 232

APPLICATION 1434

Whereas There has been deposited in the GENERAL LAND OFFICE of the United States a CERTIFICATE OF THE REGISTER of the Land Office at *Walla Walla, Washington Territory* whereby it appears that, pursuant to the Act of Congress approved 20th, May, 1862, "To secure Homesteads to Actual Settlers on the Public Domain," and the acts supplemental thereto, the claim of *Mathew Hayden* has been established and duly consummated, in conformity to law, for the *south half of the north east quarter and the north west quarter of the south east quarter of section twenty and the south west quarter of the north west quarter of section twenty one in township thirty five north of range thirty nine east in the district of lands subject to sale, at Walla Walla, Washington Territory, containing one hundred and sixty acres*

according to the Official Plat of the Survey of the said Land, returned to the GENERAL LAND OFFICE by the Surveyor General:

Now know ye, That there is, therefore, granted by the United States unto the said *Mathew Hayden* the tract of Land above described: To have and to hold the said tract of Land, with the appurtenances thereof, unto the said *Mathew Hayden* and to *his* heirs and assigns forever; subject to any vested and accrued water rights for mining, agricultural, manufacturing, or other purposes, and rights to ditches and reservoirs used in connection with such water rights, as may be recognized and acknowledged by the local customs, laws, and decisions of courts, and also subject to the right of the proprietor of a vein or lode to extract and remove his ore therefrom, should the same be found to penetrate or intersect the premises hereby granted, as provided by law.

In testimony whereof I, *Ruthurford B. Hays* , President of the United States of America, have caused these letters to be made Patent, and the seal of the GENERAL LAND OFFICE to be hereunto affixed.

Given under my hand, at the CITY OF WASHINGTON, the *fifteenth* day of *January*, in the year of our Lord one thousand eight hundred and *seventy-eight*, and of the Independence of the United States the one hundred and *second*

By the President: *R. B. Hayes*

By *B. L. Lang* , Secretary.

S. N. Clark Recorder of the General Land Office.

RECORDED, Vol. 1 , Page 284

[1885—1900]

(A-2) Mat's Declarations of Intention to Become a Citizen
of the United States

DECLARATIONS OF INTENTION.

THE UNITED STATES OF AMERICA.

Territory of Washington,
County of Whitman.

In the District Court of the Territory of Washington and for the First Judicial District thereof, holding Terms at Colfax, for the County of Whitman in said Territory.

I, *Matthew Hayden* a native of

England

do declare on oath, that it is bona fide my intention to become a citizen of the United States of America, and to renounce all allegiance and fidelity to all and any foreign Prince, Potentate, State or Sovereignty whatever, and particularly to *Victoria*

Queen of England

and that I will support the Constitution of the United States of America, so help me God.

Matthew Hayden
his Mark

Subscribed and sworn to before me, at my office, this *14th* day

of *July* A.D. 186*6*

Jno Galbreth CLERK.

by *R H Rodgers* Deputy.

(A-3) Adjutant General's report regarding Mat's pension claim

Adjutant General's Office,

Washington, D.C., July 14th, 1877.

Sir:

I have the honor to acknowledge the receipt from your Office of application for Pension No. 382,978, and to return it herewith, with such information as is furnished by the files of this Office.

It appears from the Records of this Office that Mathew Hayden was enlisted on the 3rd day of June, 1852, at West Point N.Y., to serve 5 years, and was assigned to Co. "C" 2nd Regiment of Dragoons. On the Muster Roll of Co. "C" of that Regiment for the months of November & December, 1855, he is reported a private present. Joined from Depot Dec. 21st 1855. Transf'd to Co B 1st Cav aug't 1st 1856. and Discharged from said Co. June 3 1857 Expr of Ser at Camp on Little Blue K.T. a Private.

He was on duty at Ft Columbus N.Y.H. and Jefferson Bks Mo Depots prior to assignment to Company.

No record of his having been engaged with Indians

I am, sir, very respectfully,

Your obedient servant,

S.N. Benjamin.

Assistant Adjutant General.

by D.V. Molus

The Commissioner of Pensions,
Washington, D.C.

(A-4) **Note from Father Cataldo to Mat. May 26, 1884**

R. F. Cataldo promised to M. Hayden
that One hundred dollars of the
two first installement would be remitted
as pay for the board &c of F. Joset
that for the following installement, it would
depend on how the business of the hotel
shall succeed: that if the hotel should
be closed the payments would cease
that after the term be elapsed if Mr
Hayden would remove the building on
his own ground, we would not quarrel
about it. Spokane Falls W. T.
May 26th 1884

Mr. Hayden after paying $110.00
must pay $500.00 for farm,
$75.00 for ware-house, and
$100.00 (as here above) next July,
and the same on Nov: and July after,
and so on till July 1887.

(A-5) Antoine and Anna's Marriage Certificate

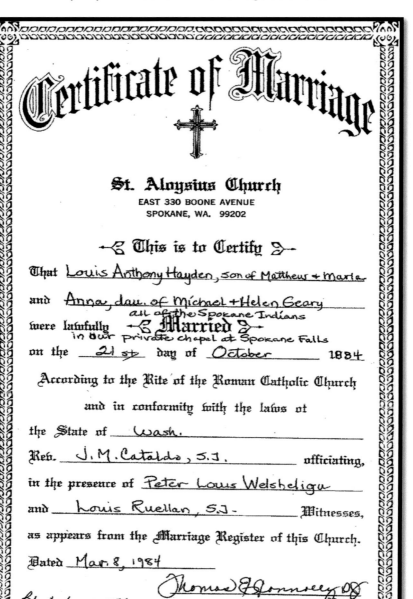

Certificate of Marriage

St. Aloysius Church
EAST 330 BOONE AVENUE
SPOKANE, WA. 99202

⟨ This is to Certify ⟩

That Louis Anthony Hayden, son of Matthew + Maria

and Anna, dau. of Michael + Helen Geary

all of the Spokane Indians

were lawfully **Married**

in our private chapel at Spokane Falls

on the 21st day of October 1884

According to the Rite of the Roman Catholic Church

and in conformity with the laws of

the State of Wash.

Rev. J. M. Cataldo, S.J. officiating,

in the presence of Peter Louis Welsheligu

and Louis Ruellan, S.J. Witnesses,

as appears from the Marriage Register of this Church.

Dated Mar. 8, 1984

Thomas J. Connolly OS Pastor

Bk 1, page 176

(A-6) Catherine Hayden, daughter of Antoine Hayden

Certificate of Baptism

✠

St. Aloysius Church

EAST 330 BOONE AVENUE
SPOKANE, WA. 99202

⸸ This is to Certify ⸸

That _Catherine Hayden_

Child of _Antoine Hayden_ ("Temsinhie")
and _Ann Chittiulshe_ daughter of Nellie
daughter of
Spokane Garry

born in _____
(CITY)   (STATE)

on the _14_ day of _Sept_ 1887

was **Baptized**

on the _15_ day of _Sept_ 1887

According to the Rite of the Roman Catholic Church

by the Rev. _Loss. Smith OJ_

the Sponsors being { _Michael Kolkolz/Kainn_

as appears from the Baptismal Register of this Church.

Dated _____

_____
Pastor

200

(A-7) A Coeur d'Alene Brewing Company[236]

(A-8) Boomtowns, gambling, saloons, and substandard beds . . . Life in a mining camp . . . An Idaho town whose streets are paved with cards . . . Whip-sawing, poker playing and thimble operating where Chinamen need not apply and idlers are few. [237]

MURRAYVILLE, IDAHO, July 18, 1884. I am in a mining camp, and a strange, curious place it is, with its crowds of sunburned, hardy men, its rows of uncouth, primitive buildings, its dilapidated streets, and its daily humdrum, monotonous life. This town is of but little more than four months' growth, but at present, it is the important place of the Coeur d'Alene region. "Curry" is the name by which it is known to the postal authorities, but no one calls it such; it is far easier to call it Murrayville, the place where Murray lived and had his claim. For a town to have two names is not uncommon out here, and it just occurs to me that Belknap, a neighboring place, is officially known as "Enterprise."

In my last letter, I said that the whole Coeur d'Alene country was a dense forest, except where the hand of man had hewn out a few small clearings. Over mountains and levels alike the thick timber extends, and there are miles and miles of it. Murrayville lies in one of the little clearings, and on a level spot, narrow and hemmed in on two sides by almost perpendicular mountains. At the base of the southern mountain, which raises its broadside abruptly to the sky for fully a thousand feet, runs the clear and beautiful stream of the gulch. The almost vertical wall is covered with a thick growth of trees, many of which have loosed their hold upon the feeble soil and stand pointing sideways and outward as if ready to hurl themselves from their loftiness and plunge into the innocent and unoffending stream below. The opposite mountain is not quite so steep nor as high. From its sides, the trees have already been stripped from upward of 200 feet, and in their places stand, here and there, scrubby-looking little houses of unconventional shape. A steep, narrow path rises to each of them, but the ascent once made, a view of the town and gulch is well worth the exertion.

Lumber for homes is very expensive, mostly shake roofs

Murrayville has one main street, from which, at intervals, are offshoots in the shape of side streets. It is about 75 feet wide and is full of the stumps of the trees cut to make room for the townsite. On either side of this main street, for perhaps an eighth of a mile, are ranged the stores. They are of every conceivable kind and shape. There are a few log houses, more tents, and tent houses, but one-story frame buildings abound. A tent house is half log or frame house and half tent; it is simply a shell of logs or boards with a canvas roof. This kind of building is very plentiful in the West and particularly popular in new towns. The canvas is not made especially for the houses; it is an ordinary tent adapted to the purpose. Their size is often considerable. I have seen them 90 by 30 feet, but the average is from 60 by 20 to 40 by 20. They are plentiful and cheap, lumber being an expensive article in a new country, but they are more comfortable than a tent. Anything covered with canvas is damp in rainy weather, and insufferably hot when the sun pours down upon it; besides light canvas is not waterproof, and here eight-ounce or bucking is used almost exclusively.

There is no seasoned lumber in the town and promises not to be for some time owing to the limited capacity of the mills of the gulch. Everything has been built of green material, and for a long time, lumber was worked into houses the same day it was sawed. It sells now for $35 per 1000 feet, and before any sawmills were put in it was at one time as high as $300 per 1,000 feet. At that time every plank was whipsawed, the amount made was small, and the demand was very great. Many thousands of feet were sold at $300, $275, $250 per 1,000 feet, and most of it was sold before it was cut. The sawmills, of course, hurt the tremendous profit of the business, but for a long time, both they and the whip sawyers coined money. They have held prices upmost persistently, but $35 per 1,000 feet is a high figure, and ought to satisfy them. The whip sawyers have not given up; they are still working and making sales.

For the benefit of those who know little of lumber, I will say that whip-sawing is done by two men. The log is placed on two uprights. One man stands above on the log; the other is below. They have a long thin saw, with handles on either end. One man is continually pushing the saw, while the other is pulling it. The man below usually wears goggles to keep the sawdust from his eyes; whipsawing is hard work and slow work, but it pays because running expenses are almost nothing. The freshness of the timber is seen most plainly in the frame houses. From those recently erected the pitch can be seen oozing in quantities. Besides this habit of oozing, the pitch has an extremely rude and unmannerly way of dropping constantly. When the inhabitants are not kept busy dodging the glistening balls, they have lively times making a general clean-up.

It is most unhealthy for the clothes to lean up against any portion of a newly built house in a mining camp, but I know of no way in which one can so easily and with so little trouble and expense experience the delightful sensation of having been in a mucilage pot. Those buildings which were erected two months or more ago are now almost open to the weather, for the boards in their drying have shrunk apart and made gaps in many places an inch wide. The floors, too, have curled up in a wonderful way, and are anything but handsome. Sidewalks are too luxurious for Murrayville or any town in the young Coeur d'Alene section, but there are in front of the store's little platforms for the benefit of those who may wish to enter. No two of these are the same height, and jumping off places is frequent. Rather than disjoint themselves, the people use the dusty or muddy street. In speaking of the houses, I forgot to mention those made of "shakes." A "shake" is a piece of cedar about three feet long and six inches wide. It is intended to take the place of a shingle but is considerably thicker. Cedar is very straight-grained, and the "shakes" are easily split out with a heavy steel-pointed knife specially made for the purpose. There are few buildings in Murrayville which have not "shake" roofs, and there are many structures in which they are used instead of boards.

Saloons are most popular business

Saloons fill more than half of all the buildings in a mining camp. The lodging houses come next in number and the balance are restaurants, stores, and shops of various kinds. The lodging houses are really half saloons, for most of them contain bars. Drinking and smoking are unquestionably the most active employments. The whisky and other liquors dealt out are bad--dreadful; the price, 2 "bits," (25 cents), for a single drink is simply outrageous. Beer and all other drinks, likewise cigars, are the same price. There seems to be an objection to using any smaller change for those luxuries, though ten-cent pieces are to be had in the country. There are two kinds of "bits," the long and the short. They are very familiar to those who have lived or traveled on the Pacific slope. The long "bit" is 15 cents, the short bit 10 cents. If one buys an article worth one "bit" and gives 25 cents to pay for it, he gets back only 10 cents. It seems to be an arrangement in favor of the seller, and its origin is due to the scarcity of small change in the West years ago.

The saloons of the Coeur d'Alene are not handsome. Many of them are in tent houses and have only a cheap bar, a dirty wooden floor, and a few chairs. Some have stoves, and some are without any bottom but the bare earth, but all have the same array of cheap liquor behind the bar. A peculiar feature of the Western saloon is that each one contains one or more gambling tables. No saloon is complete without at least one gambling table, and most of them have one or more "faro" tables, and in addition a "stud-horse poker" table. "Stud-horse poker" is like other "poker," but the cards are dealt out by a gambler, who sits on the inside of a semicircular table. On the outside sit the players, who bet among themselves according to the nature of their hands, the gambler simply dealing the cards as they are asked for, and taking a certain percentage of such a "pot" from the one who wins. The game is a sure thing for the dealer, for he takes no hand, and no matter who wins he is bound to get his percentage.

Gamblers follow from strike to strike

The gamblers in these saloons are not their own masters. They are paid to run the games by the owner of the tables; sometimes the saloon keeper owns both saloon and games, but it is more often the case that the games are run by an outside party. The usual pay of these gamblers or dealers is [$25 or $35] a week, and in addition, they are entitled to supper, all the cigars they can smoke, and all the whisky they can drink. The gamblers change off with one another as a rest and often play against the game themselves. There is no particular time for the opening of the game. From early in the morning until late in the evening, in fact, all night long, if there are any players, the game goes on, but the bulk of the playing is in the evening. In this region, and throughout the West, every gambling game is open to the public. Anyone can go in and look on who likes, and be welcome to put his money on the table if he wants to play. In most places there is a limit, but it rises or falls according to the solidity of the bank or the character of the town.

Helena, the capital of the territory, is an old mining town, and it always has been a great gambling town. Gambling is going there at a great rate today in many saloons, and it is all open and in plain sight from the streets. There is not the slightest pretense of concealment. The doors of every saloon are as wide open as if in New-York, and there is a constant stream of men, moving in and out. They look at the game a few moments and, perhaps, leave, but the chances are that they will throw down a dollar or half a dollar carelessly and watch indifferently for the result If it is swept from the board, perchance they try again, but it is probable they will walk out and down street, step into another saloon, and put the same amount on a table there. If a winning is made a chair is apt to be secured and a stay made until their money is either gone or its pile sensibly increased.

To gamble or to indulge in anything a man has a fancy for is no crime, nor even vice, in this country. If he does not steal, play the sneak, or impose upon another, nothing the worse is thought of him. Clustered around a gambling table, either playing or looking on, can be seen any evening, in any of these Western towns, a specimen from almost every class of people in the country. Tradesmen, clerks, miners, laboring men of all kinds, all indulge at times. But in the larger and more established towns, and, as a rule, throughout the country, the better class does not indulge in play--at least not before the public.

The success of the gambling tables depends considerably on circumstances. The game is more lively on some days than on others because of the changing condition of the pockets of the players. The workingmen are their chief supporters, and on days when they are paid off the tables fairly ring with the sound of coin. When the Northern Pacific Railroad was under construction the gamblers made quantities of money. They followed along as it was completed, and kept their hold upon the workingmen.

With them, too, went the loose women, who have since scattered themselves all over the country and been reinforced by numbers of their kind from either coast. There is a fraternity between them and the gamblers: where one is the other is sure to be; both are here in plenty. Confidence men are also numerous in the Coeur d'Alene country, and the tricks and devices to catch people are many. The weakest game I have seen is that in which one draws conditional prizes. A man bets three times on the running of a ball into a slot. He usually wins twice, but he wins what he has made only on condition of his winning the third time also. He never wins the third time and loses everything.

What's called the "thimble game" and "three-card monte" are also common. It requires considerable skill to be successful at the "thimble game." The operator puts three shells on his upper leg as he sits with them crossed, pushes a pea under them all in turn, and then gets someone to bet which one it is under. He always finds some smart man who can surely tell, and who readily loses his money. This is a great country for betting, and for getting things by taking all kinds of chances. People are constantly trading horses, exchanging watches for pistols, or blankets, rifles, and anything they may own for something they want more. Dice shaking for liquor or cigars is as natural to a Western man as to eat his meals. If one shakes dice for a cigar he shakes not for one cigar, but for one for himself and one for the proprietor. If he loses, he simply has to pay double for one cigar. "Shaking" is profitable for the seller.

Currency and the definition of "two bits"

Twenty-five and fifty-cent pieces are getting more plenty in the country of late; for a long time, there was a great scarcity of them. Banknotes of large denominations frequently could not be broken without great difficulty. Banknotes of small denominations are very scarce. One does not see one once a month, but the country is flooded with silver dollars. People [in the] East dislike the silver dollar, and I do not doubt that they are purposely shipped West. I know they are very plenty even in St. Paul. Anything passes out here without a question. Trade dollars, a coin with holes or other mutilation, are given their par value. Canadian twenty-five-cent and fifty-cent pieces, which are discounted in value East, pass here the same as our own money. One often sees Canadian bank bills and money of foreign countries, besides an occasional shinplaster. I presume the immigrants put the foreign coin in circulation. [Ed. note: a shinplaster was originally paper money of small value that the U.S. government printed and circulated from 1862-78. By the time of the article, a currency called shinplasters was issued privately and was considerably devalued because of inflation or questionable source.

The sale of playing cards is a very large item in this region today. Everybody, even Indians and Chinamen play. The Indians usually play for cartridges, but sometimes for horses and other of their possessions. It is hard to walk a block in any street in one of these new towns without finding half a dozen cards in the dust or mud. Often one comes on whole packs. And not alone are they found in the towns; the whole country is strewn with them. You see them in the roadside as you ride through in the cars [railroad]; you see them in the rivers as they hurl their waters by; they are in wagons, in the woods near towns, and on the trails miles and miles from any habitation. They turn up in most lonely and unexpected places, and it is hard to find any piece of ground where a camp has been pitched for the night without at least a scattering of them. The amusements in this country are absolutely none. I believe that gambling, card playing, (of course for money,) and the other vices are indulged in largely because there is nothing else to do.

Miners are nomadic and beds are miserable

The life is nomadic in the extreme. Men do their day's work or tramp their day's journey. There is nothing to amuse or elevate them after sundown; they must have a chance, and they resort to these things to pass their time and to temper existence with some excitement. Life in this country is demoralizing in the extreme for him who is weak-minded.

The lodging houses are a curious feature of the section. They are of various kinds and differently fitted up. Some contain cots, a few have old beds, but the majority have bunks ranged in tiers above one another. They resemble very much in appearance those [that are] furnished emigrants in the steerage of ocean steamships, but many are no better than those of the same character I once saw in a ten-cent lodging house in the top of a five-story Fourth Ward building. They are made of rough pine, and usually contain a very hard and roughly made mattress, a pillow covered with unbleached cotton, a pair of sheets of the same material, and a pair of blankets. The cots sometimes have sheets, a pillow, and blankets, but often one gets only blankets. The beds are grander in appearance, but I cannot speak enthusiastically of a night's rest in them. To say that all are old is enough of a description. Sometimes the sleeping apartment is in the rear of the building, and a store or restaurant in the front, but usually the whole building is given up to the bunks, cots, or beds. A cot or bed lodging house resembles very much, except in neatness and brightness, the ward of an Eastern hospital, and the rows of strangers asleep throughout it look for all the world like patients in the same hospital. Except in a few houses, there are no partitions, or even screens, between the cots; one sleeps in the midst of strangers and relies on the community at large to protect him from theft or danger.

I have so far not heard of anyone's has been robbed while asleep; theft is the most serious offense in the mines, and everyone knows it. No office is connected with these lodging houses, nor is there any place in which one can read and write. It is possible only to wander about aimlessly until confirmed absence of anything to do compels one to turn in. The only luxuries thrown in with the night's rest are a stove, a tin washbasin and a pail of water, a towel, a worn-out comb and brush, and perhaps a few cheap chromos on the walls. Fortunately, one is too tired when traveling to object to anything. After a day or two, it becomes a matter of pure indifference what he sleeps in, or where he sleeps, so long as it is indoors. He sleeps soundly and well always; it does not matter to him who occupied the bunk, cot, or bed before him, nor does he investigate its merits too closely, or question the proprietor as to the length of time since the sheets were changed.

To secure custom all lodging houses advertise outside on a grand scale. The many prominent signs announce "mattresses of wool," "spring beds of the newest pattern," "clean and comfortable cots," "the best and cheapest beds in the country," etc. And then to catch the eye of the newcomer, and to perhaps assure him that he is apt to find within someone who is at least acquainted in the town from which he came, taking names are given to the houses, such as "The Gold Dust," "Coeur d'Alene," "The Placer," "Oro Fino," "Black Hills," "Golden Gate," "Denver," and a hundred other names, chiefly of Western cities. If one stays in any of the new towns in this section and does not own a building of his own he can only live in a lodging house. The pleasure of such an existence can be easily seen.

I slept in a tent-roofed lodging house in this place a few nights ago, and I shall not forget the experience of one poor man who happened to have a cot in the middle of the building, and just beneath the joining of the two large pieces of canvas. It rained very hard all night and the drops of water trickled down on every cot. They fell on my pillow, and I had to dodge my head, but they did not wet through the blankets. The man of whom I speak was well soaked. The water rushed down upon him in quantities; but he was an old miner, and, supposing that everybody was getting the same dose, would not make a complaint. He quietly curled in his blankets and made the best of it. When he saw the opening of the canvas in the morning he was disgusted. Every man in the place took a look at his cot and the water spout above, and there was much laughter at his expense. He said he had just come into town, and thought perhaps to get such baths was a regular thing in the country. I always examine the roof now before I lie down.

Of the stores in the place, I need only say that they are like any in a new Western town, and are filled with material most adapted to the country. "General merchandise" is the best represented; the hardware stores come next, and then follow one or more of every kind, down to the barber's shop. Prices are high in them all, but not extortionate, considering the trouble and expense of packing the goods in and risk run. The days of giving things away are going by. One can now get a good meal at the restaurants for 75 and 50 cents, and there are one or two places which carry good liquors. Lodgings and meals six weeks ago cost $1 each; lodging can now be got anywhere for 50 cents, and in some places for 25 cents. Everything is getting more reasonable, and I expect before long that a good hotel will be erected.

Life is often empty, boring, and depressing. Rx: The great outdoors

Owing to its situation in the gulch and in the woods, Murrayville is or has been, very damp, and considerable sickness has resulted from it. There has been some business for the physicians, who haunt the country in numbers, but there have been few deaths in the place, and these were more from the wasted condition of the person than from the dampness. The atmosphere of the country round about is beautiful and very invigorating, and people seem to thrive on it even with little food. To live in a mining country and to travel through it are two different things. One gets used to the country very soon and does not mind it. It is perfectly safe for everybody, and I should as soon think of making a trip to this section and not seeing the mines as of going to Italy without seeing Rome.

The life of a mining camp is in the morning or evening. At these times the streets are full of men dressed in all kinds of garments. Style, cut, or shape is not considered: everyone dresses for warmth and comfort. Flannel shirts, buck coats, and trousers, leather trousers for riding, overalls, top-boots, rubber boots, and hats of all kinds except "the stovepipe" are seen. I presume a "stovepipe" hat would soon be knocked in. The men stand about in knots and smoke and talk or wander about aimlessly. At these two times can be seen the pack mules going out empty or coming in with their cargoes, the leader always wearing a cowbell, which causes tho others to follow.

A favorite amusement of the inhabitants Is In betting what the various boxes on the mules contain. It is wonderful how quiet and docile these pack animals are, for their burdens are heavy, and they are "cinched" on in a way that fairly makes them groan. To "cinch" them so hard is a necessity, for otherwise, the loads would sag to one side. Along the narrow trails, they go steadily, following the tinkle of the bell, and hurried on by the packers if they move too slowly. The average load carried by the mules here is between 200 and 300 pounds, but they do not load them often with 400 pounds. Horses are used in many instances, and one sees a few "burros," but mules are considered the best. They are no surer footed than the others but are tougher than horses, and their backs do not so easily chafe. They are more desirable than a "burro," because they are larger and can carry more.

The real-life of a mining camp is after dark when the lights are lit and the music begins in the shape of banjo, fiddle, or accordion. It is then that the people move about and the crude free-and-easy existence is best seen. Murrayville has not as many idlers now as it had. That the streets are more deserted in the daytime and full as lively at night shows that work is being done on claims, and that things are getting into organized condition. One does not see any Chinamen in these Coeur d'Alene camps. They have been prohibited from entering and a promise of death for the first one who sets his foot across the mountain. The Chinamen understand the case and make no effort to get in.

(A-9a) Sale of the Wardner Property to Mrs. L. Tilly.

Articles of Agreement, Made this .....15th..... day of ....October.....

in the year of our Lord one thousand eight hundred and ninety .....One..... Between .....
James Monaghan Executor of the Estate
of Mathew Hayden

party of the first part, and.................*Mrs L Tilly*.........................

.... party of the second part :

Witnesseth, That if the party of the second part shall first make the payments and perform the covenants hereinafter

mentioned on ....*her*..... part to be made and performed, the said party of the first part hereby covenants and agrees

to convey and assure to the said party of the second part, ~~for simple~~, by a good and

Quit Claim

sufficient ~~Warranty~~ Deed, the lot , piece or parcel of ground, situated in the County of .....*Shoshone*.....

and State of .....*Idaho*..... known and described as ....

.....*The Lots and House in the Town of*

Wardner Known as the Tilly House

and now occupied by the party

of the Second part.

and the said party of the second part hereby covenants and agrees to pay to the said party of the first part the sum of

Sixteen hundred and fifty (1650), Dollars in the following manner, viz: Upon delivery of these presents

Seven hundred and fifty £750.00) dollars

and upon the 15th day of the months

of November December 1891 and January

February March April May June

and July the sum of one hundred

£100.00) dollars

with interest at the rate of ....*18*..... per cent per annum, payable *At* maturity, on ~~the whole~~ sum remaining from time

to time unpaid, and to pay all taxes, assessments, or impositions that may be legally levied or imposed upon said land, sub-

sequent to ~~the year~~ .*Oct 15th 1891.* And in case of the failure of the said party of the second part to make either of

the payments, or any part thereof, or perform any of the covenants on....*her*.....part hereby made and entered

into, this contract shall, at the option of the party of the first part, be forfeited and determined, and the party of the second

part shall forfeit all payments made by....*her*.....on this contract, and such payment shall be retained by the said

party of the first part in full satisfaction and in liquidation of all damages by....*her*.....sustained, and....*he*.....

shall have the right to re-enter and take possession of the premises aforesaid.

And the party of the second part hereby appoints the County Auditor of said county....*his*.....lawful attorney

to quit-claim to the party of the first part, all....*her*.....right, title and interest on the premises above described, in

case the party of the second part shall fail to peform the covenants in this agreement mentioned to be performed by the

party of the second part, or shall fail to make any payment herein mentioned, when the same shall become due and payable.

It is Mutually Agreed, by and between the parties hereto, that the time of payment shall be the es-

sence of this contract; and that all the covenants and agreements herein contained shall extend to and be obligatory upon the

heirs, executors, administrators and assigns of the respective parties.

In Witness Whereof, the parties to these presents have hereunto set their hands and seals the day and

year first above written.

SEALED AND DELIVERED IN PRESENCE OF

O M Thompson

P. V. Conroy

J Monaghan [SEAL]

Executor Estate Mathew Hayden [SEAL]

Mrs L Tilly [SEAL]

(A-9b) Dec 14, 1891: The State of Idaho received $71 from Hayden Estate for Wardner Property valued at $2,000.

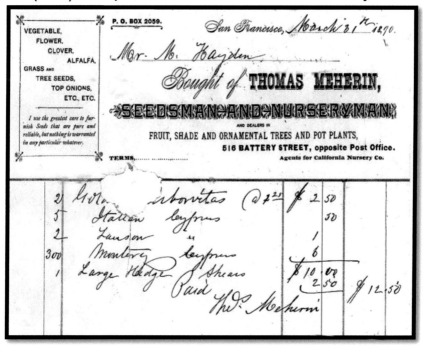

(A-10) A receipt from Thomas Meherin's Seeds and Nurseryman

(A-11) A receipt from the Dalles Nursery

THE DALLES NURSERY,
The Dalles, Wasco Co., Oregon.

...ordered to the contrary we reserve the right in all bills ...out in either one or two year old trees if we have not the ...in varieties ordered. No other substitution will be made ...es by special agreement, and aside from this any article not ...ished will be deducted from your bill.

WATERS & RAWSON,

...will please furnish to me, and deliver in good order at *Cœur d'alene* in the Fall, Spring 18 _90_., the following bill of Trees, Plants, etc., for the ...pose of improving my property.

		Age.	$	Cts.
10	B Barmarts apple	2		
10	Minnesota	2	2	00
5	Bartlett	1		
3	congress	1	1	45
2	Idaho Pear	1	3	50
5	cons Golden Drop			
5	Elton			
4	B Republican		2	55
6	Fay's Victoria currant	1	2	50
2	Quinces			50
12	English goos By	1	2	5
6	Champion			65
6	evergreen BBE			60
5	Hagloe			
5	G Fulton		3	00
10	Gloria Mondi			
5	Bailey 5 Crawford		1	80
10	Indian Quest		1	80
5	Yellow Prune		1	90
	Strawburys			

Please notify me by mail of date on which my order will be ...livered. On the delivery of this bill of Trees at the above ...amed place, it shall be considered delivered to me, at which ...ime and place I promise to pay to your order as per contract ...he sum of $ 1 4 7 and 3 75 cents, for value received. ...hould this order, by accident or otherwise, fail to arrive on ...e day set, I am to be notified again, and will receive when ...livered in good order.

Signed by ....
... 23 ... day of _July_ ...... 18 90.
...nty of _Kootenai_, State of _Idaho_
...O. _Cœur d'alene_ Location ....
...les North, East, South, West.
.... _C T Rawson_ Salesman.
...Bros., Portland.

(A-12) Mat's Citizen Papers were held at the Dead Letter Office
before being delivered. [238]

CHAS. E. METZ, CLERK.   F. A. ENGLISH, DEPUTY CLERK.

~OFFICE OF THE~

Clerk of the Superior Court of Whitman County,

WASHINGTON.

Colfax, Washington, Mar. 8, 1890

Mr
   Mathew Hayden
      Old Mission, Idaho.
Dear Sir

   I enclose you a letter returned by the Dead letter office to the writer, Reeves Ayres, in which were contained your Citizen papers – It had traveled all over the country and I trust it will find you now.

   Trusting this will reach you now, I am respectfully yours
      Chas. E. Metz
       per F. A. English
        Deputy

(A-13) Nov. 8, 1890 Letter from Dr. Cole to Mathew Hayden

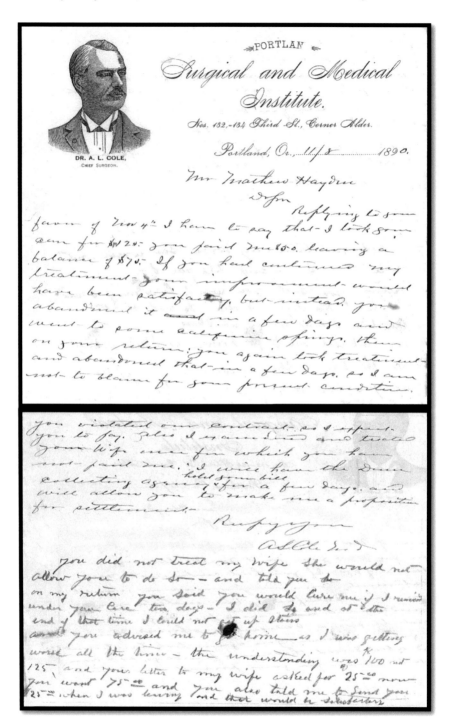

(A-14) Dr. Stoddart wrote M. Hayden on Nov. 6, 1890

Medical Staff Correspondence.—Dictated to Confidential Stenographer.

Qualified and Responsible.

DR. LIEBIG & CO., organized in compliance with California law. Diplomas procured by regular college education. Twenty years' special practice, and duly licensed in accordance with California Medical Law.

The DR. LIEBIG & CO. MEDICAL STAFF is the largest on the Pacific Coast, and the only Surgical Incorporation conducting an elegant Drug Store of their own in a Dispensary Building.

PATIENTS and LIFE MEMBERS have the benefit of a thorough Examination and Diagnosis by Dr. Stoddart, who has been Examining Physician for Dr. Liebig & Co. the past 14 years, and now President of The Liebig World Dispensary.

ARCHIBALD C. STODDART, M. D., Physician from Scotland. Late Physician at Magdalen Asylum, San Francisco. Formerly Examining Physician Ancient Order of United Workmen, elected on Medical Board of Examiners of the State of California, and late Corresponding Secretary for Medical Society of California.

MEDICAL OFFICES
—OF THE—
LIEBIG WORLD DISPENSARY
(Incorporated)
—AND—
International Surgical Institute
(Limited)

TERMS.

CONTRACTS made and curable cases guaranteed under our special advice and treatment. Letters or private correspondence can be addressed to A. CHALMERS, Esq., 405 Mason street or to the Dispensary Chemists, STODDART BROS. 400 Geary street, and they will reach the office safely.

OUR REMEDIES, when in liquid form, must be sent by express, and in name of our chemists, Stoddart Bros. An allowance of ten per cent. is made to patients who pay cash, and guarantee receipt in full is forwarded with first monthly box; also Certificate of Life Membership in the Liebig World Dispensary which entitles a patient to any extra treatment during life, without extra charge. Those who are unable to pay cash may do so in monthly installments. Any Surgical appliances required, will be arranged for at separate prices, independent of medical treatment and medicines.

The San Francisco Sunday Chronicle of Nov. 20, 1882, had the following editorial notice:

"Dr. Liebig's wonderful invigorator is a medicine that has the magic of a distinguished name, and which it is said to have honorably. Its restorative powers are said to be great, and his popularity among the business men whose physical energies have been wasted, and whose nervous systems are shattered by excessive devotion to business and the waste and hurry of city life, is great and increasing. Such a medicine has long been needed."

Call or address, Dr. LIEBIG & CO., 400 GEARY ST., Cor. MASON, SAN FRANCISCO, CAL.

Private Entrance, 405 Mason St. Letters strictly Confidential.

For the speedy and permanent cure of all Chronic Disease, call on or address DR. LIEBIG & CO.

WESTERN DIVISION, LIEBIG WORLD DISPENSARY, 400 Geary Street, corner Mason, San Francisco, Cal.

NORTHERN DIVISION, 8 E. Broadway, S. E. Cor. Main, Butte City, Mont.

EASTERN DIVISION, 301 and 303 West Ninth Street, corner Central, Kansas City, Mo.

San Francisco, Nov 6th 1890.

Mr. M. Hayden

Dear Sir Yours of Nov 1st enclosing $10 has been received and same placed to your credit on books. Thanks for remittance. I have forwarded a full months supply for your complaint. Persevere for a few months and you will be restored to health and strength. You have functional debility of several internal organs that can only be cured by persevering with the remedies for a few months. I will forward another supply in one month from now. Write in three weeks and give me all symptoms of case.

Yours confidentially
Liebig World Dispensary
Per Dr. Stoddart

(A-15) Hall and Noble Undertakers at Spokane Falls delivered a casket to the Mission for Eliza.

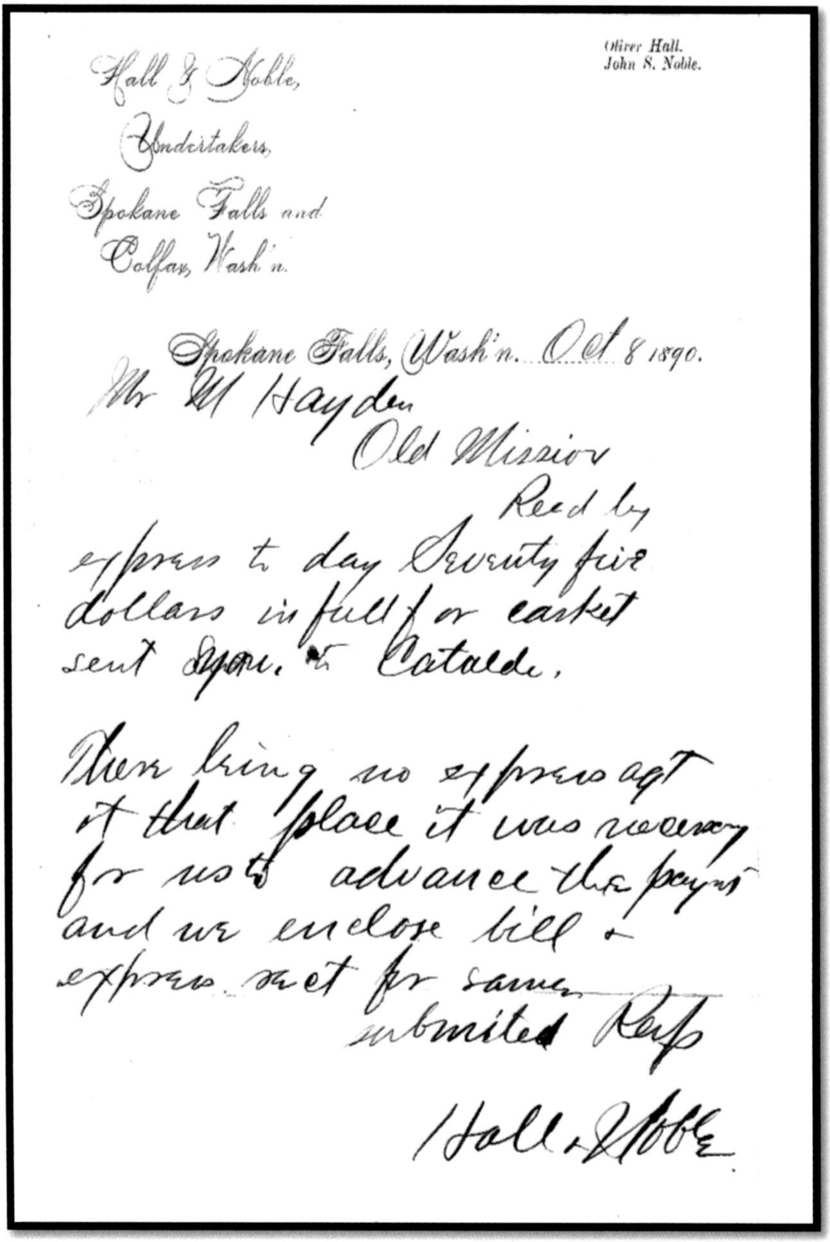

Hall & Noble,
Undertakers,
Spokane Falls and
Colfax, Wash'n.

Oliver Hall.
John S. Noble.

Spokane Falls, Wash'n. Oct 8 1890.

Mr M Hayden
Old Mission
Rec'd by
express to day Seventy five
dollars in full for casket
sent upon. to Cataldo.

There being no express agt
at that place it was necessary
for us to advance the pay't
and we enclose bill +
express rec't for same
submitted Resp

Hall & Noble

(A-16) James wrote Pat Whalen, and one of Pat's children replied:
Only a partial letter was found

January 18, 1890 Mr. Monaghan
Dear Sir,
The statement of the fowoloing goods (following)
1 Bedsted and 1 small Round Tabel
1 Bunoro (bureau)   1 stand
Buttlos man Book 1 lg Pitectur (picture) of st Josip
They killed forty chickens and 4 turkies of mine I had those chickans befoar Mr. Hayden or Lizzy Died. When I went after my Clows they would not let me have them the time Mr. Lucas tuck charge of the Place he was drunk every day and did not know what he was doing It was a shame the way he Run things a Round here. Pat worked at the Ranch 2/x at three Dollars a day and how not Reserved a sent for his work Pleas ask Mr Lucas if he sent the Mashean (machine) to Spokane to the Sisters also unkel mats pitcher is Missin Mr Lucas said you tuck it Did you send Mr Haydens things to Spokan and also Mrs Hayden things we doant kair much a bout the things but we want to know the fact a bout these things.

(A-17) Pat Whalen wrote to James regarding his $95.00 debt to Mat

(A-18) Accounting of some bills paid by James Monaghan

Funeral Expenses	$166.00
Suit of Clothes for Tom Powers	7.50
Graham account	1.25
? traders notice in paper	7.50
Fruit trees ordered by Hayden's	12.00
Baling Hay, selling and collecting	154.85
Bequest to Jesuit Fathers	100.00
Dr. C.A. Cole to settle account	30.00
Bequest to Sisters of Charity	200.00
James C Smith to settle account	46.50
Wm. Lucas to settle accounts	184.00
C.B. King & Co. to settle accts.	400.00
Expense for two trips to Mission Farm	25.00
Dr. N Q Webb to settle acct.	65.00
Fare on from Mission to Colville	49.50
Tuition for Hayden's 4 children from ? to Jan 91	1070.00
Dr. John Temple to settle Accts.	30.00
V N Sanders and Co. to settle accts	115.35
Sisters Hospital to settle accts.	27.85
Chas. Zelling to settle accts.	337.85
Total taxes pd in 1890 & 91	362.32
Holly, Mason Marks & Co.	2.16
Insurance on Wardner	100.00
Interest pd on Notes& Nego.	1069.46
Amount Pd. on Notes	1863.60
Eliza Whalen Annuity $12. per mo	216.00
John Sullivan to settle accounts	24.00
Mortgage pd on Colville farm	1000.00
Mortgage pd on Hayden Lake	500.00
Knapp Burrell & Co. to settle Acct.	10.89
Od ahloah	140.00
Payments to NP Land Co.	445.75
Assesmnt on mining claims	128.83
Tuition and board for Tom Powers	482.90
Tuition and board for John Powers	193.85

(A-19) **Personal property purchased from Mat's Estate by G. Simmons**

Mathew Hayden Personal Property

Mortgage made by John G Simmons and Lucy A Simmons Bearing interest Dec. 11th 1890 at the rate of 10% per annum	$2700.00
63 Head of Cattle	800.00
13 Mules and Horses	325.00
770 lbs of pork	24.25
2 doz chickens	25.00
3 old wagons	115.00
1 Buggy	50.00
2 (unreadable)	45.00
2 Cultivators and Plows	22.50
Lots of old Harnesses	40.00
4 Cross Cut Saws & Iron Wedges	9.00
1 Lot of tools	25.00
3 Mowing Machines	75.00
2 Horse Rakes	10.00
2 Kitchen Ranges & furniture	20.00
1 Side Saddle	10.00
25 Sacks of Flour	25.00
2 bedroom sets	35.00
2 Box stove	15.00
1 Sewing machine	10.00
1 Hay press	125.00
1 (unreadable) mill	20.00
1 saddle	10.00
1 Harrow	2.50
1 Whip Saw	5.00
22 Tons of Hay @ $3.00 per Ton	440.00
Blacksmith Tools	20.00
	5000.75

(A-20) D.K. Butler to James Monaghan about the Hayden Ranch in Old Mission, Idaho

<u>January 7, 1890,</u> The hay will be baled today the figures aren't yet run up but Smith (the man that has charge of the baling) says it will be near fifty tons. The baling will cost like the Devil but I don't see that it could be helped the days are so short that you couldn't put in more than a good ½ day and the hay was so fixed that it took a big force to get the hay to the baler. I will send you the exact result in 2 or three days. I didn't have any idea you would sacrifice the hay but hay is worth it here now. Timothy 18.00, Oats Hay 14.00, and Wild Hay 9.00. what I would know what would I sell them at these figures.

Lucas sold a considerable of the stuff left in the house and I would like to have a bill of it so as to see what's left. You didn't acknowledge Rect. 300.00 I sent you did you get it. Truly yours D.K. Butler.

<u>December 28, 1890,</u> Dear Sir. You will find enclosed checks for 300 dollars to pay on the ranch and hotel. The cattle were all in the field yesterday so I telephoned to Follet to come for them he hadn't got him yet. The baling is going on but slow. You will have very near if not fully forty tons. Lucas is here yet and sick. All hands got drunk Xmas day and aren't over it. The old woman and Whalen's wife came with the tram last Friday and took away a lot of the furniture. They told the Duch man that Lucas sent for them and the Duch Jack ass let them go taking an inventory of what they took! To any whom the women got thing worth ten cents to the estate, old chairs, some dishes and rags that you couldn't sel for enough to pay for locking them up – all I saw any good abut the house was 2 stoves, washstand and looking glass, bed stand and 12 or 14 hundred pounds flour. Them are all they get and he duchman will see; that they don't get away. Mrs. Monaghan's mare is heavy with foal so she couldn't be worked if you wish I could keep her here for the winter. I won't do to sell any more horses til the hay is bailed and shipped. I can sel the flour to a man here for the cost landed here. The groceries that were at the house will be all eat up by the balers. Lucus got the rent from Wimpy for dollars some time ago. Write me and give any instructions you think proper I will attend to them. Truly Yours D.K. Butler

<u>Old Mission Dec 30^{th,} 1890</u> Dear Sir I only got yor letter the 26th today. I don't know wheather Lucas collected any money from Follet for the cattle. He gave me no statement atall I think he went to CoeurDAlene City today on his way to Spokane. Follet sent after the cattle today and got all here but 3 calves the calves were in the brush and couldn't be fund on account of a fog. They came out themselves when it was to late but Follet says he will come down and kill them here in a day or two. Then so yet two critters birth Whalens cattle and out in the hills. The Hay will be baled this week do you wish it sold for what it will bring now. I enclose you John's Sullivans @ Will I pay @ here I get money Let me know what Follet was to pay for the cattle if you wish me to collect the money. Truly Yours D.K.Butler

<u>Old Mission January 21, 1891,</u> Dear Sir: I went to Wardner and Wallace yesterday to try to sel the hay but could only sel 10 tons of wild hay and two tons of oats hay. The oats hay I had to let go for 14 dollars and this is all I think it will fetch unless the roads get blocked you can buy a single bale in Wardner for 15 dollars per ton. Al Page wouldn't take the white horse. I sold the team of pony's

and the Duch man (living on the ranch) for 50 dollars. Then was some old hay left and I was paying the Duchman 2 bits a day for feeding it to your mare, the white horse, and a colt. If the wether gets bad I will bring them here and attend to them as it is now they are doing well. I was offered 25 dollars for the bedroom set. I think the party may pay 30. I think the set would cost in Spokane 45 dollars What will I do about it? The flat is so soft between here and Hayden's that it is imposiable to get the Hay across now to load on the cars but I look for a storm and a cold one soon. Truly Yours D.K. Bulter

Old Mission Feb 7<u>th, 91</u> Dear Sir I got the rent from Wimpy the last day of January – but about sending it to you tis out of question for I have paid it out already and twenty-five or thirty dollars of my own on the Hayden business. It cost like the Devil to bale the hay the days were short on account of the way the hay was scattered all over the fields and it took near double the hands to get it to the baler. The hands had to get 1.50 per day and found so that and so that wages, grub, and wire the bill came to $140.00. I shipped 4,730 lbs. of oats, to W. McMullen and Southerland, 8,390 wild hay to Tog Bro. and 4,089 lbs. of wild hay to Paul Hurlinger. This is all I have sold. I will go next week and try to sell more. I am now hauling the hay here so I can load a car. I will go see Al Page, the first time I go to Wardner. Sincerely yours D.K.Butler.

<u>Old Mission April 21, 91</u> I enclose you Check for fifty dollars and Rec from Wymacin and Sullivan for 34.00. I haven't collected what is out yet – no sale for Hay so far. I think thought be best to sel down that old warehouse you see Hayden took away a part of it. And so now anyone can help themselves to boards off it. I wouldnent give more than 30 or 40 dollars for it but if twas down I would use some of the lumber and could in all likely hood sel the rest say what you think is best. Truly yours D.K. Butler

<u>Old Mission Oct 6, 91</u> Dear Sir I got your letter Sunday. I am just now finishing up baling hay and helping every day so that my time is limited at present next week I will send you a statement of what I disposed of and what is on hand The baler I had no offer for nor do I think any one here wants it but Pat Whalen and he only wants to lent it I don't know wheather tis best send I to him for I don't think he would pay any thing. I owe you over 100 dollars besides the 200 dollars rent. This I will be able to ? up some time this month or as quick as I can colect it in I am able to be in Spokane in a few days and will see you.

Wimpy has paid no rent since last May he says he told you he could only pay 10 dollars a month and that he took your silence as consent. This is harsh, if the place isn't worth 20 dollars tis worth nothing. Respecetful D.K. Butler.

You were gone east before I got your 2nd letter. Telephone message Oct 11 Bailer could not be sold for more than $150 @ even at that I cannot sell it.

<u>Old Mission Oct 12, 91</u> Dear Sir Wimpy is rustling the delinquent rent and will pay it some time this week. Don't be alarmed about him giving up the Hotel. He paid ¼ year whiskey license a couple of weeks back and tis? an? you may be sure any way that a difference of ten dollars per month is sent. ? not kept him here or drive him out. I will be in Spokane Monday or Tuesday at ? of nexzt week and am in? fact that I will be able to? up with you. also wish Mrs. Monahan for the mare and colt. I had her? A dress right at the telephone for sending the mashine. The Agent at Cataldo promises me a car tomorrow morning and if he

keeps his word I will load the baler so that I will be in Spokane Wednesday. Truly Yours D.K. Butler. I have worked the Baler 2 or 3 days and twil bale 8 tons in ?? with any kind of decent handling.

Oct 13, 91 Dear Sir I just got back from Cataldo and the Agent hasn't put on the car for me but says he will get it on as quick as he can I have to load the bailer myself and he won't receipt for anything but I got it on the car so I twont do to pack it til the car arrives. I will advise you. Truly yours DK Butler

Old Mission Nov 15, 91 Dear Sir I got our letter with inventory of stuff at Hayden's I have Rented the house and potato ground to another man. All stuff left will be then turned over to the new man and I will be there so that I will be able to give you an exact a/c of what is left and what disposed of. I am loading today the last of the hay and will get paid for it next Tuesday. I only got 23 dollars from Wimpy so far and I got that by an order on me from a man that owed Wimpy and I was owing. I think you should write to him or me I can show the letter, that you would put him to troubles if he didn't hurry up you see he owed 100 dollars less 23.00 that I got and his property is good for it. You will hear from me again in the middle of the week coming. Truly Yours DK Butler

Nov 23, 91 I got your letter Saturday. Will send you a statement of what I have done tomorrow. I enclose you check for 47"50 the price of the last of Hayden Hay I got the money last Saturday. Wimpy and his wife are away for a week. The woman went to her fathers funeral and Wimpy himself to see a dying brother. There is no danger but you will get the money. I will show him your letter when he gets back. Truly Yours DK Butler

Nov 25, 91 The mail got out yesterday before I got the a/c made out. You will see by the figures I am owing you 129+53. This I will send you as soon as I can get to some bank I didn't think I owed you so much and have an idea I paid you more money if so you will know it. Then is the big stove I used it some last summer and will pay 25 dollars for it. I was never offered over 20 dollars you see the furniture is all gone. There is a horse rake I sold for ten dollars but haven't got paid yet tho the partners are good (Small and Colbey) and there is also dollars behind on hay if I can only shake the man that owes it. Wimpy buried his brother and his wife her father in the last few days. They got home yesterday and Wimpy said he would rustle all he could for you before the 28th. Truly Yours DJK Butler

Dec 3, 1891, Enclosed find check for 130 dollars I couldn't go up the country til yesterday to get the check. Wimpy is away now selling off his stock. He want to sel ranch and all and offers them cheap since his brothers death His father wants him to live with him so soon as he takes on any cash he will pay the rent Truly yours D.K. Butler

Old Mission Dec 21, 91 Dear Sir You will find enclosed a check for $300.00 I couldn't posibly go to Spokane without damage to my self. In about two weeks the rush will be over and then I will go down and square up with you. Wimpy didn't give me any money yet but he will get it as soon as he posibly can and hand it to me. He had 25.00 yesterday that he intended giving me but a butcher swooped down on him and made him pay him, money is scarce here and hard to collect but Wimpy will come out all right in a few days. Yours Truly DK Butler

Dec 17, 91 You will find enclose checks to the amt $216.50 100.00 for Mrs. Monahan for the mare and 116+50c rent of Hotel from Wimpy up to the 1st January 1892. I will be in Spokane the 21st or 22nd of this month and hope to see you. Truly yours DKButler You didn't acknowledge rect of my last letter but recken you got it.

Old Mission December 28, 1891, Dear Sir I enclose you list of what is left at Hayden's or rather what ought to be left. However, there is nothing missing but small things and 2 cicken they can be hunted up. You see I rented the tillage land to another man for the coming year and his wife is living there when the duch man moved he took such things along as he wanted and I found some more had been loaned out but as I send most all can be hunted up. The ware house has been taken down last summer and offered the lumber for 6 dollars a thousand but never sold a board. I used some of it myself and the but the majority of it is stacked up. Hayden took away a good part of the boards before his death and everyone else that wanted one helped themselves until I took it down and hauled it away. The mowers are in bad shape. You see they had taken a big part of the mashonary (machinery), out one to keep the other running, and just when they got through mowing the horses ran off with mower and broke it all to pieces. This I didn't know til I sent 3 or 4 parties over to buy at Hayden's and they never came back and I finally heard from one of them that the mowers weren't fit to use atol. The one of Hayden's harvest hands told me how they got Now you want me to make an offer on the whole thing and for me to give you anything of any account would be out of the question. For anything but the stove and I will pay you 25 dollars for that. Or give you 110 dollars for everything loose belonging to the place. I have figured if I take the old wagons mowers in fact everything in the house of mashonary get a blacksmith to work on them I may be able to get rid of them next summer and make something on them but I will have earned it or I will get this done for you if you pay me for any trouble. Truly yours D.K. Butler

List of stuff I've sold on Hayden Estate: Stove or Range, Lumber, Mowers, Wagons, block, but and 2 tables, plates, 2 chairs, Harrow, 1 draft Harness, Faning mill, Lantern, blacksmith tools, Horse rake, bed stand, and 3 milk pans. There are a few other small things that haven't listed but they don't amount to anything. The 2nd sadle young Powers got by going to the Duch man when he left the college you can charge him what you please for it. I think I got about all that was on your list-that Whalen dident get away with. Chag. Henry Pomeroy 175$ for Baler. Cr. 49.00 Freight.

Augt 10th 92 Your favor of the 8th came to hand yesterday. Wimpy paid me up to 1st July which leaves rent in your favor 80.00. I enclose check for the amt. I have got through cutting hay and am now baling as soon as I can pay the hands up. I will pay you the rent for the Hayden ranch. I would like to keep the ranch as long as I am the one farmng it. And if you wish to sell it I have an offer for the two ranches as soon as I can prefect my Titele Tis as well to have things as they are for a while and I will be liable to see you in a few days when we can have a beter understanding. Wimpy quit the hotel 1st July. There was a tirade going on between him and Frost when the old Mission Massacre happened (or rather when newspapers said it happened) and Wimpy was arrested and is up in the pen at Wardner since This demorrahsed (demoralized?) everything. Mrs. Wimpy and three young children are living in the hotel and I don't think it would be wise to bother them at present. Respectfuly your friend DK Butler

(A-21) The many letters from Dr. Sims to James demanding payment for treating Lizzie at her death

Feb 17th, 1891 Dear Sir I have just learned of the death of M. Hayden!! Late of Old Mission, Idaho, and that you are the administrator? Will you please tell me the time, place, and to whom, must I present my Doctor bill, against Hayden's Estate for treating his wife in her last Illness: by writing me, and informing me of the above sought for information you write. Very gratefully obliged. Yours truly L.M. Sims. P.S. I enclose you stamped envelope.

March 17 1891 Dear Sir I hereby enclose you my bill against the estate of late Mathew Hayden of Old Mission, Idaho. Which I hope you will please send the money as the amt. should have been paid long since. I have written to you before but cannot get any reply. I will give you a reasonable time to attend to the matter, or I will take other measures for collection of the enclosed account. Your ? in regard to my former letters I do not understand. Please let me hear from you and very greatly oblige. Your truly L.M. Sims. M.D. I send this registered so I will know that you get this. I was formally at Old Mission with Hospital there at Osborn from where I was called to attend Mr.. Hayden Family. With regards

March 18, 1891, L.M. Sims About Oct 1 To Professional Services to wife (Ms Hayden) in confinement Instrumental delivery of child) $75.00 Notary Public: A.H. Innis

March 26, 1891, Dear Sir Your letter of the 24th duly re. I simply reply to disabuse your mind of any preemptory demand for immediate payment of my bill If you will only reread my letter you will not discover any such demand, therefore your remark is very ungracious and unwarranted. I only ask you as executor to immediately acknowledge receipt of my bill, as I have written to your four times and could not get any answers from you in regard to the matter; also another object I had in asking you to acknowledge the receipt of my bill is that I am expecting any day to have to go to near Montezuma line and if I could not get any inform ? from you in regard to filling my bill, that while so near the county seat, I would go out of my way to place my bill in the hands of probate judges. I am fully aware my claim cannot be paid in other channels than through the regular process of administration of execution and therefore please correct your files as to my making immediate demand" preemptively or otherwise for the payment of my file for services rendered. I simply write this injustice to myself and register the same, so that I will know you received this. Respectfully Yours. L.M. Sims. P.

Sept 30th/91 Dear Sir: In referring to your letters some over 6 months ago. You say that you will give my claims against the Hayden Estate proper attention and co. Will you be kind enough to write me what disposition you have made of my claim? It has been nearly a year sense my services were rendered and I think it time indeed to know something about it. If you will kindly let me know at once I will be very much obliged. Your truly. L.M. Sims I can give you plenty of good references in Spokane if you need it. (written on the back: in pencil and Oct 2. Stating claim would be considered in proper time other claims more important have precedence).

No Date Dear Sir: Your letter of Oct 21, 1891, reply to my inquiring of Sep. 30th, at hand and contents noted: In reply must say, that your reply is rather vague and in defense? and not satisfactory to me. My bill is for the Medical services for Mrs. Haden *in her last sickness* and *therefore has* precedence over all other claims together which claim of last sickness and funeral expense of Mr. Haden. Now will *you please tell me* if *my* claim has been allowed by you as administrator or Ex. or not. Now I have a right to know and if not, and you do not see fit to allow my claim my recourse is to appeal to the County Courts. Now I do not want you to feel that this is in any sense a threat against you but I must look after my own interest: and all along the spirit of yourself towards me has been such that is not business or friendly towards me. Now I would prefer that you attend to this matter pleasantly and agreeably. Mr. John Nestor of your city knows me full well and know that I am in no sense a bull? dozen and all I want you to understand is that I only want my claim attended to and paid according to law. The indefiniteness of your letter is why I ask you again if my claim has been approved and I am ? to been approved and I am entitled to bo know as my bill has procedures as it is for last sickness of Mrs. Haden. Yours truly I..M. Sims M.D (written upside down on the first page). P.S. will discount my bill if pd cash if it is any to all or any past due concerned. Dr. Sims

Nov 20/91 Kalama Wash   Dear Sir: Your letter of the 16th just at hand offering me only $30 for my claim of $75 against the above estate: will say in reply that I must respectfully decline any such offer. The "letters" I have are ample proof that the Estate can and will pay 100% on the dollar. My claim is just and reasonable and unpaid. Will subpoena Doctors down from the Coeur D'Alene towns to …my claim reasonable. If you declaim to allow it in full I …a few days to hear from you or I shall put the matter in the hand of my atty in Spokan to collect. I am entitled to interest on the claim since lodged with; you. (I hope you rre? For my account sent to you months ago. Now to? any further trouble to you I will say that if you will send to the C.A. Doty Ex agent Kalama Wash $65.00; with ? for me to sign I will receipt in full. You see in this I wave the question of interest and offer a discount of $10. Now this offer is good only for a few days. Now if I have to contest the matter I shall contest for the full account of $75.00 and by all interest.

Please tell me when you will have a final settlement. You have never sent me any date. I have asked you for information but you have not as yet given it. If you and I can settle this all night if not proper authority can. I wait but a few days on the above proposition of $65.00. Truly Respectfully Yours Dr. L.M. Sims

July 28, 1892, Dear Sir In regard to my claim against the Hayden Estate. I will say I am willing to write out a ? of the case and submit it to three physicians. I choose one and you the 2nd and they the 3rd. And I will accept what they say is fair and right – that is all I want. I have been so busy I was not able to get to Spokane last month as I had arranged. Or I will make you this final proposition that if you will send me 40 - I will accept the a/c against the estate I have met you ½ way on the original amt I agreed to take of Mr. Hayden if paid before I let this Coeur D'Alene - you can send such paper for me to sign together with 40 cash (or check- crossed off) or express order to the express agent here and I will sign and return. Trusting you will accept this or either of the offer in the ? in which I will make it. I do not have my right to collect my bill of $75.00 if you do not accept this proposition. Please let me hear from you soon. Yours truly dr. L.M Sims Kalama Wash (in pencil below: amt. Aug 12 Stating nothing to have to decision of 5 F?(dc tors) ? had approved for Adm. of Estate.

(A-22) Anna and Kate Hayden leased land on Hayden Lake on Feb. 6, 1907

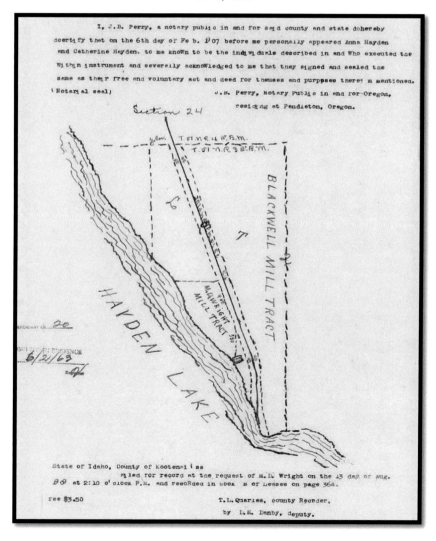

(A-23) Expenditures of the Hayden Girls

```
Statement of Hayden Estate from March 11th,1907 to Sept,10,1910.
DEBITS.
Mar, 28,    Notary fees                                      .50
Apr, 26,    Dentist bill Katie & Annie                     65.00
"   26      Geo.F.Steele,Spec.Administrator                25.00
May,  3     P.F.Quinn,Legal Services                        5.00
"     3     Recording decree                                1.50
"     3     Attorney fees a/c Estate                      120.00
"    17     Katie & Annie                                  35.00
"    21      "     "  "                                    60.00
"    29     Monument                                      187.50
June 28     Katie & Annie                                 100.00
"    28     Cash,Katie & Annie                             85.00
Aug, 28     Katie & Annie                                  40.00
"    29       "    "   "                                   20.00
Sept,11     Schacht & Riorden,bill for girls              113.00
Oct, 11     P.F.Quinn,legal services                       15.00
"    24     Katie & Annie                                  50.00
Dec, 17       "    "                                       100.00
1908.
Jan,  4     Tuition to July,1908.                         314.50
"    14     Taxes Kootenai County,                         75.03
Feb,  8     Crescent,bill for girls                        48.40
"    18     Katie & Annie                                  50.00
Mar,  5     Taxes,Stevens Co.,                            113.73
Mar, 20,    A/c Blaney's bill,                            100.00
Apr, 13     Katie & Annie                                  50.00
June 14       "    "                                        60.00
"    29       "    "                                        40.00
July 10       "    "                                        40.00
"    10       "    "                                        60.00
"    25       "    "                                        20.00
"    25,    Fare,Pendelton $12.00 Colv.$12.40              24.40
Aug, 24     Annie ,trip St.Georges                         31.00
Sept,25     A/C Blaney                                      50.00
Oct, 20     Katie & Annie                                  60.00
Nov, 24     Telegram                                         .50
"    27        "                                             .50
Dec,  5        "                                             .89
"    15     Katie & Annie                                 100.00
"    18     Doctor & Hospital,Annie,                      270.00
"    23     Taxes 1908                                    148.50
1909.
Jan, 28     Sisters St.Francis,tuition,                   144.75
Feb, 24,    Katie & Annie                                 100.00
Apr,  6       "    "   "                                   100.00
"     6     Taxes Stevens Co.,                             92.83
"     6       "   Kootenai Co.,                           132.84
"    30     Escrow                                          1.25
May,  1     Unexpired lease Jones & Co.,                  320.81
"     1       "      "    "    "    "                      346.88
            5% on sale Kootenai property                  375.00
"     4     Abstract Kootenai     "                        15.00
June  1     Katie & Annie                                 200.00
"    16     Sisters St.Francis.                           196.50
July 20     Katie & Annie                                 100.00
Sept, 4       "    "                                        50.00
"    27     Cash, by J.M. to girls in Seattle,           110.00
Nov, 27       "   "  J.M. at Tacoma,                      200.00
Dec, 20     Katie & Annie,                                200.00
1910.
Feb, 28     Katie & Annie                                 100.00
May, 26       "    "        4/26/10                        200.00
May, 28       "    "                                       300.00
July 17       "    "                                        25.00
July 27       "    "   by J.M.                            250.00
Sept, 9       "    "                                       200.00
"    10     Bal.due Jones & Co., Commission,            1125.00
TOTAL DEBITS.                                           $7565.81
```

Bed in the Forest.

In 2009, I asked friends to go look for Mat's cabin on the east side of Hayden Lake. We drove to O'Rourke Bay and Yellow Banks Creek. The old logging road meandered uphill for a mile. After two hours on animal trails and bashing our way through underbrush, we were unsuccessful and aborted our hike.

In the fall of 2010, my husband and two adventurous friends agreed to try again to find Mat's cabin. The logging road was overgrown and washed out as it twisted through the forest. The creek had changed its path over the last one hundred and thirty years, forcing us to build rock bridges to cross the stream. We crawled over dozens of rotting trees and pushed through undergrowth higher than our heads. When we neared the spot, we broke off into three different directions. I was going through an area where huge trees appeared to be thrown like pickup sticks. I would step on a log and my feet would sink through to the one below. After 30 minutes, I needed to get out. My husband called and told me to walk up a dry creek. There in the middle of the forest were two bed frames. The remnants of an old corduroy road, two stoves (one for cooking and one for heating) old jars (1950s style) a large washtub, porcelain pans, and the outline of where a cabin had stood. I assumed the spot had been used in the past by hunters and campers after Mat's death. The wind came up and rain pelted us.

End Notes

1   A Mathew Hayden is listed in 1849 arriving in New York Harbor on the Ship Affghan. The spelling of the name is correct but the years did not coordinate with his servitude and military enlistment.

2   MacManus, Seumas. *The Story of the Irish Race.* Ch. 3. Famine. p. 601.

3   The misnomer in Mat's name may have started when he began doing business in Idaho Territory. Many immigrants were often illiterate and spelled a name as it sounded. They did not have the opportunity to attend more than one or two years of school and their first language was usually a European language. Mathew Hayden is the spelling in his Military Papers of 1852. Mat's name has always been spelled as the city of Hayden is today including 1860, 70, 78, 80, and the reconstructed census of 1890. One map showed the name of the lake was Hayden's Lake. Spellings such as Heydon, Haden, Heydn, and Heyden were used to search immigration and ship records. Mats parish in Wexford Co. Ireland was not found.

4   Limpets have the flavor of clams and mussels. Most Irish did not live near the sea. The famine in Ireland lasted from 1845 to 1851. One million people starved to death and another million fled. The Irish depended upon the potato crop to meet the nutritional needs of their families. Woodcuts were used to print in the *London Times* between 1840 to 1845 and showed the world the plight of the Irish. 1886. Public Domain.

5   £ was equal to $4.35

6   Manhattan did not have a central processing center for Immigrants. By 1820 Captains submitted the passenger list. The immigrants were often preyed upon by scoundrels ready to take advantage of them.

7   Public Domain.

8   Banta, Byron Bertrand Jr. *A History of Jefferson Barracks, 1825-1860 (1981). Https.//digitalcommons.lsu.edu/gradschool_disstheses/3526. LSU Historical Dissertations and Theses. 3626.*

9   *The Company of Military Historians: Pre-Civil War.* Photo Courtesy.

10   Colonel Kearny (Kearney) Served with the US Army from 1812-1848 Dragoons in a skirmish with Plains Indians. *The Company of Military Historians: Pre-Civil War.* Public Domain.

11 Russell. Charles, Buffalo Public Domain published and registered with the U.S. Copyright Office before January 1, 1928.

12 *Battle of Blue Water*. Work before 1924 is now in the public domain and can be used freely in your work.

13 Cordley, Dr. *A History of Lawrence*. Ch. V.

14 Jim Bridger started a fur trading post in 1843 and sold whiskey and arms to Indians. This upset the Mormons and Bridger was forced to abandon the post. Fort Hall was sold becoming one of the primary restocking places and resting stops for immigrants. It closed in 1854 when a young brave stole a horse and was killed by the Ward family traveling with the wagons and twenty immigrants. The tribe retaliated by killing all but two of Ward's children.

15 Lavieille, Eugene Samuels, 1860-1869, Paris, France. Self-taught artist. .is interpretation of the outdoors and winter scenes were highly regarded. He died in poverty. Stephane Pannemaker 1847-1930 used Lavieille's sketch to make a wood engraving of the wagon train before 1900 when photo mechanization began. He died in poverty. Their works are In the Public Domain.

16 Worthington, Whittredge. *Encampment on the Plains*. 1820-1910 journeyed to the Rocky Mountains in 1865. "Whoever crossed the plains at that period the herds of buffalo and flocks of antelope, its wild horses, deer and fleet rabbits, could hardly fail to be impressed with its vastness, silence and the appearance everywhere of an innocent, primitive existence." Public Domain.

17 Lot Smith was a horseman rounding up mustangs on Antelope Island, Utah. He had married eight women and had a total of 52 children. Lot volunteered to be part of the Morman militia when he and two other men killed an elderly native man who had taken a piece of clothing. The Timpanogos retaliated by stealing fifty cattle. The militia pursued and took forty women, children, and men and sold them into slavery. They killed all the tribe members they could find. Lot was killed when he was sixty-two years old after a confrontation with a group of Navajos in 1892 that allowed their sheep to graze on his land.

18 Harper's 1858. Inside an Officers' Tent. "Forts Supply and Bridger were burned down so the Army would not have a place of shelter. The winter was more severe than normal and Johnston's troops wintered at Ham's Fork. Scurvy is diminished with dried fruits and native plants such as wild onions. The Army faced a new and strange disease the surgeons were unfamiliar with called 'mountain fever' by the Mormons. It is believed to be Colorado tick fever. The Army remained inspired, by the belief they would be welcomed by grateful women being freed from the "harems" in Utah. An anti-Mormon attitude was not limited to the rank and file. One Army surgeon, Dr. Roberts Bartholow (1831-1904), in an official report that Mormons had an expression compounded of sensuality, cunning, suspicion, and a smirking self-conceit. The yellow, sunken, cadaverous visage; the greenish-colored eyes; the thick protuberant lips; the low forehead; the light, yellowish hair; the lank, angular person, constitute an appearance so characteristic of the new race, the production of polygamy, as to distinguish them a glance."

19 The Snake River is 1078 miles long, the largest tributary of the Columbia emptying into the Pacific Ocean.

20 Gibbs, Rafe. *Beckoning the Bold*. 1976. Chp. 10. p. 125-130.

21 *The Spokan Times* was the correct spelling for the paper.

22 Hult, Ruby El. *Steamboats in the Timber*. Caxton Printers, 1953. p. 205.

23 Photographer unknown. Courtesy of National Achieves and Records.

[24] Courtesy of the Army Corps of Engineers, 1957

[25] Kane, Paul. Public Domain.

[26] Gustav Sohon, a German artist, came West as a Private being paid $7 a month with the 4th Infantry Regiment. He worked as a topographical assistant for Lt John Mullan on the maps and illustrations of the Pacific Northwest. Sohan was the first to guide a wagon train across the Rocky and Bitterroot Mountains to the Columbia River. Public Domain.

[27] Deeds: Book A. p. 412. Vancouver, WA.

[28] *The Wardner News.* Saturday, December 6, 1890. The handwritten paper was found unsigned, stating Mat owned a boarding house in the early years in Vancouver, WA. *Spokane Falls Review*, December 11, 1890. p.3, under "*A Valuable Estate*" stated that Mat owned eighty acres of pasturage six miles north of Vancouver, WA.

[29] The Spokan Times. August 28, 1880.

[30] Courtesy of Oregon Jesuits. Public Domain.

[31] Battle of the Spokan Plain. Gustave Sohan. In the Public Domain.

[32] Arksey, Laura. *U.S. Army founded Fort Colville on June 20, 1859.* History Link.org/File/7992. 8.10.2009.

[33] Fort Colville was established in 1859 as Harney Depot until 1862. It closed in 1882. Census for Harney Barracks. 1860. p. 13. Valley County Spokane, WA. Territory line 9: Mathew Hayden is listed as a Teamster Age 29.

[34] Kane, Paul. 1810-1871. Kane traveled by sled and snowshoes. The painting is in the Public Domain.

[35] *History of Washington.* 1871-1908. Ch. 2. p. 85-86.

[36] Census. 1871. Kettle Falls, WA. James Monaghan's son was listed as Monaghan, John. 4 years old. Neither James nor other family members were listed.

[37] *The Spokan Times.* November 13, 1879. Pg. 3.

[38] Fort Colvile. Buchtel and Stolte Photo. Portland, Oregon. Public Domain.

[39] Mat settled on the S1/4 of NE1/4 of SE1/4 of Sec. 20 and SW1/4 of NW1/4 of Sec. 21 in Township 35 N of Range 39. East of the Willamette Meridian containing 160 acres. Mat filed a land claim under the Homestead Act of 1862. Receipt # 1434. Approved August 7, 1877. Ratified. Jany, 15, 1878. The final certificate and proof are dated. January 15, 1878. The patent was issued on August 30, 1884, and delivered to him on September 8, 1884. Land Office, Walla Walla. W.T. Record. Vol. 1 p. 284.

[40] Final Certificate. No. 232. Homestead Application. No. 1434. Land Office, Walla Walla W.T. June 12, 1877. Sec. 20/21 Approved August 7, 1877. Ratified. Jany. 15, 1878. Record. Vol. 1 p. 284.

[41] Bounty land application based on military service. June 28, 1877. Mathew Hayden. Private #332978 County of Walla Walla, Washington Territory. A resident of Stevens Co. applied for Military Pension. Age 46. Ft Colville WT.

[42] Department of Interior. Pension Office. A letter stamped June 28, 1877, stated that Mathew Hayden, age 51, a resident of Stevens Co, was a private in Company B commended by Captain D.B. Lackett, (Sacket) in the 1st Regiment of the US. Cavalry. Commended by Col E.V. Summer in the war with Indians on the plains, but principally in suppressing riots in the border war in Kansas.

[43] Public Domain.

[44] Rickey, John. The letter was written on paper from the Treasurer's Office in Stevens Co. Washington, Treasurer. December 17, 1891, and June 16, 1891, written to J. Monaghan after Mat's death. The spelling is as written.

[45] *Spokane Daily Chronicle*. Friday, July 2, 1976. p.19.

[46] Hayden Lake was formed by the Missoula Floods 12-15,000 years ago.

[47] Photo Courtesy

[48] The land Mat purchased was the SE 1/4 SW 1/4 and lots 1,2,3,4 and 5 Sec. 19 Township, 51 North Range 3 West. Mat's home was located on the SE 1/4 Lot 6. On April 28, 1882, Mat granted James a mortgage recorded in Book B. p. 24. NE 1/4 and lot 5 of the NW 1/4 Section 19 Township 51 N. Range 3 West. On March 25, 1890, a mortgage was granted to Jon L. Farwell. Book B, p. 109. NE 1/4 and NW 1/4. Sec. 19.

[49] Spurgeon, Jack, and Evelyn. Photo Courtesy.

[50] Bozanta Tavern was sold and named Hayden Lake County Club in 1927.

[51] Watershed Improvement District. Defendant. December 19, 1989.

[52] The affidavits obtained from the Sacred Heart Mission at DeSmet were a second version of the whirlpool at Hayden Lake.

[53] Hayden Lake was known as Hayden's Lake from 1880 to 1906. The logs skidded easily over the snow into the lake to be transported to the mill on Monaghan's Beach.

[54] Mitchell, Vicki. Mining History Specialist, Idaho Geological Survey. Yellow Banks Creek showed gravel pit mining activity. The early information on mines in the area is dated 1913. Anderson, Alfred. *Geology and Metalliferous Deposits of Kootenai County, Idaho.* Bureau of Mines and Geology.

[55] Spokan Times. May 22, 1880. p 3.

[56] Schell, Mary. Photo Courtesy. On the right by the second tree is Hazel Noble, Mother of Mary Schell. In the middle front is Mr. Todd. The second woman on the right is the mother of Hazel. The man on the far left, partially cut, is William Webb, her brother. Behind him are Mr. and Mrs. Lowry.

[67] *History of North Idaho*. Part V: History of Kootenai County. p. 817-818.

[58] Clark, Lewis F. changed the name to Honeysuckle Beach in 1910.

[59] The original blueprint is in Monaghan's papers at Gonzaga University.

[60] Deed No. 793. Book C. p. 210-214. Granted September 1, 1879. SE1/4SW1/4 and lots 1,2,3,4, and 5. Of Sec 19 T 51N R3W of the Boise Meridian. A letter from the Northern Pacific Railroad Company, Land Department, Western District dated January 21, 1891, from Tacoma, WA, stated that the unpaid principal and interest of the 18th installment was due January 21, 1891, of $261.80 or $360.60 required to make payment in full. A second letter arrived September 28, 1891, stating that Mat's contract 3890 for lots 6 and 7 and S1/2 SE1/4, sec/19 Township 51 N.R.3 In arrears of $377.87. Formal notices were duly mailed to Mr. Hayden and returned to this office, uncalled for. Paul Schulze.

[61] Montgomery, Charles H. Plaintiff vs. Matthew Hayden. Defendant FO2cv #106 40CV 1883. Civil Index Kootenai Co. Idaho. Hayden defendant Stevens Co. Case 51 and Case 42. Debt Collection.

[62] Wauck, John. *Putting Asunder: A History of Divorce in Western Society*. National Review. May 19, 1989.

[63] Gonzaga University and Oregon Jesuits. Photo courtesy.

[64] John Green purchased 125 acres on the Spokane River and began his ferry business in 1890. The property was a mile west of Bananzy City on the river. When he sold the business in 1894 to the county, people could cross the river without paying a toll. The Greensferry Bridge collapsed in 1971.

[65] The spelling is correct as shown on the 1880 census. It has been confused with Bonanza City; a mining town established in 1877 in Custer Co. Idaho

[66] Bananzy City did not make the 1890 census. It was located at the end of Highway 41 near the Spokane River, where the Ross Point Baptist Church Camp is located. When the stage from Spokane stopped near Bananzy City, many people opted to continue their journey by steamer on the river. Mat's name appeared in the 1880 Non-Population Census. Agricultural Schedule at the Foot of the Coeur d'Alene Mountains.

[67] Illustrated History of North Idaho. 1903 p. 985.

[68] Greenough, Earl. *Mining Engineer. First 100 Years Coeur d'Alene Mining Region. 1846-1946.* Published, 1947. p.10. Mullan, Idaho.

[69] 1880 census, Idaho territory. Mat is listed as 41 years old. Farmer. Tom Irwin is listed as 49 years old. Partner Placer. Miner. Ohio.

[70] Lavender, David. *Land of Giants.* p. 388. Andy Prichard's story was published by the Northern Pacific Railroad.

[71] Spokesman-Review. *Hidden Pitfalls: Closed North Idaho mines are hazardous relics.* September 20, 2013.

[72] The Spokane Falls Review. April 5, 1884, referred to W. Earp as a peacemaker. *The San Francisco Examiner.* August 16, 1896, had a different opinion. 12 years later.

[73] Neuman, Betty. Coeur d'Alene, Idaho. Photo Courtesy.

[74] *Spokane Falls Review.* February 9, 1884. p. 1 Col. 4

[75] Gilmore, Fr. sketched the buildings at the Mission of Scared Heart in 1860. The on the right was used as sleeping quarters for travelers, there was a kitchen, repair shop, blacksmith and harness shop. Public Domain.

[76] Chittenden, H.M. and Richardson, A.T. *Life, Letters and Travels of Father Pierre-Jean DeSmet 1801-1873.* New York 1905.

[77] Conley, Curt. *Idaho for the Curious. A Guide.* 1982. p. 438-439.

[78] *History of North Idaho.* Part V History of Kootenai County. p. 815.

[79] Evjen, George. Photo Courtesy.

[80] *The Coeur d'Alene Press.* February 28, 1881.

[81] Tubbs, Tony and Hulda, were involved in several lawsuits between 1883 and 1907 in Coeur d'Alene, Idaho. Book of Deeds A. p. 422-423. Tony sold the hotel on August 18, 1885. Mudge, Charles F. vs. Tubbs, Tony and others, F-32 CV 186 2164 CV 1907. Mudge won the suit claiming he was the owner of Lots 7-8-9-10 Block E in Coeur d'Alene. Tubbs, Tony and others vs. Wonnacott. F-30 CV 170 2036 CV 107. Wonnacott had previously owed the Mercantile at Bananzy City and became a partner of V.W. Sanders in Coeur d'Alene Mercantile. Tubbs, Hulda vs. George Sheppard FO3 CV 146 125 CV 1886. Tubbs Hulda vs. Phebe Knight FO#CV 170 131 CV 1887 and 174, 132 CV 1887, Tubbs, Hulda and Tony, vs. John Knight F 28 CV 186 1868 CV 1906. Hulda's maiden name was Knight. Phoebe Knight or John Knight may have been related to her. A warranty Deed in Idaho Territory was made to John B. Knight and recorded in Book L. p. 470.

[82] Washington State Archives Records: Frontier Justice Civil Cases 3166, 3069, 3236 (1880), and 3525 (1881) all involved debt collection with Tony Tubbs as the Defendant. Criminal Case 3359 involved harboring deserters from Fort Walla Walla.

[83] *Spokan Times.* September 20, 1881. p. 3 Col. 1.

[84] *Spokane Falls Review.* September 19, 1884. p.3 Col.7.

[85] *Spokan Times.* August 7, 1879.

[86] Evjen, George. Photo Courtesy.

[87] Record of Citizenship. Book 4. p. 17. Kootenai County Court House.
[88] The spelling of Hulda changed on the divorce papers to Hilde. 1868 #2 1906 CV- PCR-End. Lawsuits also involved James Monaghan, C.B. King, D.C. Corbin, and Mat Hayden.
[89] County Courthouse, Shoshone Co. Idaho. Marriage Book: Vol. 1 p. 96.
[90] Warrant Deeds. Book B. p. 102.
[91] Mary was not found in census or marriage records in W.T. or I.T. Records were searched for May, Maybens, Mabus, Mebus, or Mabis.
[92] Kootenai County Court House: Film F03-CV Civil 102 Case # 113CV 1885. May 28, 1883-May 28 1884.
[93] *Spokan Times*: January 13, 1883. p. 3 Column 2.
[94] James was postmaster in Coeur d'Alene from March 4, 1886, to January 7, 1887. In June 1892, he became foreman of the Gem mine in Shoshone County and was promoted to Superintendent in August. Art Randall, 1923-2017 of Hayden said James was arrested for assaulting a minor. Art wrote a story on Wyatt Earp in Idaho. Art graduated from the University of Idaho in Geology.
[95] Fahey, John. *Inland Empire. D.C. Corbin and Spokane. 1965.* p 23.
[96] Fruchtl, Mike. In the basement at 215 Sherman in 1911. Photo Courtesy
[97] Elsensohn, Sister M. Alfreda. *Idaho Chinese Lore*. Ch. 17. Idaho. 1979.
[98] The National Achieves and Records Administration, 8601 Adelphi Road, College Park, MD 20740-6001. Homestead entry Issued on August 30, 1882, Dept. of Interior Land Office. September 25. 160 acres of land for farming. Kootenai Book A. p. 183. The Northern Pacific RR Co sent Mr. Mathu Hagden, Sept. 23, 1889, referring to yours of 17th inst. (installment) relative to land in N1/2 of SW1/4 Sec 29 Tp 49 NR 1 E.B.M. advising him the land in question is not on the market and no record can be kept of applications for such lands before being offered for sale. Due notice will be given by public advertisement in newspapers in your locality when the land referred is on the Market. Yours truly, Paul Schuylze. General Land Agent.
[99] Randall, Art. *A Short History and Postal Record of Idaho Towns.* 1994. Cataldo is known as Mission. No dates were given.
[100] *The Spokane Falls Review.* January 12, 1884. p. 4 Col. 4.
[101] *Spokane Falls Review.* February 2, 1884. p. 2 Col. 2.
[102] On January 26, 1884, the Review reported that Mat purchased hotel furnishings. Spokane regretted losing Mr. Hamilton. as he had been successful in the hotel business.
[103] The certificate of register of the property as lots 2/3/4 and N ½ of SW ¼ of Section 29 and Lot 1 Sec. 32 Twp 49N of Range 1 E Boise Meridian in Idaho.
[104] Sept. 25. 160 acres of land for farming, Kootenai. Book A. p. 183. Homestead entry on August 30, 1882. Dept. of Interior Land Office.
[105] The plows sold for $10 to $12.
[106] Pat Lucas (William/Bill) and his brother George met Mat in 1871.
[107] Mat granted a loan to L.R. Grimes on May 20, 1889. Book F. p. 183 in NE ¼ of NW ¼ Section 19. On July 27, 1893, a deed was granted to Mat. Book K. p. 604 in the NE ¼ and NW ¼ lots 6 and 7 S ½ of SE ¼ Section 19. Loan #3338 dated January 1, 1889, 1890, and 1891. $200.00 in April of 1891 and January 1892. On March 1, 1892, $508.35 was paid.
[108] The Hunt farm in Kingston. John Powers. Photo Courtesy.
[109] Lewty, Peter J. *Across The Columbia Plain, Railroad Expansion in The Interior Northwest 1885-1893*. WSU Press. 1995. p 104.

[110] Leo's Studio photo shows evidence of logging and the devastation caused to the town of Cataldo in 1933. Photo Courtesy. Betty Neuman. Reprint.

[111] Betty Neuman. Photo Courtesy

[112] DeSmet Mission Records. DeSmet, Idaho. Book 1. p. 176.

[113] Bernadette LaSarte of Coeur d'Alene Tribal Nations, Plummer, Idaho, said of Louie Antoine Hayden's name; "It's possible that the ending is not missing, but composed of sounds in Salish languages that English speakers miss."

[114] Sacred Heart Mission. DeSmet, Idaho. *Spokesman-Review.* May 31, 1943. p.11, referred to Ignace's father as Ed Hayden, who died in 1892.

[115] Connolly, Thomas S.J. Sacred Heart Mission, DeSmet, Idaho. Photo Courtesy. Joe Garry's vest with his name and intricate beadwork.

[116] Mat was from Wexford Co. Ireland. Mat Hayden is the grandfather of Ignace Garry. Mat's son, Antoine, was the father of Ignace.

[117] Dolan, Maureen. *"The Last Traditional Chief."* November 10, 2010. Coeur d'Alene/Post Falls Press.

[118] *An Illustrated History of North Idaho. Embracing Nez Perce, Idaho, Latah, Kootenai and Shoshone Counties. State of Idaho. Western Historical Publishing Company. p. 955. 1903.* There were several inaccuracies in the text on Pat Whalen's history. Pat Whalen was married with a child and lived in Haverstraw, N.Y. when his father died in 1880. Pat's father died when he was 24 years old. He was not a child. Pat married Agnes in 1877, and their first son, Dennis, was born in 1879. His mother, Eliza, was living with the couple in June of 1880. New York census p. 87 Dist. 4, June 28/29, 1880. Agnes was 44 when she died in childbirth in 1904. She had thirteen children: eleven were born near Cataldo in Shoshone County, and nine were living at the time of her death. Pat died at 67. His last years were in Coeur d'Alene with his second wife, Mrs. Anna Schmidt, who had two sons and three daughters. His mother remained in Haverstraw with his sister. Lizzie's husband, Thomas Powers was ill with lung disease. There were Jesuits, trappers, miners, and several families when Pat arrived in Cataldo in 1883. Mat began his military service in 1852 before Pat was born. Mat Hayden built the first hotel and saloon in 1884 in Mission City. The Kootenai County paper, Coeur d'Alene, Idaho, September 28, 1956, indicated that Pat Whalen had "blazed the naming of Hayden Lake and the town of Cataldo." Mat had arrived seven years before Pat Whalen. Hayden's Lake appears on maps as early as 1880. Lizzie's four children with Tom Powers arrived in 1885 in Cataldo, and she had two daughters with Mathew Hayden. Russell, Bert in the *North Fork of the Coeur d'Alene River, 1984.* p. 368. repeated that Maurice Whalen, Pat's son said, " Mr. Whalen has no uncles, aunts, or relatives that he knows of living except his children." In fact, Maurice Whalen grew up and knew many of his Snyder and Powers cousins.

[119] *An Illustrated History of North Idaho.* p. 882. 1903. The US Government told Westwood they had to change its name to avoid duplication. They chose Rathdrum in 1881.

[120] Public Domain

[121] Cherry Peak reaches 7,352 and Patrick's Knob reaches 6,837 ft.

[122] Hyndman, Pam. Great-granddaughter of Pat Whalen. Photo Courtesy. 1910 Wayside Inn, Cataldo, Idaho. Next to Pat Whalen is Malcolm McGill, log driver; Joe Dodd, laborer from Latour Creek; Myron Lightner, driver; Myron Smith; Dusty Rhodes; Al LaBranche, driver; Pat Whalen Jr. driver. 2nd row: Frank Young; Stanley Thomas, prospector at Latour Creek; Sam Murchison,

driver; Ernest Palworth; Charley Lymen Heanecraft, prospector; Tom Holland, boatman; John Hazelstein; Nate Howe; Bill Murrary, boatman; Joe LaBlane, driver; Paul Rallef, saloonkeeper. *Directory of Kootenai Country 1914-1916 Pat* Whalen's, net worth was $2,705. Cataldo.

123 Sohon, Gustave's sketch of The Mission of the Sacred Heart is in Public Domain. "Coeur d'Alene Mission was established by the Jesuit Fathers in the Rocky Mountains in 1842" provided translations, names, and notes with his drawings and paintings.

124 A later court case awarded O. Peck and Dr. J. T. Cooper from Murray one-quarter of Kellogg's Bucker Hill claim.

125 Corbin, Daniel planted 1200 acres of sugar beets in 1907 in Dalton Gardens. His first wife was unhappy in the West and moved her three children to England. He paid for his Swedish housekeeper's education at a collegiate school and later at a finishing school in New York City. He groomed Anna to become a proper gentlewoman. She attended for two years at Columbia University. He was forty when he and Anna married.

126 Peterson, Chuck. Wardner, Idaho. Photo Courtesy.

127 Stevens. http://www.historylink.org/essays/output.cfm?file_id=752

128 *Spokane Review.* Friday, September 5, 1887.

129 Historylinks.org/File/7528

130 Russell, Bert. *North Fork of the Coeur d'Alene River. p. 67.* A story said that Mrs. Shafer lived there and was very deaf. When the hall burned, she died in the fire. No information was found on her.

131 Bond, Rowland. *Early Birds in the N.W. 100 Years of Western History. 1971.*

132 W.T. Washington County of Spokane Bk. I. Deeds. p. 233. March 20, 1889.

133 Book of Deeds. H. p.163. The consideration was $1.00.

134 Munk, Ivan. Permission and Photo Courtesy of Eastern Washington University, where the original painting hangs. Munk was a former student of EWU and director and cartoonist for Easterner's student paper. He became a Spokane illustrator and worked on special projects at KHQ-TV. He was sought after to remodel Spokane's historical homes and is known for his encyclopedia knowledge of British history, and the Packard automobile.

135 Blessing, Linda. The family story is shared by the niece of Laurance Kinsolving, son of Julia Blessing Kinsolving the daughter of Titus Blessing.

136 https://www.nbcnews.com/news/asian-america/150-years-ago-chinese-railroad-workers-staged-era-s-largest-n774901.

137 Pierce, Idaho. 1870. There were 411 miners, 14 gamblers, 3 hotel cooks, 3 blacksmiths, 3 gardeners, 2 laundrymen, a trader, a hotel keeper, a merchant, a hotel waiter, a barber, a doctor, and a Chinese agent.

138 *Washington Statesman.* December 20, 1861. Volume 1. p. 4.

139 Photo in Public Domain.

140 Mortgages. Kootenai Co. Courthouse. Book B. p. 169. Filed July 8, 1886.

141 Mortgages. Kootenai Co. Courthouse. Book E. p. 61. Filed May 3, 1887.

142 Stevens Co. WA. Territory. Tuff Nut Mine Book T. A. p. 16. May 25, 1886. The mine was filed for record at the request of P. Pierce, duly recorded by W.K Bishop, Auditor. May 10, 1887. Agreement for Ore or No Ore Mine, April 10, 1888. Recording of Tuff Nutt Mine. Book A. p. 32. Salmon District- Vein deposit Quartz Stevens Co. June 12, 1888. Tough Knot. Book A. Galena District. p. 281.

143 Moen, Wayne. *Conconully Mining District Okanogan Co, WA.* Circular No. 49. WA. Dept. of Natural Resources, Division of Mines and Geology, 1973. p. 28-

30. Spokane, Washington. From 1892 Mat's estate showed he had assets of $20.00 paid by the Tuff Nut claim; $116.33 Metaline; $612.50 Okanogan; $433.00 Grant Crow and $25.00 Salmon River. Dividends were not noted.

[144] Auditor's office. Stevens Co. Book G of Quartz Records. p. 58. May 26, 1886. Amended: Tuff Nutt: Book T. A. p.37-8. August 7. 1886. Gage, 1941. p. 20.

[145] Bethume, George A. *Mines and Minerals of Washington*. Annual report of the 1st State Geologist. 1880-1892. p. 55-56.

[146] Spokane Falls Review. January 12, 1884. Column 4, p.

[147] George A. Snyder told the story that he was hired by the Sunshine Mining Company in 1923. He went down into the mine and came out at noon. He never returned, always saying the Sunshine owed him a half day's pay.

[148] Fruchtl, Mike, grandson of Xavier Fruchtl. Photo Courtesy.

[149] Mat's daughter, Kathleen Hayden, was born on January 2, 1887. Antoine and Annie named their daughter Catherine, born on September 14, 1887. Molly's sons, the Snyder boys, did not realize that Louis Antoine was Mat's son and Ignace Garry was his grandson. They joked about Mat being "the man with a fast horse," acknowledging the distance between Cataldo and Spokane.

[150] Peterson, Chuck. Wardner, Idaho. Photo Courtesy.

[151] Newman, Betty. Coeur d'Alene, Idaho. Photo Courtesy.

[152] Sporting people were prostitutes, gamblers, and drinkers.

[153] Case file F CV in the District Court of the First Judicial District of Idaho in and for the County of Kootenai. Mathew Hayden: Plaintiff.

[154] Photo Courtesy

[155] The Homestead Preemption and Commutation Proof on July 30, 1887. Pat Whalen lived at W1/2 SW1/4 Sec 34 Tp 49 N R 1 E, stating his age as 37.

[156] Sept. 25. 160 acres of land for Farming, Kootenai. Book A. p. 183. of Interior Land Office. Department and General Land Office #140782-1890 Washington, D.C. (Cataldo, Idaho). December 5, 1890, Register and Receiver, Coeur d'Alene, Idaho. Gentlemen, Under the date of November 19, 1890, the NPRRCO (through a resident attorney, W.K. Mendenhall Esq.) requested the immediate cancellation of the following preemptive filings on the ground that they conflict with the prior adverse rights of the said R.R.Co, and are therefore invalid. 1st. Pre. C.E. No. 14 Mathew Hayden made July 30, 1887 (D.S. filed May 22, 1887, alleging settlement-June 1, 1884) for the N1/2 of the SW1/4 and Lots 2,3,4, Section 29 Township 49 N. Range Sec 27. 1E. Others included in this paper were S.H. Bernard Sec. 35, W.H. Knapp, Sec.35, and Fred Hubinfield. The opposite and conterminous section of the road was definitively located on August 30, 1881, but the withdrawal was not ordered until January 7, 1888, when a diagram showing the amended fifty-mile limits of the grant was forwarded with the usual instructions. During the interim filings and entry were admitted, the Register and Receiver not knowing that they covered Railroad land and their allowance of the same was not a violation of instructions and regulations. An examination of the records disclosed the fact that the preemption entry of Hayden has been patented, thus placing the case beyond the jurisdiction of this department. I have refused the cancellation of the filing under the authority of the honorable secretary's the decision in the case of Catlin V. the N. P. (9 L.FD. 423), in which it is held that the right of a preemption settler on lands in the company's grant before notice of the withdrawal was received at the local land office is protected by the act of April 21, 1876. You will advise all parties of interest of

this decision allowing the usual 60 days for appeal, and if the preemption claimants desire to make final proof and payment you will permit them to do so on complying with the regulations governing the allowance of such entries. Mr. Mendenhall has been notified by this office. Louis Goff Commissioner. I certify the foregoing to be a true copy of the Commissioner's letter on Dec. 5, 1890. James E. Russell, Register. (Ruled in Mat's favor).

[157] *Spokan Times.* August 16, 1881. p. 1. Column 1.

[158] Morning Oregonian March 10, 1887. p. 8.

[159] Chapman, Ray. Golden *History Tales. Idaho's Coeur d'Alene Mining District.* Three miles north of Enaville, one can see the saunas. p. 86. 1992.

[160] Page, Sarah, passed away in Spokane. December 13, 1962, a few months after her 100th birthday. Sarah is buried at Riverside Memorial Park.

[161] Peterson, Chuck. Wardner, Idaho. Photo Courtesy.

[162] Gonzaga Preparatory Students and Teachers in 1887: 1. Fr. Rebmann S.J. 2. Fr. Smith S.J. 3. Mr. Brounts S.J. 4. Fr. Smith S.J. 5. Mr. Kock S.J. 6. Mr. Hand S.J. 7. Clement Haas 8. Louis Wallace 9. Denny O'Rourke 10. Constantine McHugh 11. Sam Hannon 12. Frank Denford 13. Joseph Fischer 14. Laurence Corbett 15. George Dunford 16. Michael Cleary 17. Vincent Roman 18. John Powers 19. Richard Ganahl 20. Frank Stilz 21. Robert Monaghan (son of James) 22. George Russell 23. Charles Dowd 24. John Kirk 25. Fr. Monroe S.J. 26. Mr. VanRoe S.J. Photo Courtesy.

[163] Hayden, Anna. Born June 13, 1888, and baptized at the Mission of the Sacred Heart in Cataldo on June 24, 1888. Fr. Joset officiating.

[164] The first Sanders mercantile was located on the north side at 233 Sherman (Harvey's clothing) and later on the SE corner of 4th and Sherman.

[165] The Certificate of Register in the land office described the property. Twp as lots 2/3/4 and N ½ of SW 1/4 of Section 29 and Lot #1 Sec.32. 49N of Range 1 E Boise Meridian in Idaho.

[166] Fruchtl, Mike. The bakery was owned by W. Wagner and located between 3rd and 4th on Sherman Ave. Photo Courtesy

[167] Spurgeon. Jack and Evelyn. Postcard Courtesy.

[168] Public Domain

[169] Monaghan, James purchased lots 7 and 8 in Block 22 Second Sinto Addition in Spokane from Mat for $1100. Mat originally purchased the property from O.M. Kent for $1250.00 on the 13th of December, 1889. Kent purchased the lots for $1700 but knew he could not pay the remaining $850 with 10% interest before April of 1890 to Newberry and D.M. Drumheller.

[170] *Puget Sound Weekly.* Cure for Consumption. p. 6. Col 5. June 14, 1878.

[171] Sims, Dr. L.M. was the Doctor who attended Lizzie. Louise Shadduck's book. *Doctors with Buggies, Snowshoes, and Planes One Hundred Years and More of Idaho Medicine. 1993.* p. 231 mentions Dr. W. S. Sims as the physician who renovated the Wallace Hospital in 1891. He hired the first black man in Wallace, David Strouder, who helped him with operations, general nursing, and cooking. The hospital was under Dr. W.S. Sims' supervision in 1915.

[172] Frank Quinn attended Fulton College in Illinois in 1860. He worked on the Milwaukee Railroad and later in Portland on the streetcars. Quinny (as he was called by Mat's family), became the director of schools in Cataldo for five years. His parents were Peter Quinn, born in Ireland on May 21, 1833, in Crossmolina, Mayo, Ireland, and Eliza Dixon, born about 1839. They lived in Rockford, Illinois. Frank was the oldest of three brothers and two sisters.

[173] The white lilac planted on Lizzie's unmarked grave at the Cataldo Mission remains today. Elizabeth "Eliza" Whalen, wife of Dennis was buried next to Lizzie on June 8, 1895. The small iron fence that encircled the graves has not been replaced, though money was collected in 2000 for repairs.

[174] Mat's estate book shows that payments of $30 and $50 were made for a stone for Lizzie. James Monaghan, having to care for six additional children, raising his own large family, and being involved in several business ventures, may have forgotten to check if the stone was installed.

[175] Dennis Whalen, the father of Lizzie, was working in North Carolina in 1880 as a veterinarian on a plantation when he was kicked in the head by a horse and killed. His burial place was not found.

[176] Mat is believed to have been born in 1832, making him 58 years old when he died. Mathew's first name was misspelled with two t's in the paper.

[177] Fruchtl, Mike. Photo Courtesy. Outside mass was held in 1887 at Fourth and Indiana during the summer months. Catholics in the area attended church at the fort's chapel and shared the building with the Protestant congregation. Father Joset and other priests held mass at the fort beginning in 1886. As the congregation grew and the chapel was not available, the parishioners met in homes or at log school at First and Wallace. Father Smith encouraged the people to raise money to build a church.

[178] Dunnigan, Loretta. *Early History of Coeur d'Alene* states that the money was raised and the first Catholic Church was built at 4th and Indiana. Its first service was on November 23, 1890. Mat died on November 27th and his services were on Sunday the 30th.

[179] Evjen, George. Photo Courtesy. Grandson of George Winter.

[180] Eastern Washington State College. Father Mackin was paid $25.00 for Mat's services. Estate Book. p.5. December 8, 1890.

[181] James Monaghan purchased a monument for Mat on May 29, 1907, for $187.50. It marked Mat's grave at St. Thomas Cemetery in Coeur d'Alene.

[182] Evjen, George. Mortuary owned by T. E. Hedal. The carriage was driven by George Winter, the great-grandfather of George Evjen. Photo Courtesy

[183] Class of 1891 Gonzaga University. The students listed from left to right are: 1. Frank Butler 2. John Shannon 3. Dan Muga 4. Ed Finnegan 5. Frank Henry 6. Jessie Loop 7. James Hanley 8. Wm. Charbonneau 9. Ed Butler 10. Arthur Knoll 11. Mr. Taelman S.J. 12. Dick O'Shea 13. Ellis Morrigrau 14. Dick Sullivan 15. Earl Mayer 16. Ed Mayer 17. Wilfred Prouly 18. Humprey Sullivan 19. Joseph Prouly 20. Theo Knoll 21. Mr. Goller S.J. 22. William Cunningham 23. Ed O'Shea 24. **Thomas Powers** 25. Thomas O'Hanlon 26. John Goodwin 27. Ralph Mayor 28. John Murphy 29. Oscar Keneck 30. Joseph Farrell 31. Denny O'Roucke 32. Anthony Fisher 33. William Reynolds 34. John McGinn 35. Wm. Hughes 36. Albert Keneck 37. Bishop Bondel 38. Gerald Ronan 39. James Farrell 40. Stephen Sullivan 41. James Breen 42. Frank Burke 43. John Gogart 44. Ambrose Sullivan 45. William Finnegan 46. Robert Hamell 47. Theo Rocque 48. John Tattan 49. Felix McGinn 50. Paul Shannon 51. Pat Graham 52. Vincent Ronan 53. James D'Arcy 54. Thos. Meagher 55. Fr. Rene S.J. Photo Courtesy.

[184] Sister Mary Oswalde was given a Chevrolet to replace her horse in 1921.

[185] *Spokane Daily Chronicle.* March 25, 1970. The orphanage closed on July 7, 1982, after 90 years. Father Joseph Cataldo donated the land for the orphanage in the Sinto Addition. The orphanage was located at N. 1016 Superior St., Spokane, WA.

[186] *Inland Catholic Register*. July 18, 1965. Charles C. Finucane is the grandson of Charles Sweeney. His farm is known today as the Finucane Farm in Hayden, on the corner of 4th and Honeysuckle.

[187] February 17, 1920. An influenza epidemic struck many at the orphanage.

[188] The paper states that Mat's Hotel was at DeSmet, it was in Mission City.

[189] The Spokesman reported that Mat's valuable estate consisted of a large hay ranch in Kootenai County, a farm in Stevens County, four houses and lots in Wardner, the hotel at DeSmet Mission, two lots in Coeur d'Alene City, 80 acres of pasture six miles north of Vancouver, Wa, four lots in Spokane Falls, and various mining interest in Washington and Idaho. The estate is valued at $120,000.00. He desired to leave $12 a month to his mother-in-law Eliza Whalen. His stepson, John Powers, chose $500 in lieu of two more years of schooling. The proceeds of the Hayden Lake farm will be divided between the remaining three stepchildren, Parick, Thomas and Mary. In the event of the death of his two daughters, Anna and Kate, the estate will revert to the Jesuit fathers. James Monaghan will be the guardian and with absolute authority to dispose of the estate and its income without an order of the court. Mat's will originally left the Hayden property to Molly, Tom, and Pat Powers. James felt it was best to give them the property at Cataldo because he believed that area would be more prosperous than Hayden being so close to Coeur d'Alene.

[190] Paul Hurlinger owed bills to the Hayden estate of $60.02. Mr. Kellinger 86.00. Mr. Samuels 28.00. Jas Tilley 90.00. Mr. Bass 25.00.

[191] Frank Quinn took the Hayden children shopping. They purchased two suits for $3.00, 1 suit of underwear for $2.50, a dozen pair of socks for $1.00, 2 pair of boots, and three hats for $3.25. They were loaded down with their purchases when they stopped to buy a lantern with two globes, twenty candles, paper, pens, and ink totaling $12.40. Molly received new overshoes and four pairs of hose for $5.25, two vests, and two pants. With expenditures for freight, lunch and railway tickets, the day's excursion came to $129.68.

[192] $500 was paid for 12 ½ months labor, and receipts totaling $346.16 included $100.00 to VW Sanders Mercantile, labor for Thompson, $88.25, J. Hardy, $11.55 and Peterson $16.00, potato seed $6.35, and horse medicine $1.00. John Sullivan was paid $1.50 per day for 16 days of work at the Mission Ranch, $24.00. Pat Lucas was kept busy collecting some of the money owed to Mat. He collected $32.16 from John Wieman. Sarah Page paid a bill of $55.00, and Al Page later paid $72.70. J.A. Wimpy paid $25.00 for rent for the Hotel and Mr. Furbush $10.00. He tried to collect $95.00 from Pat Whalen but Pat said it was not owed.

[193] Follet and Harris purchased livestock at auction from the Hayden state offering the family a fair price. Mat had always been fair in selling his cattle. Pat Lucas held the auction at the ranch. He sold 2 heifers for $45.00, 2 cows $ 50.00, 1 cow $22.00, 2 poor cows $30.00, 2 cows $40.00, 1 yearling $ 15.00, 1 bull $ 15.00, 2 cows $40.00, 3 calves $30.00, 2 yearlings $ 30.00, 5 calves $ 30.00, 1 calf $ 9.00, 1 very poor bull $5.00, 6 calves $48.00, 3 yearlings $36.00, 1 poor cow $ 15.00 and 674 lbs. of pork at 71/2 cents a per pound for $50. 63.

[194] Eastern Washington State Historical Society. Research Library. Book M. Hayden. Estate Records. 190-197.

[195] Including $4.00 for a pair of boots and $19.45 for tobacco.

[196] March 1891. James paid Clement King $20.00 to transport 3000 pounds of potatoes from the Hayden Ranch to Spokane. He sold the hay baler and

other farming implements to Henry Pomeroy of Colville for $300.00 and agreed to pay the freight of $50 from the Mission to Chewelah, WA.

[197] Bills paid: Fuel $26.90, Feed $5.60, Laehousel ploughing $15.60, Walsh $119.00, and laborer P.F. Grace $249.60.

[198] November 24, 1891. James wrote a check for $548.00 to the Sister's Orphanage for the children's tuition at the Traders National Bank. A note in Mat's Estate book: $40 per month. $80 tuition, board January–June $39.00. Taxes paid in Spokane County. $15.25. Stevens County, $77.74. Clark County, $21.36. Shoshone County, $149.11 and Kootenai County, $76.61. James received a letter from John J. Costello, the Kootenai County Assessor, telling him he could not assess the Hayden Estate because orphans are exempt in Idaho.

[199] Estate Records 1890-1897. Northwest Museum of Art and Culture, Eastern Washington Historical Society, Spokane, Wash. MSSC. p. 67.

[200] Butler purchased livestock and some of the farming equipment at $225.00 which included two old wagons, the fanning mill, the sleigh and other sundry articles. A notation was made with the sleigh $7.50, hayrack $10.00 and produce $7.00.

[201] All four properties in Wardner were rented and payments were collected from C.T.P. Bass for the rent and the post office building. The twin cottages were rented to Mrs. L. Tilley for $420.00 and later sold the house to her for $1650.00. Frank Quinn was paid for his services.

[202] This is the only mention found that Mat's Hotel was named Denver.

[203] He said plans were made to construct flumes and ditches to supply water for irrigation of the land. The water was to be taken from Hayden Lake in consideration of $1.00

[204] Mat purchased land from the NPRRC, on Hayden's Lake No. 1850 W. Receipt No. 443 NPRR,1905. May 18, the contract was duly performed in 1886. Lot six and seven S1/2 of SE 1/4 S10 TS 51. On February 24, 1887, Mathew Hayden and Louise Hayden his wife of the County of Kootenai, Idaho Territory, and L.R. Grimes $50. Mortgage the tract of his Hayden Lake property known as the Saw Mill track. Mathew signed with his mark X and his wife as Lizzie Hadyn. The girls received notice on February 16, 1892, the NPRR attempted to convey to Mathew Hayden the parcels of land described and the deed did not convey title to said premises that the estate of a deceased person is not competent to take title. The NPRR acknowledges the released and quitclaim deed onto the said parties its right title and interest known as the saw-mill tract. If Mr. P. A. Blackwell shall be in default in the payment of any installment of rent for a period of 30 days. This lease can be terminated and the owners upon five days' notice can take advantage of said option. Witnesses were James Monaghan, Guardian, Anna Hayden, Katie Hayden and P.A. Blackwell. F.A. Blackwell, the principal stockholder of William Land and Lumber Co, arrived in 1901. When the land was auctioned where Fort Sherman stood Blackwell gave the land for the city park. Blackwell helped establish the CDA and Spokane Electric Line. Katie (18) and Anna (17) Hayden were both living in Oregon, on November 29, 1905. Filed for the request of M.L. Wright on the 27th day of Oct 1909 Recorded in Book B. Leases on page 372-373 $2.50 Lot 1. 45.90 2. 18.90 3. 31.02 4. 41.20 5. 32.80   Total: 169.52 acres of land. Lot 6. 52.60 acres and Lot 7 29.50 acres. Section 19 on the S. side of Hayden Lake, Lease B Lot 2. p. 364. Blackwell, F.A, (Grantor) to M.D. Wright (Grantee) August 12, 1909. Assigned Lease. Book B. p. 220. Lot 2. Hayden Estates to Blackwell. Grantor: Kathleen

and Anna Hayden to Grantee: M.D. Wright August 13, 1909. October 27, 1909, lease. Book B p. 372. Lot 2. James Monaghan to Arthur D. Jones Nov. 30, 1909. Accnt. Book W. p. 549. Lots 1-2. Northern Pacific RR Co. Grantor to Grantee: Hayden Estate December 18, 1909. Deed Book 36. p. 327 Lots 1 through 7. Hult, Rudy El. *Steam Boats in the Timber.* p. 87-88. Grantor: Kathleen and Anna Hayden to Grantee: M.D. Wright August 13, 1909. Lease B Lot 2. p. 364. Blackwell, F.A, (Grantor) to M.D. Wright (Grantee) August 12, 1909. Assigned Lease Book B p. 220. Lot 2. Hayden Estates to Blackwell.

[205] The Edison Company arrived in Spokane Falls in 1885. Thomas Edison had invented the first iridescent light bulb and by 1883 the first transmitter illuminated over 500 homes in lower Manhattan. It was an exciting time for people all over the nation and the country was quickly changing. (History Links: Washington Water Power/Avista).

[206] Appelquist, Wm. O. Granted on November 22, 1897. Deeds Book O, p. 535. To Washington Idaho Improvement Company on Mat's Hayden property to build ditches for irrigation, giving water rights. James Monaghan, Executor Grantor to Grantee Wm. O. Appelquist on January 8, 1898. Book R, p. 311 signed over the job of Executor of Mat's Estate to Appelquist.

[207] Kathleen Hayden et al to Arthur D. Jones May 11, 1910, Deeds 37 p. 327.Arthur Jones Grantor Deed p. 327, June 1, 1901. In consideration of 41.00 and other valuable consideration paid by part of 2nd part Lots 2-34-5-6-7 S ½ of SW ¼ and S ½ of SW ¼ and S ½ of SW ¼ Sec 19 TS 51 NR 3 also all of Lot 1 Sec 19 TS 51 N. Known as Finch. Beginning at the meander line of Hayden Lake crossed Sec 18-19 in 51 NR 3 to point 20 feet East of SW corner drawn parallel with West section line of Sec 19, 800 ft. Drawn at right angles with the West line of Sec 19. Lot 1. 45.90 acres. Free of all encumbrances except leases to F.A. Blackwell dated November 25, 1905, and M.D. Wright dated February 6, 1907, and James Garvey from Washington May 1910. p. 328. George Steele appointed and acted as administrator of Mat Hayden Estate to sell lands described without any court. Deed p. 219. December 31, 1903, in Rathrum. The records showed a reidué of $3140.87 with closing costs of $150.00 leaving $2960.87. All 194 Appelquist, Wm. O. Granted on November 22, 1897. Deeds Book O. met p. 535. To Washington Idaho Improvement Company on Mat's Hayden property to build ditches for irrigation, giving water rights. James Monaghan, Executor Grantor to Grantee Wm. O. Appelquist on January 8, 1898. Miscellaneous. Book R. p. 311 signed over the job of Executor of Mat's Estate to Appelquist. On the expenses paid. Miscellaneous Records V. p. 147-148 # 27234 Kootenai County. (Residue, according to a will, "leave the rest and remainder of my estate." John Finch paid $2,200 for Lot 1 consisting of 45.90 acres, his widow Charlotte S. Finch sold the 45.90 acres for $100.00. Deed p. 309310. June 20, 1906. Today this area is known as Honeysuckle Beach. Mat's Cataldo ranch was divided between Molly, Pat and Tom, his stepchildren. March 27, 1907. December 14, 1922. p. 418 and filed on January 18, 1923. Book 77. p. 417. $100. And other property Lot 4 Sec 16 1.02 acres NE1/4 of SE1/4 TS 51. John A. White and Arthur D. Jones. $1000. Quitclaim. Lots 1 through 7 SE1/4 SW1/4 S1/4 S1//4 Sec 19 TS 51 NR3. Deeds Book 32. April 30, 1909. p. 525. Quitclaim to Hillyard Townsite Company. Deeds Book B 37. June 10, 1909. p 328 $1.00 Lots 2-3-4-5-6-7-S1/2 SW1/4 and S1/2 of SW1/4 Sec 19 TS 51 NR3. All of Lot 1 known as the Finch crosses Sec 18 and 19 meandering lines of said Hayden Lake filed May 11, 1910.

[208] The Spokesman-Review, Spokane, Washington. April 23, 1895.

[209] On the death of the Samoa King, his rival, Mataa who was supported by Germany, returned from exile. The US and British consuls opposed him and backed the dead king's son. Fighting erupted in Apia, the capital city. The monarchy was eventually abolished. Germany received the western islands, and the United States received the eastern islands. The British withdrew recognition rights of Tonga and the Solomon Islands. Twenty-seven Mataafans, three Britons, one American, and one Samoan warrior died.

[210] The cost of closing was $150.00, and the estate was left with $2,960.87.

[211] Leases Vol. B. p.364. Filed: August 13, 1909. March 24, 1881. p3. Col 5.

[212] File No. 3153. August 4, 1909. Judgment, February 8, 1910, p. 18-22. The Drainage District No. 2 of Stevens Co. through William Miller, D.J. Burk, and William Compton, its Board sued A.N. Haskins and Mrs. Haskins, including the Defendants named, alleges that the construction, maintenance, and operation of said proposed drainage system is necessary that the plaintiffs have acquired the right of way for the drainage ditch or canal of which it is proposed to effect said drainage over and across the property. The defendants, A.N. Haskins and Mrs. Haskins, Peter and Mary Rhoads, Stephen and Marguerite Bonnett, George S. Morley, Mrs. Morley, and Sister Mary Julian, represented by an attorney, would benefit $5,750.

[213] Hines, D.D, Rev. H.K. An Illustrated History of the State of Washington. The Lewis Publishing Co., Chicago, IL. 1893, p. 303.

[214] The Monaghan home is the Gonzaga University Music Building today.

[215] Lis Pendens: Document No. 50317, and Complaint No. 6571, dated May 27, 1919. Filed for Record May 27, 1919, at 1:30 p.m. recorded in Book D of Lis Pendens, p. 161. George L. Ryan and Anna E. Ryan, husband and wife, Plaintiffs vs. James H. McCool and Kathleen McCool, husband and wife, Defendants.

[216] July 19, 1919. Document No. 51304. Filed 10:50 a.m. Bk. 57 Deeds. p. 346.

[217] Greenwood, WA. is south of Kettle Falls where Clara's family farmed.

[218] Benedict Arnold was commander of West Point and a spy for British intelligence. He planned with Major John Andre to capture West Point for £20,000. John Powers had come out to Idaho Territory with his mother and grandmother. He wrote the letter to his nephew Ted Snyder in 1942 and then added a postscript to Ted's wife, Cleo. She was a school teacher in Cataldo and Post Falls.

[219] An inventory of supplies used in a school year: beef 200 pounds, salt 160 pounds, bacon 225 pounds, bread 7,960 loaves, beans 200 pounds, potatoes 325 pounds, vegetables 259 pounds, coffee 275 pounds, tea 152 pounds, sugar 740 pounds, butter 150 pounds, lard 750 pounds, rice 320 pounds, and 380 pounds of soap.

[220] Public Domain.

[221] http://www.em.gov.bc.ca/mining/Geolsurv/Minfile/mapareas/ 2eswcov.htm

[222] James Monaghan purchased new clothing and blankets for the children on August 7, 1894. Expenses from DeSmet to Camp McKinney were $15.00. Clothing was purchased for John Powers for $11.84.

[223] Tom Graham, a nephew of James Monaghan, was at Camp Fairview not long after the robbery and events at Camp McKinney. Tom was to ship a gold brick by stage and return to Camp McKinney when a woman posing as a clairvoyant and water diviner asked him if he would take her to Camp McKinney. She remained a few days at Camp McKinney. People believed

she was Mrs. Matthew Roderick. Several thought she found the bullion and made her way to Spokane and later to the Yukon.

[224] Miller, Charlotte. Family Achieve. Photo Courtesy.

[225] The Jew's harp is one of the oldest musical instruments in the world. It originated in China and the tribes of Turkey in the 4th century B.C.

[226] Kay Miller Proctor was the daughter of Henry and Christine Miller.

[227] Bounty Predatory Animals. Grazing associations in Idaho offered bounties from January 1st, 1915 to July 1st, 1915. Bounties paid: Coyotes $3.00: Coyote Pups $1.50; Wolves $25.00; Wolf Pups $5.00; Wild Cats $4.00; Wild Kittens $2.00; Mountain Lions $25.00; Lion Pups $5.00. Premature Pups were not included. CONDITIONS: Full fresh pelts be presented. Affidavit as to where and when animals were killed. The inspector would remove both hind feet. May 7, 2021, https://www.thewildlifenews.com/. Current bounties paid $1,000 per wolf. Bounty hunters are allowed to use night-vision goggles and aircraft to exterminate 1350 wolves (90% of the population).

[228] The mine tailings were dredged from the river six months each year, 24 hours a day from 1932 to 1967. The "dredge fund" was established by the local mines that dumped the tailings into the river. It helped to appease the people of the Coeur d'Alenes, who were concerned about the hazards of the mine waste. The Mission Precinct was chosen as the site where the river is almost level with the lake's high water. Cataldo floods nearly every year.

[229] Hayden, Kathleen. School scores: Christian Doctrine 72, Bible History 65, Spelling 89, Penmanship 92, Drawing and Perspective 93, Arithmetic 88, Algebra 92, Modern History 94, Composition 87, and Typewriting 97. Her optional classes were Instrumental Music 97 and Painting 98.

[230] Refectory: where meals are served in a college or institution.

[231] A waist is a woman's dress's bodice. (the top half).

[232] Terry Rohe Cooper said her Aunt Kate Hayden made dresses that looked like they came from the finest store in town! Or the finest store in a finer town!

[233] 1900 Spokane census. St. Joseph's Orphanage. Sister Eugenia, 50 was a Superior from France, and Sister Ladislous, 46, was from Germany.

[234] The Owl Tavern in Cataldo was later called the Mission Inn and is now the Timbers Roadhouse. It was built by Molly's youngest son, George. He later moved his family to Post Falls and sold the property to his brother, Tom Snyder. Tom owned the Tavern until 1976.

[235] Russell, Bert. North Fork Of The Coeur D'Alene River.p.371.

[236] Fruchtl, Mike. Photo Courtesy.

[237] Wilkerson, Frank. New York Times. July 28, 1885.

[238] Foley Library. Gonzaga, Spokane, Washington. Monaghan #1873-5.

The Author

Susan Lee was born in Wallace, Idaho, attended school in Post Falls, and graduated from the University of Idaho earning a Bachelor's and Master's. She taught in Boise, Idaho for one year and then found herself in Guantanamo Bay, Cuba teaching for the Department of Defense. She continued teaching for DOD in Stuttgart, Germany, RAF Lakenheath, and London, England. She married an Air Force pilot in England. Fate took her to Fayetteville, North Carolina, and next to Wichita, Kansas. Seeking new adventures, she moved to Malaysia and taught at the International High School and Elementary School of Kuala Lumpur. Upon returning to North Idaho, it was time to write about a man with a fast horse. She had grown up hearing stories about him. A lake, streets, and gulches have been named for Mat Hayden. Molly was her grandmother.

Made in the USA
Middletown, DE
30 January 2024

48791184R00142